Youth Power in
Precarious Times

DUKE UNIVERSITY PRESS Durham and London 2020

Youth Power in Precarious Times

MELISSA BROUGH REIMAGINING CIVIC PARTICIPATION

Printed in the United States of America on acid-free paper ∞
Designed by Aimee C. Harrison
Typeset in Warnock Pro and ITC Franklin Gothic
by Westchester Publishing Services

Library of Congress Cataloging-in-Publication Data
Names: Brough, Melissa, [date] author.
Title: Youth power in precarious times : reimagining civic
    participation / Melissa Brough.
Description: Durham : Duke University Press, 2020. | Includes
    bibliographical references and index.
Identifiers: LCCN 2020008194 (print)
LCCN 2020008195 (ebook)
ISBN 9781478007708 (hardcover)
ISBN 9781478008071 (paperback)
ISBN 9781478009085 (ebook)
Subjects: LCSH: Youth—Political activity—Colombia—Medellín. |
    Digital media—Social aspects—Colombia—Medellín. |
    Mass media and youth—Colombia—Medellín. |
    Communication—Political aspects—Colombia—Medellín. |
    Social media—Colombia—Medellín.
Classification: LCC HQ799.2.P6 B768 2020 (print) |
    LCC HQ799.2.P6 (ebook)
DDC 323/.04208350986126—dc23
LC record available at https://lccn.loc.gov/2020008194
LC ebook record available at https://lccn.loc.gov/2020008195

Cover art: Graffiti art by Perrograff (2018)

To my family,

+ to all *guerriller@s simbólic@s*

fighting for a better world.

CONTENTS

ACKNOWLEDGMENTS

This book has benefited enormously from the tireless support of many, first and foremost my family. I am also indebted to my mentors Clemencia Rodríguez (without whom this project would not have happened), Sarah Banet-Weiser, Manuel Castells, Henry Jenkins, Josh Kun, and Doe Mayer. I am grateful to Angela Garcés Montoya and Gladys Acosta Valenica at the University of Medellín for being crucial collaborators, and to many other Colombian friends and co-conspirators, including Camilo Pérez, Melba Quijano, Jair Vega, Monica Pérez, Rafael Obregón, and the audiovisual collective Pasolini en Medellín, which provided an intellectual and creative home away from home.

I would also like to thank: Alexandra Halkin, Jose David Medina Holguin, Yesid Henao Salazar, Rafael Augusto Restrepo Agudelo, Daniel Acevedo Gómez, Jose Arellano, Ángela Panesso and the Subsecretaría de Metrojuventud, Victor Daniel Vélez Vélez and the office of Planeación Local y Presupuesto Participativo in the Secretaría de Cultura Ciudadana, Sergio Fajardo, Alonso Salzar, Jorge Melguizo, Nectalí Cano, Jairo Foronda Cano, Adriana Zafra Kiasúa, Clara Inés Restrepo Mesa, Santiago Leyva Botero at the Universidad EAFIT, the Educación en Ambientes Virtuales research group at the Universidad Pontificia Bolivariana, Alex Correa Velez and Lina Mejía of Platohedro, Orlando Lujan Villegas and the Instituto Popular de Capacitación (IPC), Libardo Andrés Agudelo, Diego Andrés Río Arango, Jeison Alexander Castaño Hernandez, Alexandra Castrillón Laverde, Daniel Felipe Quiceno, Jhon Jaime Sánchez, Jhon Fredy Asprilla Jave, Ingrid Joana Bonilla Jaramillo, Natalia García, Álvaro Ramirez, Gabriel Jaime Vanegas

Montoya, Diego Fernando Gómez, Henry Barros, Ana María Cardona, Kelly Múnera and the other members of Hiperbarrio, Jorge Blandón, Juan Guillermo, Miguel Ángel Bedoya, Mauricio Cadavid Restrepo, Gerard Martin, Juan Pablo Ortega, Yan Camilo Vergara Gallo, Andrés Montoya, Rafael Aubad, Germán Franco Díez, Delio Aparicio, Paula Marcela Moreno Zapata, Juan Carlos Flechas, Orley Duran, Amparo Cadavid, the Emisora Comunitaria San Vicente Stereo, Jesús Martín Barbero, and—especially—members of La Red de Hip Hop La Elite, Son Batá, and Ciudad Comuna.

I am indebted to my friends and colleagues who read earlier versions of these chapters and offered their invaluable feedback, including: Zhan Li, Camilo Pérez, Sonya Fierst, Gerard Martin, Charlotte Lapsansky, Daniela Gerson, Julian Sefton-Green, Mizuko Ito, Laura Portwood-Stacer, Kari Hensley, Sohinee Roy, Aimee Carillo-Rowe, and Pilar Riaño-Alcalá. I also want to thank Kathryn Sorrells and my informal writing group in the Department of Communication Studies at California State University, Northridge, and my fantastic research assistants Eddy Lorena Cuartas Graciano and Adilene Uriostegui.

This research benefited from the generous support of the following institutions: the Fulbright U.S. Student Program, the Annenberg School for Communication and Journalism and the Graduate School at the University of Southern California, the Stark Foundation, the Annenberg Program on Online Communities, and the Mike Curb College of Arts, Media, and Communication at California State University, Northridge.

Ultimately, I am most indebted to the youth who participated in this study; they taught me, motivated me, humbled me, and humored me. I experienced both profound inspiration and great sadness working in Medellín. During or since my time there, several youth—including one of my interviewees—have been killed in the dynamics of armed violence that I describe in the following chapters. I dedicate this book to their memory, and to the youth of the future, including my daughters.

INTRODUCTION

This book is a response to a defining contradiction of our times: the mainstreaming and commercialization of discourses of participation with the rise of social media on the one hand, and the ongoing political and economic disenfranchisement of the majority of youth worldwide on the other. "Participation" has become an integral part of the cultures, practices, networks, economies, and powers that increasingly structure the contemporary relationship between youth, society, and social change. As the view from the Global North—particularly Silicon Valley—would have it, a participatory zeitgeist swept much of the globe in the last two decades as a defining characteristic of digital communication and of the era more broadly. Some saw this as empowering (e.g., enhanced ability to self-publish and to organize collective action) and others as exploitative (e.g., free labor prone to extractive corporate and government surveillance practices). A casual observer might even conclude that participatory media was invented with the Internet, or at least with Web 2.0, which Tim O'Reilly famously characterized as an "architecture of participation."[1]

Of course, this is not true. Participatory media and communication have been central organizing concepts in Latin America and other parts of the globe for decades, despite often dramatic disparities in technological access. The question of participation is not (and never has been) just about our communication technologies. The productive question of participation lies more broadly in how we cultivate ecologies of participation—which includes communication platforms, practices, cultural and political norms, and institutions that support meaningful participation in public life. This book is about a city attempting just that in a context of great precariousness and instability—two words that aptly describe the state of much of the world today.

In the contemporary moment, thanks in large part to the far-reaching tentacles of corporate social media, the concept of participation has become so commercialized and institutionalized that, as Christopher Kelty describes, it has become "like a monument one passes every day—so routine, so common it's hard to remember just why it is there."[2] Drawing on the *Oxford English Dictionary*'s definition of the term, he notes that participation implies an effect; it is "the process or fact of sharing in an action . . . esp. one in which the outcome directly affects those taking part."[3] The benefits and drawbacks of participation may be experienced by the individual participant and/or a broader collective or entity of which that participant may or may not be a part—and therein lies the slipperiness of the term.[4] This "slipperiness" makes it rhetorically useful to a wide array of sectors and applications (e.g., participatory marketing, participatory mapping, participatory research, participatory development, and participatory art, to name just a few). The use of the term typically implies agency, empowerment, and some form of democratic practice—whether or not these are actualized.

The episteme of participation was central to the marketing of social media but also reflected a larger international imaginary about the promises of a more democratic digital age. However inaccurate or simplistic, terms such as "Facebook Revolution" or "Twitter Revolution," used to describe social/political movements in the Middle East and elsewhere, captured the predominantly optimistic spirit of the global technological imagination in the early days of social media.[5] There are of course several significant examples from across the globe of civic and political engagement being amplified by the use of online platforms. These include, among others: the high participation of youth in electing the first African American president of the United States (2008); the One Million Voices Against FARC protests in Colombia (2008); the international Occupy Movement (started in 2011); the overthrow of governments in several countries, including Egypt (2011) and the Ukraine (2014); the Me Too movement's elevation of issues of sexual harassment and assault (since October 2017); and the student-led movement March For Our Lives (2018). As Manuel Castells observed, digitally networked communication technologies have helped spawn a "new species" of social movements by offering new infrastructures for faster, more interactive, and more autonomous communication.[6] Additionally, the free/libre and open-source software (FLOSS) movement has helped bring about an unprecedented (if unequally realized) opportunity for the participatory design of these communication platforms.[7] Indeed, in much if not most of the world, the possibilities for participation in public life are arguably more diverse and more widespread than ever before.

Yet, we can no longer be naive about the fact that social media platforms can be as antisocial as they are social, and that they not only enable but also constrain and curate participation in public life in much of the world today. Social media can be used to mislead and manipulate political participation; and digital algorithms can, however inadvertently, help to perpetuate inequality and further polarize people's political views. In hindsight, cyberoptimist visions of a more participatory age brought about by digitally networked platforms seem not only technologically deterministic but somewhat quaint.[8] However, as the pendulum of public and scholarly opinion swings from general optimism to pessimism about the possibility for digital communication to enhance participation in public life, there is a risk of losing sight of the middle ground. While some scholars suggest that participation has been rendered a nearly useless concept with its widespread proliferation and should perhaps be abandoned,[9] this book contends that it is crucial to recuperate its analytical and practical utility in order to work toward more equitable, just societies. What is at stake is not only the conceptual utility of participation but, more importantly, our ability to understand and better support youth engagement in public life today, and the individual and societal benefits of doing so effectively.

The literature to date has generally failed to connect adequately what we already know about participation from a range of non-digital historical and cultural contexts with what we are learning in the digital media landscape. In this book, I make some of these connections by bridging learnings from the theory and practice of participatory communication (developed in Latin America and elsewhere over the second half of the twentieth century) with more recent work in digital media studies primarily from North America and Europe. I do this through the lens of youth engagement because of the many ways young people in particular have been both willingly and unwillingly inscribed by discourses and practices of participation across government, intergovernmental, commercial, and civil society sectors—and how in some cases they are forging alternative visions of participation.

In most countries, the proportion of adolescents using the Internet exceeds that of the general population.[10] Despite a rapidly growing body of research on this topic, we still lack analytical tools to understand the nuanced relationships between young people's participation in the digital realm and participation in the material lives of their communities. All too often, adults still tend to approach these as distinct or even disconnected spaces.[11] The aim here is not to characterize youth participation definitively in the ever-changing digital age but rather to develop a productive way of thinking about and supporting it in an era of global discord and precarity. To be clear, this book is not a(nother) proselytizing of participation; nor is it a wholesale, cynical dismissal. It is an effort to identify the analytical and practical value of participation in a way that does not merely perpetuate a Northern universalizing of the concept but rather investigates the cultural and political work of this trope—and its implications for contemporary policy and practice—by drawing on Latin America's longer history of critically theorizing participation.

Toward that end, in this book, I develop a definition of *participatory public culture* based on scholarship from the Global North and South,[12] particularly from studies of participatory communication in Latin America and digital media studies of participatory culture and participatory politics/ civics in North America and Europe. I argue that we need to think about participation ecologically, and that we can use the metaphor of polyculture to describe the potential for mutually beneficial relationships between grass-roots and institutional modes of youth participation, or what I call *polycultural civics*.[13] While I focus in this book on the implications of these ideas for youth engagement, they apply to questions of citizen engagement more broadly at a time when both grass-roots and institutional participation are being questioned—and in some cases intentionally undermined— on a global scale.

Medellín, Colombia A Model Participatory City?

In 2013, Citigroup, the *Wall Street Journal*, and the Urban Land Institute named Medellín, Colombia, "Innovative City of the Year":

> Few cities have transformed the way that Medellín, Colombia's second largest city, has in the past 20 years. Medellín's homicide rate has plunged, nearly 80% from 1991 to 2010. The city built public libraries, parks, and schools in poor hillside neighborhoods and constructed a series of transportation links from there to its commercial and industrial centers. . . . The local government, along with businesses, community organizations, and universities worked together to fight violence and to modernize Medellín. . . . In addi-

tion, Medellín is one of the largest cities to successfully implement participatory budgeting, which allows citizens to define priorities and allocate a portion of the municipal budget. Community organizations, health centers, and youth groups have formed, empowering citizens to declare ownership of their neighborhoods.[14]

From a city known for Pablo Escobar's drug cartel and for having the world's highest homicide rates in the early 1990s to one known for its urban renaissance by the early 2010s, the "transformation" of Medellín is now world famous. Despite marked socioeconomic inequality and continued, though significantly reduced, street violence the government, commercial, and media sectors have branded the city as a model for urban renewal and citizen participation, drawing international attention from researchers, policy makers, corporations, artists, architects, tourists, and the press.

In this same period, Medellín's business, technology, and political leaders were working to fashion the city as a leading digital hub of Latin America. International corporations such as Hewlett-Packard opened regional offices there, in what developers hoped would become one of Latin America's largest information technology districts. The city invested in cultivating "digital citizens" with major government commitments to bridging the digital divide and promoting digital literacy and e-governance.

Medellín is also home to a vibrant citizens' media movement, in which ordinary citizens collaborate to produce locally relevant media both on- and offline. Colombia has been a nexus of such participatory media and communication since the middle of the twentieth century. Its practitioners and scholars (among them, Orlando Fals Borda, Jesús Martín Barbero, Pilar Riaño-Alcalá, and Clemencia Rodríguez) have contributed significantly to international debates about citizen participation, and have developed a diverse range of participatory practices using both old and new media technologies to promote civic engagement and social justice.[15]

The first time I visited Medellín in 2009, I was struck by the myriad ways participation was being invoked by different actors across the city, from grass-roots hip-hop activists to city and state officials. Later, one afternoon in January 2011, I found myself sitting on the corner of a couch in the San Javier Park Library, one of five similar structures renowned for their impressive architecture intentionally located in some of Medellín's poorest neighborhoods. The building had become a recreational and educational meeting space for local youth; they filled the computer labs and appropriated the outdoor patio for break dancing. The wall of windows in front of me looked out at the heart of Comuna 13 (Subdistrict 13)—a part of the city made notorious by the media for its history of violence and ongoing gang activity. Just down the hill was the end of the metro B line and the beginning of the San Javier Metrocable, one of three gondola lift systems in Medellín that climb through the uppermost reaches of the city's shantytowns. Together, the library and the gondolas stood out against the backdrop of ramshackle brick housing. Heavily branded with the insignia of the Alcaldía de Medellín (the Mayor's Office of Medellín), they were dramatic signs of the local government's efforts to make its presence more visible and impactful in neighborhoods where the rule of law had been trumped by gang and paramilitary politics. The fervor with which the Mayor's Office branded such initiatives was striking, often using taglines such as "*Medellín, un espacio para el encuentro ciudadano*" ("Medellín, a meeting space for citizens") and "*Medellín, gobernable y participativa*" ("Medellín, governable and participatory").[16]

Next to me on the couch sat the hip-hop artist and activist known as JEIHHCO (a stage name combining his first name, Jeison, with hip-hop and Colombia), age twenty-five, and the local graffiti artist known as El Perro (The Dog), age twenty-one.[17] JEIHHCO was sporting classic hip-hop attire: wide pants, a baggy T-shirt, and a large, stiff baseball cap. El Perro carried a backpack of aerosol paint cans and other art supplies. JEIHHCO and El Perro were members of one of Colombia's most active and widely recognized youth-run hip-hop networks at the time, La Red de Hip Hop La Elite (The Elite Hip Hop Network, known as "La Elite"). They joined the network as teenagers and had since devoted the majority of their time each week to organizing the network and developing their skills as both hip-hop artists and activists for peace. In their own way, they had become as iconic of Comuna 13 as the famous Park Library and Metrocable; they were known by many across the city and beyond for their promotion of nonviolence and youth empowerment through the arts of hip-hop.

This was my first meeting with them, and as we concluded our conversation about hip-hop activism in Comuna 13, JEIHHCO did something that I had started to experience as a pattern in Medellín: he offered me the cell phone numbers of senior officials in the municipal government. What I found surprising was that rather than the researchers, nongovernmental/ civic organization staff, or other professionals I spoke to, it was most often my youth interviewees who offered to put me in contact with the local government, challenging my assumption that youth—especially youth from marginalized neighborhoods such as this one—had little access to centers of institutional power. As JEIHHCO explained, "If I want to speak with the

San Javier Library Park, Comuna 13, Medellín, Colombia. Source: Alejandro Rojas.   I.1

Participación. Graffiti art (artist unknown), Medellín, Colombia. Source: author.   I.2

Secretaría de Cultura Ciudadana [Office of Civic Culture] or Metrojuventud [the municipal department of youth programs], I can call them, they'll pick up their cell phone. This doesn't happen in Bogotá, or almost anywhere else for that matter. . . . [H]ere, there's an administration that is close to [grass-roots projects] but furthermore, La Elite pulls a lot of weight in this city, in the political realm. And this means that our spaces, our process, and our voice are more often heard."

This is true. During my time in Medellín in 2010–2011, I witnessed, for example, how the murder of a young hip-hop artist by a local gang prompted a conversation between hip-hop activists and government officials via Facebook, which resulted in government support for a memorial march and concert that materialized only a few days later. I found all this surprising in a city where youth from places such as Comuna 13 had been heavily stigmatized since the height of narcotrafficking violence in the 1980s and early 1990s. In my fieldwork, I learned that such relationships between youth organizers and the municipal government were not necessarily an exception (even though La Elite had a particularly strong relationship with certain branches of the government) but rather a product of the city's public and political culture at the time. The following chapters explain, among other things, how it is that young hip-hop artists from one of the poorest, most violent areas of a highly segregated city came to hold political and cultural sway as social change agents. It becomes clear this was not (just) about cell phones or Facebook; more importantly, it was a set of relationships and actions between grass-roots youth organizers and institutional actors that made this possible—a phenomenon that I describe as polycultural participation.

A City of Contrasts

Lodged between the Andes Mountains in the northwestern Aburrá Valley, Medellín is Colombia's second largest city and the capital of the Department of Antioquia.[18] It is home to approximately 2.5 million people. Nearly 45 percent of the population is under the age of thirty, down somewhat from the late 1990s, when this segment accounted for approximately 53 percent of the total population.[19] The city is divided into sixteen administrative subdistricts referred to as *comunas* and five surrounding rural *corregimientos* (towns/villages).

Medellín has a dramatic topography and a very segregated urban landscape, which ranges from well-appointed shopping malls, luxury car dealerships, and high-rise condominiums to the shantytowns in the mountainsides encircling the city. While approximately 80 percent of the population belongs to the three lowest of Colombia's six socioeconomic strata, Medellín is one of Colombia's wealthiest cities and home to some of the country's richest landowners and industrialists.[20] With vast natural resources in the surrounding region and an industrious culture, Medellín has historically been a prosperous, largely self-sufficient city. Its economy first boomed from gold mining in the late nineteenth century, followed by coffee and textile exports; in the mid-twentieth century, it led Latin America as the largest textile exporter.[21] Yet, by the second half of the twentieth century, the city's infrastructure was unable to keep up with the flood of rural migrants coming to the city out of economic hardship, or displaced by natural disasters and the national armed conflict. Informal settlements crawled up the mountainsides, with many residents organizing to demand official recognition of their neighborhoods and the provision of public services.[22]

Medellín has a long history of community organizing, as well as a long history of exclusion. It is a city where, as Mary Roldán describes, "paternalism, civic duty, a tradition of non-partisan public service, and ascent based on merit have always coexisted with exclusion, discrimination, parochialism and selective repression."[23] *Paisas*, as native residents refer to themselves, are known among other things for their local pride; they will often distinguish their history from that of the rest of Colombia, starting with the settlement of the area by Spanish Jews in the late sixteenth century. This different cultural identity is strongly asserted as normatively white, despite the hundreds of thousands of Afro-Colombians and other people of color living in the city.[24] As I discuss in Chapter 3, this is one of several intersectional dynamics that shape participation in Medellín's public culture.

By the 1970s, the rapid decline of the textile and manufacturing industries, which had been weakened by global competition, led to rising unemployment, and the number of unemployed male youths between the ages of twelve and twenty-nine became the highest in the country.[25] The situation was exacerbated by the neoliberal policies of the 1980s and 1990s that further opened Colombia's manufacturing to global competition and mandated public-spending cutbacks through economic restructuring. The weakened economy and high unemployment fueled the growth of narcotrafficking and other illegal markets. The lack of economic and social opportunities weighed heavily on Medellín's working-class youth, approximately half of whom came from single-mother households. Some of Medellín's youth (particularly boys and young men from poorer neighborhoods) joined the growing number of street gangs and played a key role in the criminal organizations in charge of the cocaine business.[26]

In the 1980s and early 1990s, Medellín became known internationally for its drug cartel, led by the notorious narcotrafficker Pablo Escobar, and for having homicide rates forty times higher than the United Nations' marker of an epidemic.[27] While circumstances have changed significantly since the 1990s, armed violence remains Medellín's unshakeable shadow—a determining yet elusive characteristic that is ever changing, and one that the vast majority of its citizens long intensely to overcome. Violence is one of the first topics many of my interviewees raised, and yet the last thing for which they want their city to be known. It has profoundly shaped youth subjectivities and their struggles for livelihood, empowerment, and dignity in the city. This is especially true among the lower socioeconomic strata, which comprise the vast majority of the city's population.

Medellín's history of armed violence has been widely stigmatized, sensationalized, and commodified in both journalistic and entertainment media in and outside of Colombia; the resulting reputation has had many negative economic and social consequences for the city's inhabitants.[28] To be clear, the history of violence is not the only factor that has motivated or affected youth participation in Medellín. Although youth have organized around civic, political, recreational, and cultural topics largely independently of the issue of violence, it has significantly shaped the context of much of this organizing. It is also one of the factors that helped to constitute and spread a pervasive discourse of participation. While I do not wish to overemphasize it, this story of participation requires addressing the historical context of violence at both the local and national level. Over the course of this book, I trust readers will see there is far more to learn from Medellín beyond the topic of violence, particularly as societies around the world face their own contexts of precariousness.

Armed violence in Medellín is imbricated in the longer history of Colombia's civil war, which, from the period known as La Violencia (The Violence, 1946–1958)[29] to a tenuous peace agreement reached in 2016, drove hundreds of thousands of displaced people from the countryside to Medellín and Colombia's other cities. Decades of ongoing conflict over land disputes and political control between state (dominated by the elite), right-wing paramilitary, and leftist guerrilla actors—most notably the Fuerzas Armadas Revolucionarias de Colombia (Revolutionary Armed Forces of Colombia, FARC) and the Ejército de Liberación Nacional (National Liberation Army, ELN)—rendered Colombia home to the largest population of internally displaced people in the world until it was surpassed in 2014 by Syria.[30] This has increased rates of unemployment and strained public services and urban planning in Colombia's cities. Rather than offer a comprehensive review of this long and complex history of violence in Colombia, I focus here on the period that most heavily shaped the contemporary context of youth participation, the time frame stretching from the rise of narcotrafficking in the 1970s to 2011, the end of the second Compromiso Ciudadano (Citizens' Commitment) administration (and the year in which I carried out the majority of my field research). This period encompasses a fracturing, reshaping, and rehabilitation of public life in the city, in which young people played key roles.

Starting in the 1970s, Colombia's internal conflict was exacerbated by the prolific rise of narcotrafficking. Through networked partnerships between smugglers such as Escobar and North American mafia organizations, by the mid-1980s, Colombia had become the epicenter of narcotrafficking and the primary supplier of cocaine to the North American market.[31] The culture and politics of narcotrafficking (which included bribery, kidnapping, and murder to exert power) caused a crisis in Colombia's political and justice systems. Crime bosses such as Escobar gained control of parts of the police forces and justice systems through bribes and the threat or use of violence. They also infiltrated the political system through traditional means at several levels; in 1982, Escobar was elected to parliament in his effort to fight legislation permitting the extradition of narcotraffickers to the United States. He was expelled shortly thereafter due to efforts by the Minister of Justice Rodrigo Lara Bonilla and influence from the U.S. government.[32]

Youth, mainly poor youth, became central protagonists and victims of the armed violence, some as gang members and hired hitmen, others as innocents caught in the crossfire. By the end of the 1980s, more than 150 gangs were officially documented in metropolitan Medellín, and the actual number was likely significantly higher.[33] Yet, narcotrafficking and gangs were not the only drivers of armed violence. From the mid-1980s onward, the power of state institutions continued to erode in the face of increasingly complex webs of allegiances between a variety of armed actors vying for control. As the social and political fabric weakened, gangs, urban militias, and paramilitary activity (classifications that sometimes blurred and overlapped) proliferated. In the 1980s, urban militias were primarily comprised of youth and children associated with left-wing guerrilla groups such as the M-19, FARC, and ELN, and justified their activity as a response to community demands for security. Urban militias began carrying out "social cleansing" campaigns, acted as a de facto police force in the poor parts of the city, and solicited bribes from local business owners in exchange for their protection.

Also during this time period, right-wing paramilitary groups developed across Colombia through various alliances between local businessmen, politicians, drug traffickers, and others interested in curbing the power and influence of leftist guerrillas. They carried out targeted murders and death squads, and enforced conservative values in the areas they controlled, often in collaboration with state actors. In Medellín and elsewhere, paramilitary groups also became involved in drug trafficking, ultimately controlling much of the drug trade after the fall of Escobar's cartel.[34] They frequently operated through existing criminal gangs primarily of youth and children; this made it possible for authorities to deny the presence of paramilitaries in the city and to blame the violence on youth gangs.[35]

The corruption and social cleansing campaigns themselves spawned other "self-defense" (vigilante) groups. The lines between criminal gangs, militias, and paramilitaries increasingly blurred—as did the distinction between private and public security forces, as off-duty, rogue policemen perpetrated masked killings and accusations of politicians' links to illegal paramilitary activity became frequent.[36] Gerard Martin reflected, "It was as if another Pandora's box had been opened, in addition to narcotrafficking, *la guerrilla*, and the paramilitary phenomenon. In reality . . . all of these phenomena ended up interconnected in one way or another."[37] The result was that, according to Ana María Jaramillo and Alonso Salazar Jaramillo (who was also Medellín's mayor from 2008 to 2011), "in this period one can't speak simply of the absence of the state, but [rather] of its illegitimate presence. The levels of corruption implicated [the state] as yet another factor in the conflict. The configuration of a *parainstitutionality*, which carried out a marginal 'justice,' transformed the state into an enemy of the citizens."[38] In many ways, this applied at both the municipal and national levels; the police force in Medellín was run by the national government, and corruption and *debilidad institucional* (institutional weakness) could be found at all levels of government.[39] On the other hand, in some cases, Medellin's drug lords, namely Escobar, financed recreational activities, housing, schools, and other infrastructure in their local communities, partially filling certain roles neglected by the state. Escobar was seen as an altruistic *patrón* (an almost saintly patriarchal figure) in certain neighborhoods of the city; narcotrafficking brought resources to these communities that the state had failed to provide.

Escobar was ultimately killed in a gun battle with the Colombian National Police in 1993. In the years leading up to his death, his cartel had been weakened by government and paramilitary activity and by the fact that paramilitary networks (and some guerrilla networks) had come to control an increasing portion of the illegal drug trade. The fall of Escobar shored up the strength of narco-paramilitary bosses and their hold over the majority of the drug-trafficking business in Medellín, which resulted in a period of declining homicide rates as their power went relatively unchallenged.[40]

Yet, by 2000–2001, the influence of the national armed conflict was felt locally in Medellín, as guerrillas and narco-paramilitary factions fought for territorial control of strategic parts of the city, such as key transportation and trade routes. This has been described as the urbanization of Colombia's armed conflict.[41] Again, youth were a heavily recruited asset, as they represented potential fighters—many already trained—who had local knowledge and were accustomed to a culture in which life was seen as expendable. Territorial struggles between guerrilla groups and the paramilitaries who eventually dominated also became battles over—and between—youth gangs as the violence escalated again. In 2000, some estimated that roughly eight thousand youth were linked to gangs in Medellín.[42]

State or state-sanctioned violence played a central role in these dynamics.[43] Most dramatically, in the early 2000s, a series of operations were carried out by the Colombian military, the goal of which was to eliminate the guerrilla groups the FARC, the ELN, and the Comandos Armados del Pueblo (People's Armed Commandos) from their strongholds in the city. These operations became notorious for the excessive use of indiscriminate force against civilians. One of them—Operation Orion—was launched in October 2002. It was carried out under then-President Álvaro Uribe, a native of Medellín who had previously served as the region's governor. Operation Orion took place in Comuna 13, the epicenter of the conflict in Medellín at the time, and home to JEIHHCO and El Perro.

These incidences of indiscriminate violence inflicted by the state in densely populated, urban residential zones were particularly traumatizing to residents and further fueled their distrust of the state.[44] Not surprisingly, these operations were frequently referenced by my youth interviewees from Comuna 13 as a milestone in their politicization. Operation Orion eradicated the primary competitors of the paramilitary crime bosses, whose networks and associated gangs filled the subsequent power vacuum. By 2003, narcotrafficking had shifted from the organizational structure of the cartel to more localized, low-profile paramilitary bosses-cum-drug lords operating more covertly.[45] Due in part to fewer challenges to their control, and to a controversial demobilization of some paramilitaries, the city experienced a period of relative peace in the years 2003–2008, with homicide rates falling significantly.[46] In 2008, the extradition of the crime boss known as Don Berna and several other powerful narco-paramilitary commanders to the United States left another power vacuum; territorial struggles once again escalated, doubling the homicide rate. However, homicide rates remained lower than they were in the 1990s.[47]

From Precarious to Participatory

Medellín had historically been ruled by a small and close-knit group of political and economic elites engaged in clientelism and paternalism. Yet, the failure of the local government and its traditional party leaders to stem the violence in Medellín propelled the need for citizen—particularly *youth* citizen—participation to the forefront of policy discussions at both the local and national levels in the 1990s, where it came to be understood by many as key to reducing the violence and created opportunities for nontraditional actors to be more directly involved in governance.[48]

Youth organizing had surged in the 1990s in response to the impact of the violence on young people and the absence of effective local government in the most affected parts of the city. With a heightened interest in the role that youth could play in rehabilitating the city's social fabric, governmental, international nongovernmental, business, and local civil society organizations partnered in various ways to help develop infrastructure and programs for youth in poor parts of the city, and to strengthen civil society. This included the Consejería Presidencial para Medellín (the Presidential Council for Medellín), created by President César Gaviria (1990–1994) to weaken the ties between the Medellín cartel and the city's low-income youth, to foster more legitimate political participation, and to strengthen civil society.[49]

The involvement of local civil society organizations in these efforts set a precedent for their participation in local governance and helped to foment a political movement led in part by some of the civil society participants. This ultimately formed the base (and much of the leadership) of the independent party Compromiso Ciudadano, which was a unique alliance of local business leaders, academics, student leaders, and other grass-roots activists. Sergio Fajardo and the Compromiso Ciudadano party won the 2003 mayoral election on a platform based largely on discourses of civic participation and education; the first of five "strategic lines" in its develop-

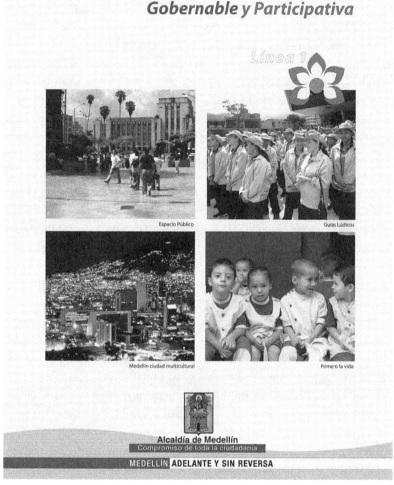

Medellín»
Gobernable y Participativa

Espacio Público

Guías Lúdicos

Medellín ciudad multicultural

Primero la vida

Alcaldía de Medellín
Compromiso de toda la ciudadanía

MEDELLÍN ADELANTE Y SIN REVERSA

"Medellín, governable and participatory," Medellín Mayor's Office Development Plan 2004–2007. Source: Alcaldía de Medellín.

I.3

ment plan for the city was entitled *"Medellín, governable y participativa."*[50] It was the first time an independent party had held the mayor's office. The crisis thus created a political opening for new actors independent of traditional party politics to enter into local government.

Fajardo's administration was composed in large part of former grassroots organizers and other nontraditional power holders who had extensive experience in participatory practices. Fajardo himself was an academic whose relative political neutrality helped him to lead the diverse coalition that comprised Compromiso Ciudadano. Alonso Salazar, his successor from the same party (2008–2011), was also a scholar, journalist, and community activist; he had written extensively about youth in the context of narcotrafficking and was active in civic movements in the 1990s.[51]

Addressing socioeconomic inequality was a central agenda of this coalition. Yet, instead of this being seen as a threat to the business class of Medellín, the crisis caused by the inequality—and its expression through narcotrafficking—meant that addressing it had become a pressing necessity, even for traditional economic elites, some of whom joined the Compromiso Ciudadano administration. Compromiso Ciudadano explicitly aimed to appeal to citizens of all classes, and emphasized bridging the divide between the local government and Medellín's middle and lower classes without alienating its elites. They developed a discourse of *corresponsabilidad* (shared responsibility) for the city, emphasizing transparency and good governance, as well as inclusivity and citizen participation—thus appealing to some members of the elite business and political classes, as well as their popular base. Fajardo stated, "The point was to bring together a fragmented society and show respect for the most humble."[52]

Under these two Compromiso Ciudadano administrations (and, in some cases, building on initiatives started under previous administrations), the municipal government partnered with both the private and public sectors to implement a variety of initiatives to stabilize the city, strengthen public culture, promote government transparency and citizen participation, and restore the public's faith in local governance.[53] This approach was dubbed "social urbanism," which, according to Kate Maclean, struck a balance between elite and more progressive interests.[54] (From the perspective of its business elites, the rhetoric and investments of Medellín's social urbanism would help lead to, among other things, greater foreign direct investment, which in fact they did.[55]) Youth participation was also a strategic focus of several of these initiatives, and was seen as an indispensable resource for reducing violence. The administration launched a citywide participatory budgeting process through which residents aged fourteen and older help determine how a percentage of the city's annual budget would be allocated for the development of their neighborhoods, which I analyze in Chapter 4.

The administration also invested heavily in public education, allocating approximately 40 percent of the entire city budget to improving access, infrastructure, and teacher training.[56] Through public–private partnerships, they expanded public Internet access and created impressive physical public spaces with computer labs, such as the *parques biblioteca* (library parks), in some of the most impoverished and violent sectors of the city. In addition to a gondola lift system (developed under the previous mayor, Luis Pérez, but opened during Fajardo's administration), outdoor escalators further solidified Medellín's growing reputation as an innovative hub of urban planning that was using public infrastructure to help stabilize the poor neighborhoods on the periphery and integrate them with the city center.

Analysts disagree on which factors were primarily responsible for the significant reduction in violence that corresponded with the Fajardo administration (2004–2007), when homicide rates were at their lowest in decades; most seem to agree that an important factor was Don Berna's continued control of Medellín's underworld and the lack of a significant challenge to his network, rather than the controversial 2006 demobilization of paramilitary groups or the investments of social urbanism alone.[57] What is clear is that the reduction in violence was one of several conditions that made it possible for the administration to carry out the large public works projects that helped Medellín earn its reputation for innovation and transformation, and to create spaces for greater public participation.

The case of Medellín thus offers many angles from which to understand participation as a multivalent resource in the digital age. Several global discourses about (youth) citizen engagement, digital and participatory cultures, democratization, and social change converged in Medellín. This book focuses primarily on the years between 2004 and 2011, which correspond to the two Compromiso Ciudadano administrations, when most of Medellín's so-called transformation took place and when the public focus on youth and citizen participation was at its height.

This book does not reduce the case of Medellín to an ideal or easily replicable model for urban transformation or youth participation. The city's particular history—including its relative (albeit highly concentrated) wealth and its history of violence—makes it exceptional in several ways. However, gang dynamics, poverty, and the disillusionment of youth with traditional political institutions are conditions faced by numerous major cities worldwide, in both the Global North and South.[58] Therefore, this book navigates a path from Medellín's contextual specificity, and its particular struggles and successes, to broader lessons that can inform challenges faced across the globe.

Methodological and Analytical Notes

A common problem in discussions of youth participation in the digital age is that participation is easily conflated with interactivity online, resulting in analyses that are technologically deterministic and overly celebratory of social media and other digital communication, while under-attending to the surrounding social infrastructures, cultures, practices, and relations of power that shape their use and imbue them with meaning. Describing digital media platforms as "participatory media,"[59] for example, conflates the technical capabilities for interactive networked horizontal communication with the actual human act of participating—anthropomorphizing communication infrastructures that may or may not be used in participatory ways. This may seem a semantic splitting of hairs, but we risk diluting the utility of the concept of participation for promoting the social, cultural, political, and economic practices that can advance democracy and social justice.

I first learned about participatory media in Chiapas, Mexico. Chiapas became famous on the world stage as the site of the 1994 uprising of the Zapatistas, an indigenous rights movement that pioneered Internet activism. But older communication technologies also played an important role in that movement. I was drawn there in summer 2000 by the opportunity to intern with the Chiapas Media Project, an organization that supported Zapatista-affiliated indigenous communities to produce their own video documentaries. In this pre-social media context—and for decades prior— the term "participatory media" typically referred to a collaborative process of media production used by community-based organizations and social justice advocates, among others, to involve disenfranchised groups in conceptualizing, producing, and sharing their own media. Participatory media was being used in communities around the world to put communication technologies in the hands of those whose perspectives were rarely, if ever, represented in commercial broadcast media or in institutional decision-making processes. In Chiapas, participatory videos documented, for example, the government-backed privatization of land farmed by indigenous communities, indigenous women's experiences of gender inequities, and Zapatista communities' collective organic coffee farming for economic autonomy.[60]

Only a few years later, I was surprised to find that independently of this history, the terms "participatory media" and "participatory video" were becoming part of mainstream and commercial Web 2.0 discourse in the Global North. One of YouTube's first advertising initiatives was called Participatory Video Ads. The company's 2006 press release read, "The new Participatory Video Ad is a user-initiated video advertisement with all of the YouTube community features enabled. Consumers can rate, share, comment, embed, and favorite advertising content that they find interesting, informative and entertaining. Rather than interrupt a consumer's experience, we have created a model which encourages engagement and participation."[61] This was certainly a different deployment of the concept of participatory media than what I'd witnessed in Chiapas. Suddenly, everything was seemingly "participatory," even advertising.

As a scholar and practitioner of participatory media for several years prior, I found these developments both exciting and troubling: exciting because I knew from experience that participation in and through communication media can be empowering to marginalized individuals and communities, and troubling because with the commercialization of discourses of participatory media and culture, the critical valence of participatory media was dissipating—and yet remained as important as ever. The analytical tools needed to support youth participation productively in public life today require a careful parsing of the capacities potentially afforded by digital media platforms from the actual human practices in and around them that determine the modes and impacts of participation. This is one of the central aims of this book. This book resists binary debates that see digital technology as having revolutionized or destroyed public participation. Instead, the following chapters invite readers to reimagine participation in public life, inspired by the case of Medellín.

Participation has most often been studied in disciplinary silos, focusing on political participation (e.g., in political science), civic participation (e.g., in sociology, political science, urban studies, or development studies), cultural participation (e.g., in cultural or media studies), or communicative participation (e.g., in digital media studies, development communication, communication for social change, or participatory communication). This book traverses these fields in search of a more nuanced and at once more powerful understanding of participation for the contemporary moment.

As Florencia Enghel and Martín Becerra note, the fields of communication studies and media studies in the Global North have tended to take a patronizing view of Latin American scholarship, positioning it historically as an "offspring of its Western predecessors" rather than valuing it on its own terms.[62] What's more, the burden of cross-regional scholarly engagement has tended to fall on the Global South. While a comprehensive review of relevant Latin American scholarship is not the aim of this book, I consider how Latin American understandings of participatory communication can inform digital media scholarship in the Global North and, reciprocally, how digital media scholarship from the United States and other parts of the Global North can inform the Colombian/Latin American context. I also draw from Latin American science and technology studies, although this book does not perceive technology (alone) as determining of public participation in the contemporary moment. The long history of theorizing and practicing participation in Latin America, despite deep structural inequalities and technological divides, attests to this.

Indeed, one of the aims of this book is to push back against techno-centric discussions of participation that have become predominant in the last decade in both the academic and popular press in the Global North. It pushes readers to think about participation in a multidimensional, non-binary way in which digital communication technologies are but one resource within a sociopolitical ecology. To that end, this book takes more of an ecological perspective than is typical in studies of digital media or participatory communication. Ecological approaches in the social sciences often aim to account for the multilevel, complex relationships between different actors, systems, discourses and values, resources, technologies, and so on that constitute and structure a given environment.[63] Similarly, I analyzed discourses and practices of youth participation in Medellín across multiple sites and levels of society—from the grass roots to the city government, as well as the national and international context—and how these were inter-related. This included discourses and practices that were noninstitutional (i.e., grass roots) or institutional, and on- and/or offline. In other words, I tried to understand the cultural, political, economic, and communicative life of youth in the city across different societal levels and sociocultural geographies as an interconnected system. An ecological approach helped me to think about participation as a resource that is constituted by a system of actors, institutions, and networks—a resource that can be wielded as a form of governmentality or resistance.[64] I found that these two are not necessarily mutually exclusive. For example, one of the factors that made youth activism in Medellín potent was the existence of some governmental and other institutional entities that facilitated youth participation in public life but did not overly try to control or appropriate it.

Over the course of a year spanning 2010–2011, I studied participation in Medellín using several qualitative methodologies, primarily ethnography. I carried out more than a hundred semi-structured, open-ended interviews (including some group interviews) with members of grass-roots youth groups, civil society organizations, and city and national government (in Bogotá, Colombia's capital).[65] I took extensive field notes and photographs, and reviewed existing research and other materials, including graffiti, videos, and songs produced by the youth collectives in Medellín. I attended formal/public events, such as conferences (including the annual conference of the Asociación Latinoamericana de Investigadores de la Comunicación, the Association of Latin American Researchers of Communication, ALAIC), participatory budgeting meetings, a hip-hop festival, and a protest march. I complemented these with other methods, including an audience survey, observations of youth collectives' activities, and participatory research workshops led by local researchers at the University of Medellín.[66] My understanding of the longer period of 2004–2011—the focus of this book—is informed by all of these methods, as well as a review of historical documents and existing scholarship by primarily Colombian scholars. I studied several more cases of institutional and noninstitutional youth participation than I had room to include in this book; I included here the cases that offer the most significant insights about participation, those that challenge dominant assumptions and/or that helped illustrate how participation functions as a resource within a broader sociopolitical ecology.

My analysis here is greatly informed by research published in Spanish by Colombian and other Latin American scholars. In most cases, translations of their work are my own, except where noted. I carried out nearly all interviews in Spanish, so excerpts that appear in this book are my translations. I asked my Colombian friends and colleagues to review many of these translations; any remaining errors are my own.[67] Language (especially local vernacular) and cultural differences were undoubtedly a barrier to my understanding certain nuances and their historical and contextual significance. In other cases, my foreign status facilitated the research. For example, my appearance as a foreigner meant that crossing the "invisible borders" patrolled by armed gangs in some parts of the city was less perilous for me than it might have been for some local residents who could be perceived as having conflicting affiliations. Additionally, many of my youth and other interviewees were eager for outsiders to acknowledge and study their lives and work, and for exposure outside of Medellín. They were therefore generous with their time, and conscientious in sharing information and offering their own analyses. My analyses reflect these invaluable contributions.

Critical anthropologists (such as James Clifford, Clifford Geertz, Elizabeth Bird, and Renato Rosaldo) problematize the subject position of the foreign researcher and the ways in which power is (re)produced through the creation of scholarly knowledge. This understanding emerged in response to the problematic history of ethnographic practices and its roots in colonial ideology, which upheld the Western white male as the author of knowledge about peoples and places entirely foreign to him, silencing indigenous voices and reinforcing relations of marginalization and subjugation.[68] To address some of the epistemological, political, ethical, and translational problems of being a foreign researcher, I collaborated with Colombian researchers from the University of Medellín, the University of Antioquia, and the University of the North (Uninorte). They informally advised me on my selection of cases, helped me to understand the Medellín context, directed me to invaluable existing research, generously shared their contacts, and invited me to collaborate with them on some participatory research workshops that informed my analysis.

Henry Giroux writes that thinking across porous intellectual and cultural borders "allows one to critically engage the struggle over those territories, spaces, and contact zones where power operates to either expand or to shrink the distance and connectedness among individuals, groups, and places. . . . At stake here is the possibility of imagining and struggling for new forms of civic courage and citizenship that expand the boundaries of a global democracy."[69] This study represents multiple, though not exhaustive, border crossings, including geographical, cultural, linguistic, and intellectual. My "partial view"[70] is informed not only by my privileged subjectivity as a white, highly educated researcher from the United States, but also by my background as an advocate and/or practitioner of participatory media and communication for social change in the United States, Kenya, Tanzania, Mexico, and other postcolonial contexts. It is also informed by my more recent work as a professor at a Hispanic Serving Institution and an Asian American, Native American, and Pacific Islander Serving Institution with a large percentage of low-income, first-generation college students. Lastly, it is shaped by my commitment to participatory research, which informed some of my fieldwork.[71] Working across this range of contexts has forced me to reckon with the complex relationship(s) between voice and privilege, two factors that greatly shape participation and its outcomes. This book is in part a product of that reckoning.

Throughout this book, my use of the terms "citizen" and "citizenship" are not confined to the legal status conferred by nation-states. Rather, I share Chantal Mouffe's position that we must constantly challenge normative conceptualizations of the citizen as a unified subject, and instead see it

as a fluid, historically contingent, and contested articulation of social relations.[72] Similarly, in this book, I use a broad definition of "politics," which
incorporates not only traditional, institutionalized forms of politics but
also discourses and actions explicitly concerned with relations of power
and representation.

Overview of Chapters

In Chapter 1, I trace the proliferation of participation, focusing on digital
media and international development as two of the sectors most heavily
invested—both economically and discursively—in participation. I argue
that scholarship has tended to frame participation within binary debates
about empowerment versus exploitation and authenticity versus co-optation,
and that the proliferation of discourses of participation has weakened
its analytical and practical utility. This necessitates a rethinking of public
participation in general and of youth participation in particular. I propose
the concepts of *participatory public culture* and *polycultural civics* as analytical tools for doing so, and demonstrate their application in subsequent
chapters.

Chapter 2 illustrates that digital technologies and other tools used to
enhance participation in public life will not be effective unless they are
understood and implemented ecologically, which includes paying attention to the power relations that shape participation. This is evidenced by a
comparison of two vastly different approaches to cultivating digital citizenship in Medellín: Ciudad Comuna, a grass-roots citizens' media project,
and Medellín Digital, the municipal government's digital citizenship initiative. Contrasting these cases shows how participation and digital citizenship can be enacted in distinct ways, with different power implications. The
ideologies, practices, networks, and even software choices (i.e., open vs.
closed platforms) of these initiatives result in different conceptions of digital inclusion, citizenship, literacy, and participation that have fundamental
implications for how we cultivate participatory public cultures.

There is an undercurrent of historical amnesia in digital culture that
incessantly fixates the frame of reference on the future rather than acknowl-
edging what we can learn from the recent or even distant past. Chapter 2—
and the book as a whole—resists this tendency and shows how the past
can, and should, continue to inform our understanding of the digital present. Bridging decades of learnings from participatory communication with
more recent digital media studies, I argue that analyzing three qualities in

particular (horizontality, dialogue, and openness) helps to uncover relations of power and locate agency in the design of projects that enlist the digital to enhance public participation. Chapter 2 illustrates how digital communication is one resource that can function as a sort of "fertilizer" in an ecology of participation.

In Chapter 3, I consider how youth collectives offer alternative visions of youth citizenship, forged in the context of disillusionment and the delegitimization of traditional institutions and spaces of participation—contexts all too familiar to youth in many parts of the world today. I analyze some of the conditions that enable prosocial participation in public life, and how these can be cultivated by youth themselves as they develop their own tactics of participation. I focus first on the case of the youth-led hip-hop activist collective La Elite and the grass-roots tactics they have developed for promoting youth participation in public life. I explore how their tactics challenged the social and cultural dynamics of violence that had constrained public space, public life, and public participation for many young people.

Chapter 3 also shows that participation cannot be defined homogenously or fostered in just one way; efforts to achieve impactful participation must take into account historical, cultural, economic, and other differences between participants. This is illustrated by the Afro-Colombian cultural collective Son Batá, whose youth participants experience a marginalized, peripheral citizenship with particular barriers to participating in public life. Their participation necessarily began with a resignification of their subjectivities as youth citizens.

Widening the lens on this ecology of participation, in Chapter 4, I consider relations of power and the productive tensions between these grass-roots youth groups and state strategies of participation. In particular, I examine the case of participatory budgeting, a governing process that is increasingly popular internationally that invites citizens—including youth aged fourteen and up—to take part in deciding on local resource allocation. Participatory budgeting in Medellín shows how the institutionalization of participation may serve as a form of governmentality but may *also* expand participatory public culture, particularly for youth. The synergies and productive tensions between state strategies and grass-roots tactics of participation form a robust civic polyculture. This finding challenges overly simplistic binary claims that position grass-roots participation as "authentic" and institutionalized participation as "co-opted."

In Chapter 5, I review what these cases tell us about cultivating youth engagement in public life and the role of digital communication in supporting participatory public culture and polycultural civics. I take stock of the extent to which these grass-roots tactics and state strategies did in fact promote a more participatory public culture (especially for youth) in Medellín between 2004 and 2011, and the key factors that contributed to this—in particular, the degree of synergy and interdependencies between grass-roots youth participation and institutions of the state and civil society during this period. While Medellín's cultivation of polycultural civics can inform and inspire efforts to do so elsewhere, I note that the branding of Medellín's "transformation" has been somewhat hyperbolic; the city continues to face many of the challenges that have historically constrained youth participation in public life. Youth/citizen participation clearly is not a panacea for all of the challenges of structural inequality and violence. Yet, all of the youth interviewed for this study had experienced positive outcomes of their public participation, across individual, group, and community levels. I discuss the broader relevance of all of these findings that could be applied in other contexts, in both the Global North and South, to cultivate impactful youth participation.

Beneath the Buzzword

Youth Power in Precarious Times challenges techno-universalist discourse in the Global North by centering practices and perspectives from the so-called periphery, where innovation transpires that is often and necessarily driven by different contexts and values.[73] At a time of rapid change in communication architectures, it is urgent to find ways for knowledge produced outside of the techno-elite and other privileged circles in the Global North to inform more directly how participation is conceived and how it is either limited or enabled through various communication platforms.

Existing studies of Medellín that consider public participation tend to focus on whether government initiatives to promote it have been successful at reducing armed violence in the city; their findings are mixed.[74] This book does not focus exclusively on the question of violence, nor does it see public participation as determined primarily by institutional strategies. Instead, it highlights the indispensable role of citizen (particularly youth) networks in helping to cultivate participatory public culture, and focuses on the relationships between these grass-roots tactics and institutional strategies.

This book reflects my experiences as both a practitioner and scholar of participatory communication and digital media. It is the result of my efforts to grapple with the slipperiness of the concept of participation, and to find an antidote to the technocentrism of much of the rhetoric of youth empowerment in the digital age. It is my hope that it not only advances debates about youth participation, but is also, as my Colombian friends might say, *propositivo* (proactive, proposing action). I offer this to help recuperate and redefine the concept of participation, digging beneath the buzzword to see the conditions that enable prosocial participation in public life and how it might bring about more equitable and just societies.

Chapter One

From Participation
to Polycultural Civics

I n a 2009 video address to Facebook users, founder and CEO Mark Zuckerberg announced, "The Facebook community has grown a lot over the last few years, and at 200 million, this population would be the fifth largest country in the world, just ahead of Brazil. A community that large and engaged needs a more open process, and a voice in governance. That's why a month ago, we announced a more transparent and democratic approach to governing the Facebook site."[1] Zuckerberg's address was a call to Facebook users to participate by voting on new "governance" policies for the Facebook platform. And yet, to this day, Facebook (which in 2018 reported more than 2.2 billion monthly active users) remains a key example of a social media platform that highly constrains user participation in decisions about how the platform is designed and managed.[2] Ironically, in April 2018, Zuckerberg found himself testifying before the United States Congress about the company's lack of transparency in how the personal data of up to eighty-seven million of its users was shared with the political strategy firm Cambridge Analytica, which used the data to influence the outcome of the 2016 U.S. presidential election.[3]

Capitalizing on participation is central to most social media business models; a great deal of social and economic capital has been wielded through the trope and its implied connection to democratic practice. Consider, for example, participatory marketing, which harnesses consumers' free labor for the development of brand content and even new products.

The marketing agency Flock Associates' description of their 2010 participatory marketing campaign for Mountain Dew—dubbed "Dewmocracy"—was as follows: "We proposed that the brand give the people their due—it was to be the ultimate Dewmocracy . . . with the ultimate goal of creating an elixir that will restore choice to the people. [Online game] players worked together to design the color, flavor, and feel of their elixir that will ultimately become the next Mountain Dew product. . . . The people's voices were heard. . . . Consumers not only voted once a day but . . . Band Digital brought forth on this continent a new Dew, conceived in liberty."[4] This kind of rhetoric conflating consumer interactivity with democratic participation, voice, and empowerment has been a hallmark of social media marketing.[5]

"Participation" has been fashioned a new communicative norm in the digital age. It has been used to describe practices ranging from crowdsourcing solutions for reality TV show challenges to solutions for real-life civic problems; from providing citizen journalism for CNN broadcasts to youth media projects with social justice agendas; and from fan remixing of pop culture content to "participatory marketing" of products such as Doritos chips. Even surveillance has become "participatory."[6] Such practices often target young people in particular, and they frequently conflate a loosely defined sense of participation with democratic practice.

Use of the term "participation" has thus become increasingly ahistorical and imprecise, particularly in commercial contexts, but also in the fields of media studies, communication studies, and international development. Participation is not inherently good in and of itself, nor does it stand outside of history, culture, and relations of power. Participation has become—to borrow from George Yúdice's work—an *expedient* concept utilized as a discursive and practical resource across a range of contexts. In other words, invoking participation has become a useful way of justifying and legitimating particular economies and relations of power.[7] In particular, the ways in which participation has been easily sutured with neoliberal ideology and taken up by commercial interests is a concern for those who see—and use—it as a tool for promoting social justice.[8] What's more, the revelations of Edward Snowden, WikiLeaks, Mark Zuckerberg, Cambridge Analytica, and others regarding the security and privacy implications of participation in an age of globalized digital surveillance have cast shadows over the so-called participatory zeitgeist.[9] Yet, it remains a crucial concept for understanding, structuring, challenging, and reconfiguring relations of power.

The concept of participation is not a product of the twenty-first or even twentieth century, but has a much longer history that can be traced back to the earliest forms of democracy.[10] In the late 1960s and 1970s, participation served as a central organizing concept for leftist social movements in both the Global North and South—from pro-democracy movements and struggles by ethnic minorities for greater inclusion and equal rights, to campaigns for workers' rights; from alternative and community media, to such theater and art movements as Dadaism and Situationism, the community arts movement, and other countercultural movements.[11] In these cases, participation was wielded as a challenge to existing relations of power. Youth participation also became a key concern of the late twentieth century, particularly in the West; in 1989, the United Nations' Convention on the Rights of the Child enshrined that both children and young people have a fundamental human right to participate in matters affecting them within the context of schools, local communities, and civic and public institutions.

Several factors help explain why the episteme of participation has proliferated in the West. These factors include the growing disillusionment with traditional politics and government institutions, especially among youth; the international dominance of neoliberal ideology; and the resulting reduction of public services and institutions in much of the Global North and South, disproportionately impacting the poor. In the wake of more than three decades of the dominance of neoliberal capitalism globally, the growth of surveillance culture, and the widening gap between the rich and the poor, the proliferation of discourses of participation is perhaps not surprising.[12] Economic, educational, and political disenfranchisement are the norm for hundreds of millions of youth—and many other people—today. While nearly half of the world's population is under the age of thirty, less than 6 percent of its parliamentarians are under thirty-five years old.[13] Against the backdrop of these contradictions, participation has emerged as a salient concept across many sectors, particularly those aimed at or concerned with young people.

In 2012, Christopher Kelty wrote, "We proliferate ways of governing ourselves and others as we proliferate these tools, technologies, platforms, or networks and in the process change what it means (and meant) to interact, vote, and protest. Participating in Twitter, or Facebook, or Free Software is not the same thing as participating in democracy, but it does change what democracy will become."[14] Kelty's words read differently and with a more ominous valence since the 2016 U.S. presidential election. Yet, as the techno-elites of the Global North continue to proliferate new "ways of governing ourselves and others," his assessment is still apt. Now more than ever, we need robust analytical tools for critically understanding these discourses, practices, and platforms of participation, as well as their nuanced relationships to power—analytical tools that account for views and experiences from the so-called peripheries, which are often the most dramatically impacted by them. This chapter argues for the recuperation of participation as an analytical and practical tool, through the concepts of participatory public culture and polycultural civics.

The case of Medellín prompts us to think about on- and offline modes of participating in public life, ranging from grass-roots to institutional initiatives—and the complicated but often productive relationship between these. Within this ecology, discourses and practices of participation function as resources for different actors and agendas. Upon scrutiny, what emerges is not a binary between good and bad, empowering or exploitative participation, but rather productive tensions whose promises lie in the gray area in between. Participation can operate as a hegemonic strategy as well as a counter-power tactic, and the relationship between the two can enable (or hinder) participation in public life.

Participatory Public Culture

Michel de Certeau used the terms "strategies" and "tactics" to analyze power and resistance in everyday cultural practices. In de Certeau's sense, the term "strategies" describes mechanisms of institutionalized power, such as those of the state. He uses the term "tactics" to describe noninstitutional (or even anti-institutional) efforts by those outside of established positions of power: "The space of a tactic is the space of the other. Thus it must play on and with a terrain imposed on it and organized by the law of a foreign power. . . . It takes advantage of 'opportunities' and depends on them. . . . It must vigilantly make use of the cracks that particular conjunctions open in the surveillance of the proprietary powers. It poaches in them. In short, a tactic is an art of the weak."[15] De Certeau was not specifically theorizing participation; this is my adaptation. I use these terms dialectically rather than as a binary, understanding tactics and strategies as mutually constitutive. Their boundaries are porous and constantly negotiated in relation to each other; their enactments shape and reshape the terrain of power and participation.[16]

Similarly, public cultures are also porous and contentious; they are not unified, bounded spheres. Public cultures reflect the commonly held meanings that shape a society; they are produced through the discourses and practices that give meaning to social, cultural, civic, and political life. They legitimate particular institutions and relations of power. They are terrains of struggle over meaning and power among multiple, diverse publics.[17] Drawing on theoretical and practical insights from studies of participatory communication, participatory culture, and participatory politics/civics in both the Global North and South, I characterize a *participatory public culture* as one with *significant opportunities for horizontal decision making, based in practices of dialogic communication with low barriers to participation, through which issues of public consequence are negotiated. It is one in which the voices, interests, and participation of non-hegemonic groups are valued.* Cultivating participatory public cultures requires lowering barriers to participation (particularly for marginalized groups), developing the skills and capacities to participate, and creating spaces and cultures of participation. Once youth (and other citizens) are engaged and have a space to express their voices, it is crucial to consider the extent to which these voices can have a direct influence over decisions that affect their well-being, and how to strengthen that influence. The relationship between public institutions and (youth) citizens plays a significant role in determining this.

The role of institutions as gatekeepers of public knowledge and participation has been rapidly changing. In Western societies, the weakening of traditional social, political, and cultural institutions and the fragmentation of media markets in late twentieth-century Western societies has led to, as W. Lance Bennett put it, "different conceptions of membership, identification, and commitment."[18] Whereas previous generations often turned to institutional membership such as leagues, unions, and political parties to express their public selves, in many of today's democratic societies, contemporary youth engagement in public culture often appears less related to government or civic institutions and more to personal interests, social networks, and cultural activism. It is frequently enacted through informal, noninstitutionalized, non-hierarchical (horizontal) networks enabled by digital communication.[19] It is clear that we can no longer—if indeed we ever could—constrain our understanding of public participation to institutional participation such as voting and party or organization membership without missing large swaths of the picture of public culture today. But this is not to say that these institutions have been rendered irrelevant to youth participation in public life.

In Colombia, studies of youth engagement reflect trends similar to those seen in the United States and globally: youth's trust in government and public institutions is relatively low, as is membership in formalized civic organizations. Their skepticism of traditional political and government institutions, and their disenchantment with the country's clientelist political culture, runs deep.[20] In Medellín, this was the result of many factors, including the government's failure to contain narcotrafficking and other forms of violence; controversies over ties and pacts between state and paramilitary actors; clientelism, corruption, and elitism; military operations that indiscriminately affected civilians; and widely criticized initiatives to demobilize paramilitary fighters. The legitimacy of the state and perceptions of formal political processes were severely compromised, which required—and catalyzed—a new approach to the role of local government institutions in public life.[21] That new approach was one of the factors that helped cultivate a more participatory public culture in Medellín.

Public participation is largely shaped by communicative practices. The Brazilian educator and philosopher Paulo Freire described participation as being "an exercise in voice, in having voice, in involvement, in decision making at certain levels of power . . . a right of citizenship."[22] Heavily shaped by Freire's work from the 1970s onward, participatory communication was practiced in various settings around the world as a dialogic, transformative process of collective communication starting at the grass roots and aimed at solving problems in a community. These practices are distinct from traditional development communication because of their emphasis on the collective rather than the individual, on horizontal over vertical communication, on consciousness raising over persuasion, and on amplifying voices that are not typically heard or valued in public decision-making processes.[23]

In Latin America, the field of participatory communication emerged first in the late 1940s in the form of community media and then evolved as a critical response to the dominant modernist paradigm of development that was advocated by multinational development and financial institutions from the Global North.[24] In 1994, Juan Díaz Bordenave published "Participative Communication as Part of Building the Participative Society," arguing that in Latin America, "We have witnessed the gradual movement from an almost exclusively *diffusion [transmission] approach* to a *group communication* approach and, more recently, to a *participative approach*, not in the commercial media, but in what is called *popular communication*." Arguing that media participation should not be reserved solely for professionals, he emphasized that "Communication media can act as tools for diagnosis . . . [and] problem articulation among persons, groups, and communities."[25]

Robert Huesca calls this movement "the Latin American challenge" to top-down approaches to development communication.[26] A central concern of participatory communication in Latin America and other parts of the Global South since the mid-twentieth century has been to reconfigure relations of power in and through the communication process—specifically, through horizontal, dialogical, and participatory processes that emphasize citizen (especially marginalized) voices.[27]

Participatory communication exemplifies what Nick Couldry describes as a commitment to voice as a strategic value; individual and collective expression is understood to be part of building strong and just communities.[28] This is particularly important in the wake of neoliberalism, which has damagingly privileged economic logic over voice, democratic participation, and other values. Couldry argues that neoliberalism created a "crisis of voice," or what Jan Servaes and Rolien Hoyng call "voice-denying rationalities," characterized by a lack of opportunities for citizen voices to directly impact policy making.[29] Equating voice with empowerment implies that voice can be—and is—*heard* by hegemonic networks of power, enough to influence their decision making. Medellín's two Compromiso Ciudadano (Citizens' Commitment) administrations (2004–2011) represented remarkable, if varyingly successful, strategies by some state actors to listen to and increase the impact of marginalized voices. At the same time, marginalized groups were using participatory communication and culture to amplify their own voices and exert influence.

There are, of course, limits and obstacles to inclusion and "voice" in public culture. Particular voices (often linked to particular types of bodies, such as those of color or female bodies) face particular obstacles to expressing viewpoints from positions of marginality. Accordingly, they face particular obstacles to participation in public culture. Marginalized voices must rely on modes of representation readable within dominant discourse. Self-representation (and therefore participation) is shaped by hegemonic systems of meaning,[30] though these can also be appropriated and repurposed for resistant practices.

From Ladders of Participation to Polycultural Civics

How do we know if citizen participation is working? Scholars and practitioners of participatory communication and participatory development have tended to define degrees, levels, or "ladders" of participation to distinguish "pseudo" or "minimalist" versions of participation from "authentic" or "maximalist" versions of participation.[31] In Sherry Arnstein's classic ladder of participation model, each rung represents a greater degree of participant control over decision making and resources that affect their well-being, ranging from participation as "manipulation" to full "citizen control."[32] Similarly, Andrea Cornwall's spectrum model ranges from "functional participation," in which participants are positioned as "beneficiaries" in order to secure compliance and legitimacy, to "transformative participation," in which participants are positioned as "citizens" and treated as agents of change.[33] Such models pit purportedly authentic, empowering, and counter-hegemonic participation against co-opted, pseudo participation that is seen as exploitative and hegemonic.[34] These models are useful for identifying relations of power in broad strokes through a simple schematic, and for making certain definitional distinctions between different degrees of participation. However, such models are linear and one-dimensional, and can be overly normative—reducing the scope of how participation can be enacted and contested, and how it may serve as a resource differently for different actors. The same is often true for efforts to understand participation in digital media studies. These newer models for analyzing participation continue to rely on a binary of strong or weak participation rather than exploring the multivalent relationships between different mechanisms of participation.[35]

Studies of digital media and youth make the important observation that youth participation works best when it is interest driven; that is, valuing youth's interests, identities, and social and cultural relationships is crucial to encouraging their civic/political engagement.[36] A key influence on this work, Henry Jenkins's concept of "participatory culture" helped catalyze a rethinking of the relationship between young people's consumption of popular culture and their civic/political engagement.[37] Jenkins and his colleagues have documented, for example, how some youth are drawn in to civic/political engagement through pop culture fandoms, or remix popular culture content for political and counter-hegemonic meaning making.[38] They define a participatory culture as one with low barriers to entry, strong support for creating and sharing one's cultural work, informal mentorship, and social connection.[39] This work spawned the concepts of "participatory politics" and "participatory civics," which are understood in this instance to be more interactive, peer-based, horizontally networked, and less tied to formal institutions than manifestations of political and civic engagement prior to the digital age.[40] Examples might include the movement to defeat the Stop Online Piracy Act, the Harry Potter Alliance, the Occupy movements, the Indignados movement in Spain, the protests in the Middle East dubbed the Arab Spring, and the Black Lives Matter, Me Too, and March For Our Lives movements in the United States, among others. Researchers of participatory politics note a significant relationship between youth's interest-driven online activities (which connect them to peers with shared interests and introduce them to causes) and their civic/political engagement.[41] This work has been largely U.S.-centric, however, and framed by a focus on digitally mediated participation.

Young people's interests in hip-hop, dance, storytelling, and other social activities have certainly played a role in Medellín's participatory public culture, as I explore in Chapter 3. Yet, while helpful in many ways, none of the approaches just described were comprehensive enough to explain the case of Medellín and what it can teach us about cultivating participatory public culture in the digital age. Participation in public life can be enacted in both hegemonic and counter-hegemonic ways (sometimes simultaneously); we need to understand better how these are interrelated and the productive tensions between them. In other words, we need to think about participation more ecologically to understand the ways in which relationships between multiple actors structure the possibilities and limits of participation. It is these relationships that may determine the outcomes of participation, and it is these relationships that are the focus of this book, through the lens of *polycultural civics*.

In agriculture, polyculture (as opposed to monoculture) farming is the practice of cultivating multiple, distinct crops in the same space in ways that enhance the overall ecosystem.[42] We can think about the productive tensions in the relationships between noninstitutional/grass-roots tactics and institutional strategies of participation as—potentially—polycultural. I adapt this term here to understand participation as a resource within a sociopolitical ecology, one that can be cultivated in different ways at multiple levels of society from the grass roots to institutions—and through the relationships between these.[43]

As an analytic, polycultural civics avoids technological determinism by not confining the analysis of participation to digital cultures or technologies alone, but instead identifying the kinds of participation that shifts in the mediascape may support in relation to cultivating a more participatory public culture. In some instances, different cultivations of participation may be in tension with each other, and in other instances, they may be compatible or mutually reinforcing—even symbiotic. I found both cases in Medellín, with a noteworthy degree of synergy between some institutional strategies and grass-roots tactics. For example, discourses and practices of participation in Medellín's participatory budgeting process operate as a form of governmentality or social control that contains particular forms of citizenship, knowledge, and power relations and bolsters the legitimacy of the state. At the same time, the youth groups I describe in Chapters 2 and 3 tactically engaged in this institutionalized space of participation, challenged it in ways that offered alternative forms of citizenship and public participation, and, in so doing, strengthened their positions as cultural and political change agents. This is one example of the potential of polycultural civics. To understand polycultural civics in Medellín, we must first consider why youth came to play such a key role in its ecology of participation.

Youth Power and Participation in Medellín

The concept of "youth" itself is a socially constructed, fluid category that is culturally and historically contingent. As a demographic category, youth typically refers to young people between the stages of childhood and early adulthood, often correlated to a range of ages between fourteen and thirty.[44] This range changes by context. In Medellín, the category of *juventud* (youth) legally refers to "a social group between ages 14 and 26 years . . . whose members are defined as rights-bearing subjects with their own characteristics that are not only biological, psychosocial and cultural, but also those that are constructed from political, social, and economic factors that influence their recognition and forms of appearing in the public sphere."[45] This is a compelling definition for reasons that will become clear over the course of this book.

Beyond a demographic signifier, the category of youth is a social imaginary vested with meanings that differ across societies and change over time.[46] Since the postwar period, these imaginaries in the United States have ranged from youth as vulnerable, corruptible, and delinquent to hip and trendsetting; from a group that should be sheltered from society to a key market demographic; and from a threat to political and economic stability to the hope for the future of nations.[47] These imaginaries are also racially constructed; they manifest differently for white youth than for youth of color. Soo Ah Kwon traces how youth of color in the United States have been paradoxically inscribed both as "at risk" and as key agents of change by state and civil society institutions. She points out that both these imaginaries have served as forms of social control to manage the problems (though not necessarily the root causes) of poverty, racism, and other structural inequalities.[48]

Similar logics underlie some of the strategies of the municipal government of Medellín and its efforts to counter armed violence. Medellín's urban youth—particularly poor, male youth and youth of color—have been ascribed similar subjectivities, not only stigmatized by the media and the criminal justice system as likely criminal gang members, but also targeted as potential change agents by youth development initiatives. Neoliberal logics of self-governance and "responsibilization,"[49] and the so-called war on drugs that boomed in the 1980s and 1990s, have thus had some parallel impacts on poor, urban youth in both countries despite the differing contexts. Rossana Reguillo further notes that the conditions that shape the subjectivities of Latin American youth today include structural poverty and rising unemployment, the increasing dominance of the market, the explosion of communication technologies, globalization, migration, narcotrafficking, organized crime, and the disrepute of traditional institutions (including political parties, churches, and unions).[50]

Just as there are many conceptions of the category of youth, there are many different reasons why scholars, policy makers, and others see the civic/political engagement of young people as important. Several start from the instrumentalist question of what engaged youth can offer society. In democratic theory, a healthy democracy requires at the very least the electoral participation of those citizens who are of legal voting age, and youth participation in organizations and community service during adolescence has been found to predict adult political behaviors, including voting.[51]

While youth participation may function as a form of social control, it may also help to enhance political and socioeconomic equality. Without their direct participation in public life, the particular interests and needs of youth are unlikely to be well represented. From a more youth-centric perspective, then, participation may also be conceived as a basic human right (as in the UN's Convention on the Rights of the Child) and/or as a tool for social justice and protest. Young people's lives are often greatly impacted by public policy, but their ability to influence it is relatively limited. This is of particular concern for youth from marginalized groups (e.g., urban youth of color, low-income immigrant youth, etc.), who are more likely to suffer prejudices and criminalization through public policies.[52] Yet, there is also a higher opportunity cost for youth with limited resources to participate in public life, as they must dedicate more time to paid employment opportunities. Youth are clearly not a homogenous group with a consistent set of public concerns and equal opportunities to address them—and disparities in opportunities for public participation can further perpetuate existing inequalities.[53]

Disengaged youth are a societal concern for several reasons. At the state level, higher numbers of disengaged youth tend to correlate with dysfunctional, less representative government. At the community level, communities with higher rates of engagement are more likely to be better at problem solving and self-governing. At the individual level, civic engagement in adolescence tends to correlate with successful personal development, sense of self-efficacy, and leadership skills.[54] When we consider that there is disproportionately high population growth in this age demographic globally, low rates of youth engagement raise concerns across all these levels, as well as on an international scale.[55] So, while the justifications vary, the significance of youth participation in public life is a topic of global concern and one that has gained renewed attention in the twenty-first century, given the rapid changes in forms of social organization brought about by globalization and the rise of digitally networked communication technologies.

In Colombia, the participation of youth and other citizens in public life has become a central concern to actors across various levels of society, ranging from the grass roots to the government.[56] This is even reflected in the Colombian Constitution of 1991; Article 45 mandates that "the State and society guarantee the active participation of youth in the public and private agencies that are responsible for the protection, education, and advancement of youth."[57] The historical antecedents that help explain this remarkable focus on youth/citizen participation in public life, including the history of Colombia's internal conflict and how this undermined the authority of the elite-run state, are detailed in the Introduction and Chapter 4.

In Medellín, led by Mayor Sergio Fajardo, the Compromiso Ciudadano administration (2004–2007) faced the legacy of distrust of the state by positioning citizen participation as central to reestablishing the legitimacy of the government and making the city more governable—thus prioritizing technologies of participation over force.[58] They rebranded the city as a participatory one in which all citizens—including and especially youth—would actively be engaged in, be responsible for, and benefit from its development.

Seeing this institutionalization of participation as purely a strategy of the state, however, is problematic. The structures and boundaries of states are not monolithic but porous and changing; they are comprised of particular people holding particular ideologies, in particular configurations of power. The two Compromiso Ciudadano administrations were composed largely of community organizers, academics, and activists (rather than elites from the two traditional political parties), whose mere presence in the municipal administration signified a marked shift in the political culture. Many of them made an intentional effort to reduce the gap between grass-roots organizing and government institutions.

In certain cases, this facilitated greater inclusion of youth in civic/political spaces. For decades prior, youth participation in public life had been dramatically constrained by armed violence related to narcotrafficking and the urbanization of Colombia's national conflict, particularly in lower-income neighborhoods. In many instances, youth "participation" in public life was enacted through armed violence. Gang members typically between the ages of fifteen and nineteen (and sometimes younger) were hired as *sicarios* (hitmen) by narcotraffickers.[59] They were dispatched to kill journalists, politicians, judges, human rights workers, activists, and others who had become enemies of the drug cartel by exposing, prosecuting, or otherwise challenging their operations. The phenomenon spread beyond narcotrafficking as a range of actors, including politicians and citizens, hired *sicarios* to settle feuds through the *mercado de la muerte* (death market).[60] While these gang members were a minority of Medellín's youth, the impact of their actions dramatically affected youth across the city and society at large.

In April 1984, two young *sicarios* hired by the Medellín drug cartel murdered the Minister of Justice Rodrigo Lara Bonilla in a move to stop the Colombian government's legalization of the extradition of narcotraffickers to the United States. One of the assassins was killed; the other, sixteen-year-old Byron de Jesús Velásquez, was captured and became the media's poster child for a new youth subject—the narco hitman. Representing both the increasingly visible impact of narcotrafficking on Colombian society and the protagonism of poor youth within it, this was a pivotal moment in a trend toward "public and media representations of youth as social threat and criminal *other*."[61] It was also one of the justifications for the Colombian government's subsequent war against the Medellín cartel. A negative imaginary of youth from lower socioeconomic strata was perpetuated by local, national, and foreign media; as Pilar Riaño-Alcalá describes, young *sicarios* had become the public face of death.[62] Youth bodies—particularly poor, male bodies, but also plastic surgery-perfected female bodies—became commodified within a market of death, territoriality, and media spectacle. For their part, some young women seeking financial resources and social prestige increasingly altered their bodies to appeal to the growing esthetic of narco-culture bling.[63]

Fear and silence came to characterize much of public life in Medellín by the late 1980s/early 1990s. Many community-based organizations disappeared as armed gangs increasingly controlled life in Medellín's *barrios* (neighborhoods, typically referring to low-income neighborhoods).[64] In the poorer neighborhoods of the city, those youth not directly involved in the violence were often unwillingly inscribed in it through family or other social connections, or through their physical addresses. Neighborhoods were divided into gang territories, and *fronteras invisibles* (invisible borders) were enforced by warring gangs with the threat of death. The physical mobility of youth through the city—even between adjacent neighborhoods or blocks—was severely restricted, making it even more difficult to pursue formal employment and educational opportunities. Some youth found it necessary to leave their homes and birthplaces to avoid danger by association. While the landscape of narcotrafficking and violence has changed significantly and homicide rates are much lower than their peak in the early 1990s, this dynamic of restricted mobility (and even displacement) continued and was evident at the time of my fieldwork in 2011. The *fronteras invisibles* were repeatedly cited by my young interviewees as a limiting factor in their lives, and were often a motivation for their civic/political participation.

To get a sense of what it was like to live through these dynamics as a low-income youth, I will quote one of my interviewees at length. He grew up in a low-income neighborhood in the northeastern part of Medellín. He was twenty-six years old at the time of the interview in 2011.

> From age 12 or 14, I was involved a lot with problems in the neighborhood, like violence, gangs, drugs; this was characteristic of where I lived ... but I felt that it wasn't my spirit. . . . At this age, in adolescence, I felt the need to find a place, a *referente* [example or role model] and for many of my friends, it seemed that the *referente* was the gang leader, who established themselves as paternal figures. . . . I am an only child, without a father and my mother was always working so it was also about finding paternal male figures in them, emotionally. . . .
>
> Various members of our family had gotten heavily involved in the violence and the conflict; five of my cousins were murdered . . . and the average life span of my cousins, for example, was between seventeen and eighteen. The last who was killed, which was about fifteen days ago, made it to twenty-nine.

At times, I have flashbacks of my life, of moments of violence in the barrio. For example, I remember clearly once when I was a kid, I was sleeping at home, in my room, where there was a window onto the street. One day a group of *milicias* [militia] arrived, which is like a sort of urban guerrilla, and started shooting at the house. I was in the first bed next to the window, and I woke up and saw the bullets passing by. My mom grabbed me and dragged me away. . . .

When I was finishing high school, something really bad happened in my neighborhood, more specifically in my family. . . . [T]wo cousins were sent to prison, but they had had a certain power in the barrio, in the area, they were part of a gang. When one of them got out he was murdered right outside of the prison, killed with another four people including his sister. . . . [W]hen they fell, we lost the protection of the family; because they'd been involved [in the gang] they had protected the family, but this protection can also become a threat. . . . [Y]ou start to become recognized as family members of the gang leader . . . so we no longer had their protection and started to be threatened. . . . By the time I started university, there was a lot of pressure, and I had to leave the barrio for four or five years, until last year I went back. The situation was so bad I had to change my appearance. . . .

In the university, I got involved with leftist movements, with very subversive and leftist factions of the country, like one of the groups that operate in the country as guerrillas, and I was very involved in the student movements. But for me, it was an intense experience because various of my friends who left [to join guerrilla activities outside of the city] ended up dead, so I realized that that wasn't the route either, even though I wanted to promote social change. . . . [B]ut in the end I said to myself, "If I left such an intense problem in the barrio, which was because of the use of arms, why do I have to be confronted with it here?" So I distanced myself from it.

Ultimately, he took up photography and joined a youth-led organization that used participatory video and photography to *desarmar mentes* (disarm minds, or change mentalities conducive to violence). These were his methods of coping with—and advocating against—the violence that had so shaped his life.[65]

Because of these kinds of dynamics faced by youth in Medellín's low-income neighborhoods, peaceful, prosocial youth participation in public life came to be seen by many as a key resource for stabilizing and developing the city. For example, at the government level, Acuerdo Municipal No. 2 de 2000 (Municipal Accord Number 2 of 2000) stated that a primary objective of the municipal government was to "strengthen the civic engagement of youth so that they become strategic actors in the city's development."[66] This fueled government and civil society initiatives working to create much-needed alternatives to gang membership for many young people. As adult-led institutions—from international nongovernmental organizations to certain government offices, to community-based organizations—attempted to organize spaces of youth participation, alternative spaces of autonomous, youth-led organizing also proliferated at the grassroots level. Cultural resistance became a primary form of youth and social movement organizing at the grass roots. The stigmatization of poor, male youth became a motivation for cultural struggle over the terms of their own representation. Some of this struggle was initiated in the poorest parts of the city by youth themselves. Together, these initiatives (ranging from religious to recreational, artistic to political) burgeoned in the 1990s; by 2007, there were nearly three hundred documented youth groups in Medellín, the majority of which had a cultural/artistic focus.[67] Medellín's crisis thus positioned youth not only as perpetrators and victims of the violence, but also as crucial agents of change in the city's development, spawning a vibrant ecology of youth organizing.

Medellín and Colombia more broadly have a long history of youth organizing through both adult-led institutions and autonomous, youth-led groups or *colectivos* (collectives). In the 1960s and 1970s, political and social movements, particularly student movements on the left, were the most visible spaces of youth political engagement.[68] The student movement in Colombia (as elsewhere) became a primary space of youth politicization and a recruiting ground for other leftist movements. Influences such as the Cuban Revolution, anti-American sentiment in response to the Vietnam War and U.S. intervention in Latin American countries, the Marxist leadership of Camilo Torres Restrepo and the growth of leftist guerrilla movements, and resistance to interventions by international financial institutions of the Global North all fueled opposition to the individualist hegemonies that were seen as propelling the stark inequalities in Colombian society. Emphasis on collective rather than individual interests gained cultural significance.[69] This collectivist orientation toward public participation was widely evident in youth groups in Medellín. What was also evident was that in several instances, the support offered to youth organizers by certain adult organizations, institutions, and the Compromiso Ciudadano's administration was crucial—when they did not try to overly control or appropriate these projects.

Participation in Medellín was not without its problems, contradictions, and limitations. My interviewees still leveled numerous critiques of policies, programs, and institutions—even, and perhaps especially, at the municipal government that had made noteworthy efforts to support youth development, participation, and leadership. Networks of violence continue to undermine forms of youth participation in public life in the city today. Yet, nearly all of my youth interviewees expressed that they had experienced a more participatory public culture in the city as a result of both grass-roots and institutional mobilizations of participation, and that this had positively benefited their lives.[70]

Recuperating Participation

In 2001, Bill Cooke and Uma Kothari published their scathing collection *Participation: The New Tyranny?*, which suggested that citizen participation in development most often amounted to co-optation and obfuscation at best, and exploitation at worst.[71] By the 1990s, "participation" had not only become central to critiques of top-down international development initiatives, it had also become mainstreamed within these same institutions and initiatives. Participatory communication was adopted by the very financial institutions, such as the World Bank, that many of its theorists and practitioners had aimed to critique and challenge.[72] Cooke and Kothari's collection offered analyses of how participation had become a sort of institutionalized orthodoxy in the field of development, illustrated by cases in which practices of participatory development maintained existing power differentials rather than challenged them. Participation, in these cases, was more of a public relations facade for multinational agencies and funders rather than a paradigm shift in how development was conceived and enacted—a critique one could also levy against many uses of "participation" by social media marketers and corporations.

In response to this book, Samuel Hickey and Giles Mohan published their collection *Participation: From Tyranny to Transformation?* in which they argued that the concept of participation can be redeemed by critically focusing on the relationships of power and inequality that structure it.[73] Hickey and Mohan contend that some of the structural conditions necessary for participatory processes to yield meaningful, positive outcomes include a state that is responsive to its citizenry and that promotes citizen–state engagement; strategies that are "multi-scaled and span political arenas," and "employ dialogic political methodologies along the lines of Habermassian deliberative democracy"; and the centering of a radical democratic and inclusive notion of citizenship.[74] Medellín presents a rare opportunity to study some of these conditions and possibilities.

To this day, the field of development is characterized by a binary debate in which advocates insist that participatory approaches are empowering and perhaps the only ethical approach to development, while critics argue that such approaches have been co-opted and repurposed by the international financial and development institutions of the Global North to help maintain their legitimacy and global dominance.[75] Far less attention has been paid to how grass-roots or noninstitutional, non-hegemonic actors may in turn co-opt institutional forms of participation to serve their own needs (in the vein of James Scott's *Weapons of the Weak*), or to the nuanced and sometimes productive tensions between these different manifestations of participation—a central focus of this book.

In digital media studies, we see a similar divide between the so-called cyberoptimists celebrating expressions of more participatory politics/civics by today's youth, while cyberpessimists see these activities as "slacktivism," "net delusion," or exploitation in a media landscape increasingly defined by data mining and surveillance.[76] Early, technologically deterministic optimism that social media would promote greater prosocial public participation has been replaced by a growing awareness that the opposite may also be true.[77] Examples are mounting and include: the reinstatement of a military dictatorship in Egypt shortly after the so-called Arab Spring; the increase in ethnic/religious violence in Sri Lanka, Myanmar, and India fueled by inflammatory content circulated by Facebook users; Edward Snowden's and WikiLeaks's revelations of unchecked Internet surveillance by the U.S. National Security Agency; and the distribution of disinformation and fake news via phony social media accounts and bots to influence elections in the United States, Europe, and elsewhere.[78]

What's more, the promises of digital participation have often been realized along existing lines of privilege and power rather than significantly challenging these. Numerous researchers have pointed out that social hegemonies, disparities, and segregations offline are frequently mirrored online. This, of course, has significant implications for the possibilities of digital citizenship and participatory public culture. The online explosion of user-generated content on platforms such as Twitter, YouTube, Instagram,

Snapchat, and Facebook does not necessarily mean that more, and different, voices are being *heard*—and when they are heard, the question is by whom and with what effect. A flood of expressions can amount to noise that ultimately drowns out voices—particularly minority voices—rather than amplifying them.[79]

Yet, it is still true that the increasingly networked mediascape affords unprecedented interactivity, mobility, searchability, speed of connectivity, the possibility of global reach, and relatively open systems of communication. These attributes of the digital mediascape have been effectively incorporated into or wielded by contemporary social and political movements and civic practices around the globe.[80] The case of Medellín offers a departure from binary debates that see digital technology as having revolutionized or destroyed public participation.

"Participation" has become at once so commonplace and variously used as to render it often meaningless. Reclaiming the utility of participation as a concept to promote more participatory public cultures necessitates less binary, more ecological thinking. It also requires reconsidering the relationship between institutions, (youth) citizens, and activist groups. The following chapters demonstrate how polycultural civics can cultivate more participatory public cultures. Participation certainly cannot be summoned into being by digital platforms alone, but digital communication technologies can function as a key resource in an ecology of participation, as I explore in the following chapter.

Chapter Two

Digitizing the Tools
of Engagement

Since the mayoral administration of Sergio Fajardo (2004–2007), Medellín, Colombia, has received global attention not only for its urban planning and citizen participation, but also for a growing digital sector. Under Fajardo, the municipal government invested heavily in cultivating "digital citizens" as a strategy to increase social inclusion and public participation, and as part of its broader development agenda to become a "digital city."[1] By 2011, major corporate actors in the Information and Communication Technology (ICT) sector, such as Microsoft and Hewlett-Packard, had taken notice of Medellín's transformation and brought some of their business operations there. Under Fajardo's successor Alonso Salazar (2008–2011), Medellín began developing what they hoped would become Latin America's largest technology district and incubator for local and international tech entrepreneurs, in an area that spans three neighborhoods near the center of the city. Some predicted Medellín might become the "Silicon Valley of Latin America."[2]

Amanda Third and Philippa Collin have argued that "digital citizenship policy and practice discourses, as they currently circulate in the Western world, work to foreclose the meanings of children's and young people's digital practices, proscribing a narrow, adult-centric and biopolitical form of citizenship for children and young people."[3] Indeed, mainstream uses of the term "digital citizenship" generally refer to norms of "appropriate" digital technology use, often implicitly or explicitly targeting children and young people to discipline their online behavior and/or to protect them from others.[4] This reduces digital citizenship to online etiquette and safety, and detaches the concept from notions of citizenship that encompass civic/political participation. A somewhat more substantive definition is offered by Karen Mossberger, Caroline Tolbert, and Ramona McNeal, who argue that digital citizenship is "the ability to participate in society online . . . [the] capacity, belonging, and the potential for political and economic engagement in society in the information age."[5] This understanding links digital citizenship with public participation. Engin Isin and Evelyn Ruppert take the concept further and argue that we should understand digital citizens as "those who make digital rights claims" through practices such as connecting, sharing, witnessing, and hacking that can be understood as acts of political struggle.[6]

Writing about citizenship more broadly, Chantal Mouffe urged us to challenge all normative conceptualizations of the citizen as a unified subject, and instead see the citizen as a fluid and contested construct, reflective of social relations and structures of power.[7] From this perspective, citizenship becomes a lens through which to explore critically how public participation is conceived, structured, policed, and contested—and how particular notions of citizenship are baked into the digital architectures of contemporary communication platforms. Digital citizenship is a polysemic and contested term that holds much at stake in how it is defined and practiced. Net neutrality debates, for instance, are not simply struggles over telecommunications policy but also over the Internet as a public sphere(s) and the terms and parameters of digital citizenship.

Medellín's municipal digital citizenship agenda took form in various ways. Most significantly, through Medellín Digital—renamed Medellín Ciudad Inteligente (Medellín A Smart City) in 2013—the local government aimed to integrate digital communication tools and practices into all of the city's public schools and into some of its processes of governance. On the other end of the spectrum, grass-roots actors, such as citizen bloggers, online community radio, and other alternative media also shaped the relationship between digital communication and participation in the city. One example is the Corporación para la Comunicación Ciudad Comuna (a double entendre that translates roughly to the City Community Communication Organization, referred to as Ciudad Comuna), a local youth-driven citizens' media project that used a variety of new and traditional media for social change. Ciudad Comuna reflects both Latin America's history of participatory communication, as well as innovative tactics in the use of digital media to promote citizen engagement. The vast differences between the institutional strategies of Medellín Digital and grass-roots tactics of Ciudad Comuna reflect divergent conceptions of digital citizenship and participation that resulted in distinct communicative architectures and practices.

Critical questioning of the dynamics that structure relations of power in the digital age has often been secondary, if not lost in techno-utopian rhetoric of participation. Too often, digital participation is conflated with meaningful participation in public life, glossing over important qualifiers such as who participates and how, who sets the parameters of this participation, and how these spaces of participation are structured. This chapter attends to these questions. It also asks more specifically what kinds of communicative practices and spaces—especially but not exclusively digital platforms—may help to promote participatory public culture. I draw on contributions from Latin American science and technology studies, though I have intentionally avoided framing my analysis of participation in this book through a primarily technological lens.

Building especially on insights from participatory communication and digital media studies, scholarship that has developed largely in isolation from one another, this chapter identifies three key potential qualities of (digital) communication that can enhance participation: horizontality, dialogue, and openness. Using these three concepts as analytical tools can help avoid technological determinism and account for power and agency in how we understand digital citizenship and participation. I illustrate this through the cases of Medellín Digital and Ciudad Comuna, showing how the horizontality, dialogue, and openness that digital communication may afford render it a sort of "fertilizer" for enhancing ecologies of participation—if digital technologies are integrated with attention to the particular local context and relations of power. Lastly, although the institutional strategies of Medellín Digital and the grass-roots tactics of Ciudad Comuna were largely disconnected, I argue that "polycultural" relationships (see Chapter 1) are possible and would help cultivate a more participatory public culture.

Although the cases of Medellín Digital and Ciudad Comuna are not comparable in scale, I contrast them in order to highlight fundamental differences and the implications for (digital) citizenship. The emphasis in subsequent chapters on participatory cultures that are not focused primarily on the digital public sphere serve as a counterpoint to the potential technocentrism of this discussion, calling into question the tendency to equate social media capacities with participation or to assume that digital citizenship is inherently participatory.

Participatory Communication in the Digital Age

Colombia, in particular, has been a nexus of participatory communication for decades, using both old and new technologies to promote individual and community empowerment, civic engagement, and social change. Participatory communication spread in Colombia and Latin America more broadly in the context of growing socioeconomic disparities, globalization, corruption, crises of legitimacy of the state, militarization, and widespread perceptions of the failure both of representative democracy and of neoliberal economic restructuring imported from (or mandated by) the Global North. Media activists pressed for democratization of the Colombian airwaves in the 1980s and 1990s, ultimately securing community media licensing policies that have enabled the growth of one of the most rich, diverse ecologies of citizens' media in the world. This activism influenced the Colombian Constitution of 1991, which—ratified well before the advent of social media—enshrined that all Colombians have the right to create their own mass media.[8] Yet, the broadcast media landscape of Colombia is largely privatized, concentrated, and elite driven. So, the Internet is—or has the potential to be—a particularly important platform for community media, political movements, and other forms of participation in public life.

Participation, as it has been theorized across many fields—from participatory communication to urban planning and development to media studies[9]—almost always implies or presupposes two-way or multidirectional *dialogue* (as opposed to one-way transmission of information) as one of its central dynamics. Well before the proliferation of the Internet, proponents of participatory communication advocated horizontal, dialogical modes of communication to promote democratic practices, more locally relevant solutions to development concerns, and greater social equity and inclusion.[10] Part of what makes participatory communication *participatory* is an emphasis on helping to amplify grass-roots and marginalized voices that are not typically heard or valued in decision-making and development processes. A frequently cited example is the Bolivian miners' network of radio stations founded in 1949, which were initiated, owned, and operated by and for local community members to share information.[11] Participatory media and communication in Latin America has developed relatively independently of any particular technology—and relatively disengaged from digital media studies—although a great deal of work has in-volved radio, video, and theater. For example, Augusto Boal pioneered the use of Brechtian, interactive theater to work with groups to solve problems in their communities by having a group act out the problem and encourag-ing the audience to intervene and play out their own ideas for solutions—a dialogical approach to community development and social change.[12] What advocates of participatory communication understood was that communi-cation is the process through which we articulate and share the meanings that shape our realities. As such, social equality requires the participation of many, rather than a few, in public communication; a society in which only the voices of the powerful are heard is clearly not a participatory society.

In the younger field of digital media studies, *horizontality* is also high-lighted as one of the most defining characteristics of digital communication and one of its most promising attributes for promoting participation.[13] The term "horizontality" in this context may refer to the openly networked struc-ture of the Internet or to particular online platforms based on what Yochai Benkler calls "peer mutualism"—"voluntaristic cooperation that does not depend on exclusive proprietary control" or on hierarchical/vertical struc-tures of command.[14] He offers Wikipedia and free/libre and open-source software (FLOSS) as two examples of peer mutualism.[15] What participatory communication historically reminds us is that horizontality is not just a technological feature of an online platform; it is also a cultural and com-municative practice that can challenge relations of power on- and offline.

If horizontality is arguably central to participatory public culture in the digital age, so too is *openness*. While digital studies scholars typically use the term to describe a technological feature of software or the Internet as a whole,[16] openness can be analyzed at three levels: content, communicative architecture (including the technologies used), and management. Open-ness in terms of content may mean being receptive to public participation in the production and editorial processes, as well as openness to a variety of thematic content and a diversity of viewpoints. Open communicative ar-chitecture may mean public administration of a website or the use of open-source software for decentralized design, coding, and management, or a communication tool such as theater, which has relatively low barriers to entry and relatively high transparency in terms of how it functions. Here again, participatory communication reminds us that openness can describe a social process, not just a technological feature. In terms of management, openness may mean public participation in key decision making for a com-munication initiative or platform.

Ample research has debunked the widespread myth that greater Internet connectivity will inherently bring about greater equality and promote democratic practices—a basic premise of many digital divide initiatives.[17] However, the capacities of digital communication systems can make possible more horizontal, open, and dialogical exchanges within and across publics, and can support subversive practices that aim to challenge less open, more hierarchical hegemonies.[18] Yet, simply expanding the technological capacities for civic/political practices to take place in the digital sphere does not guarantee a more participatory public culture.

Latin American science and technology studies have critiqued the techno-utopianism or techno-fundamentalism of Information and Communication Technology for Development (ICT4D) and corporate-backed transnational digital divide initiatives that aim to disseminate technologies from the Global North in the Global South—as in the case of Nicholas Negroponte's One Laptop Per Child initiative, the majority of which was rolled out in Latin America.[19] Beyond bringing "connectivity," technologies from the Global North also bring with them particular ideologies and possibilities baked into their design. Furthermore, these same technologies can be used to facilitate practices of censorship, surveillance, and corruption; the social practices around these technologies shape their impact. Put another way, we need to understand both the social shaping of technology (in the vein of Raymond Williams) and the ways in which these technologies embody and perpetuate a certain politics (in the vein of Langdon Winner) within particular ecologies of participation.[20]

Analytical tools such as the concepts of horizontality, dialogue, and openness are necessary to analyze critically the extent to which—and how—particular digital communication platforms and practices enhance youth/citizen agency and participatory public culture. As the following cases illustrate, the specific configurations of (digital) communication platforms for participation can and do vary widely, as do the surrounding practices of digital citizenship—and these differences determine who gets to speak, who is listening, and how power operates through these communicative spaces.[21]

Medellín Digital

In 2007, Fajardo's administration launched Medellín Digital with the aim of increasing free access to computers and the Internet in public locations.[22] The hope was that by increasing access to digital technologies and providing capacity-building trainings, Medellín Digital would promote greater social inclusion and foster entrepreneurship. This was outlined in the government's 2004–2007 Plan de Desarollo (Development Plan) to encourage "the construction of a *'Governable and Participatory Medellín'* . . . promoting citizen participation to help improve living conditions; a *'Socially Inclusive Medellín,'* contributing to the quality of education and social inclusion through access to technology; a *'Productive, [and] Competitive . . . Medellín'* . . . [to meet] the competitive demands of the global economy; and a *'Medellín Integrated with the Region and the World,'* allowing Medellín to interact with the world through ICTs."[23] Despite having the second-largest economy in Colombia (after Bogotá), Medellín was only the sixth highest in terms of computer use at the time.[24] It was ranked second-to-last out of twenty-five major Latin America cities in terms of having "digital citizens," conceived in that instance as a populace with easy access to, and making regular use of, digital communication technologies.[25]

A 2013 global study of public access to ICTs in low- and middle-income countries found that more than 50 percent of survey respondents' use of computers would decrease if public access venues were not available. For many, free public access venues provided their first opportunities to use computers and the Internet, and were seen as the most important places for developing their computer and Internet skills.[26] Medellín Digital's initial focus was on infrastructure for citywide public access to broadband connectivity. Through contracts with Microsoft and later Hewlett-Packard, Medellín Digital created computer labs with high-speed Internet connections and Microsoft software called *aulas abiertas* (open classrooms) in public schools that were meant to be open to both students and the broader community, and installed computers with free Internet access in public libraries, business centers, and government locations. Medellín Digital then began to offer digital literacy trainings, which typically included Internet browsing skills and the use of Microsoft programs such as Word, PowerPoint, and Excel. In some instances they also taught publishing and multimedia skills, such as blogging or basic digital animation, primarily to students.

Medellín Digital also developed online platforms and content, including what they described as "a network of portals that supports the construction of the digital city through the development of content and services for citizens, and active participation through the use of ICTs."[27] The five portals included one for education, one for entrepreneurship, one for culture, the network of public libraries, and Medellín Digital's own portal containing municipal government content, including "e-government" services, such as online tax payment forms and procedures, and vehicle registration. Online "tools for the digital citizen" included services such as filing for passports and citizenship cards; digital literacy trainings (e.g., a guide to browsing and searching the Internet, and creating an email account); and information on employment and educational opportunities.

To familiarize citizens with the portals and to reach some of the outermost neighborhoods of the city that still lacked broadband access, Medellín Digital launched El Circular Digital (the Digital Circular, or Digital Circuit), a mobile computer lab on a bus, which traveled what they called a "route of inclusion." Through basic training in computer and Internet use, as well as e-government and other services available through the portals, the Circular Digital aimed to help "convert [users] into digital citizens."[28] Despite undoubtedly good intentions, such rhetoric is reminiscent of what some have called "digital colonialism."[29]

So, what precisely is meant by "inclusion" and "digital citizens" in this context? In 2008, Medellín was awarded first place for "e-Inclusion" by the fifth Premio Iberoamericano de Ciudades Digitales (Latin American Digital Cities Prize). Organizers explained that "for a Digital City to have meaning, citizens should have digital access, that is, they should have rapid, easy access to diverse telecommunications networks."[30] This vision of a digital city reflects a techno-fundamentalist view, conflating access to digital technologies with development and citizenship, and ignoring the cultures and practices of use that imbue such technologies with their meanings and ultimately determine their impacts.[31] Similarly, in a 2009 study of twenty-five Latin American cities by Motorola and Convergencia Research, Medellín was ranked first (tied with five other cities) for "participation," defined as "actors using technology to voice opinions, participate, propose ideas and express themselves. In the case of public administration websites, it consists of citizen participation, whether entering into discussion forums or surveys about municipal services, or the existence of blogs and other Web 2.0 tools."[32] The specific modalities of citizen participation and the goals or ideal outcomes of this participation remained undefined; the existence of Web 2.0 tools was taken to represent participation—with little detail of the purpose, actual use, and outcomes of using those tools.

As is frequently the case in technocentric (and particularly in commercially driven) discourses of digital media and democratization, participation was simplistically conflated with technology use and hollowed of its political significance, as well as of any discussion of the communicative practices

2.1   Medellín Digital's mobile computer lab *El Circular Digital*. Source: Eliana Patricia Orrego R.

and the structures of power within which it is embedded. Medellín Digital was not a participatory communication initiative, but citizen participation was one of its stated aims—specifically, "the active participation [of citizens] through the use of ICTs."[33] And yet, as Nico Carpentier points out, these kinds of digital divide initiatives often focus primarily on access to technology, whereas participatory communication initiatives tend to focus on equalizing relations of power in decision-making processes.[34] The use of a rhetoric of participation to market Medellín Digital was in some ways misleading about its actual impact, particularly if we understand participation as tied to more equalized relations of power. An analysis of Medellín Digital through the concepts of horizontality, dialogue, and openness reveals a quite limited conception of participation.

According to Medellín Digital, its culture portal provided "participatory tools" and a "space for dialogue."[35] Yet, Medellín Digital's portals tended to function most often as channels for mass communication, with far fewer opportunities for horizontal communication or dialogue. Medellín Digital's e-government services offered citizens information and provided instruments to ease bureaucratic processes within existing government services, but they did not enable two-way or multidirectional communication with

government representatives.[36] Nor did they create spaces of citizen participation in governance. For example, the portals offered little in the way of
digital tools to support Medellín's participatory budgeting beyond providing limited, basic information about the process. This was surprising, since
participatory budgeting was one of the city's flagship examples of citizen
participation, and elsewhere such practices have been enhanced with digital communication technologies.[37]

By 2012, the existing data on Medellín Digital's programs showed mixed
results. In an interview in early 2012, a senior Medellín Digital staff person
expressed that they were still hoping for a greater number of unique users,
and that interactivity in the portals was not yet as significant as hoped.[38]
The staff person attributed this in part to technical glitches in the portals,
as well as a lack of a culture of *produsage* in Medellín—the latter justifica-
tion being debatable, given the significant number of citizens'/community
media projects in the city.[39] Medellín Digital had had the greatest impact
in the realm of education, but indicators remained limited to the number
of people trained and the skill levels attained, rather than how these have
affected the use of the technologies outside of the trainings or participation in civic/political life. Independent researchers found that beyond students, the broader community was the least impacted by Medellín Digital's
programs, and only about 9 percent of the *aulas abiertas* users were non-
student community members.[40] Further, approximately just one third of
teachers who had benefited from trainings reported being able to use independently the e-government services intended by Medellín Digital to enhance
digital citizenship.[41]

The extent to which Medellín Digital succeeded in converting Medellín
into a "digital city" with more "digital citizens" was thus debatable, further
complicated by the lack of clear and consistent measures of what either
concept entails. The initiative increased free connectivity to the Internet,
primarily for those with small businesses, teachers, and students using
the *aulas abiertas* at public educational institutions.[42] However, by 2011,
Medellín's ratio of Internet users per capita nearly exactly paralleled that
of the Colombian population as a whole, signaling that Medellín did not
yet stand out in Colombia for having an exceptionally digital populace.[43]
Further, these measures say very little about the actual digital capacities
and activities of the population, and nothing about the extent to which it
enhanced participation in public life. Through various trainings on the use
of online tools for creating user-generated content and digital animation,
Medellín Digital encouraged content production by users rather than just

the consumption of information, though not to the extent of citizens' media projects such as Ciudad Comuna.[44]

Furthermore, the ways in which decisions were made about Medellín Digital's platforms were relatively vertical and closed. Carpentier distinguishes between *content-related participation* (e.g., posting user-generated content) and *structural participation* (e.g., having a say in the management and policy of communication/media platforms or organizations). Structural participation entails greater participant control over the system (not just the content), and as such, it can be considered a more "maximalist" version of participation (i.e., participants have control over the architecture, administration, and management of the media platform).[45] Structural participation in the development and/or management of Medellín Digital's platforms would have allowed participants some degree of control over the terms and spaces of their participation, in addition to its content. Although the *aulas abiertas* were managed to an extent by local committees at each site rather than centrally by Medellín Digital, overall, decisions about Medellín Digital's content and strategies remained centralized, with limited participation by members of the communities they served.

Despite using social media tools that enabled multidirectional communication, Medellín Digital's platforms and content thus tended toward unilateral vertical communication and the delivery of information (the transmission model), rather than horizontal communication, dialogue, and openness (the participatory communication model). In Chapter 1, I defined participatory public culture as one that values the voices, interests, and participation of non-hegemonic groups, and has significant opportunities for horizontal decision making based in practices of dialogic communication with low barriers to participation. In terms of cultivating the conditions for a more participatory public culture—including lowering barriers to participation, developing skills/capacities to participate, creating spaces and cultures of participation, and connecting voice to influence—Medellín Digital's approach during this period was limited. Providing free Internet access and computer labs helped reduce the barriers to public participation for those who were able to access its locations. The initiative did less to create spaces and cultures of participation, and its trainings focused on limited technical capacities rather than a broader set of communication skills needed to participate meaningfully in public life. It did very little to connect citizens' voices to influence over issues of public concern. The grass-roots tactics of Ciudad Comuna stood in stark contrast to Medellín Digital's strategies.

The citizens' media initiative known as Ciudad Comuna is based in Comuna 8, one of Medellín's 16 *comunas* (subdistricts), situated at the eastern edge of the city. In 2011, Comuna 8 was comprised of eighteen or thirty-four neighborhoods, depending on whom you asked, some of which were informal settlements of people forcibly displaced from the countryside in the last twenty years. Such areas are known in Medellín as *barrios periféricos* (poor neighborhoods on the periphery of the city), marginalized from the center of the city geographically as well as politically and economically. Of its roughly 150,000 residents, nearly 40 percent were categorized as living in the lowest of Colombia's six socioeconomic strata, and another 40 percent in the second-lowest strata. Best known for the violence it witnessed during the urbanization of Colombia's armed conflict in the late 1990s and early 2000s, Comuna 8's reputation for gang and paramilitary violence was made internationally visible in the dramatic 2005 documentary *La Sierra*.[46] But there are many other stories to be told about Comuna 8, and Ciudad Comuna's participants were motivated in part by the desire to re-signify their marginalized subjectivities, thus challenging hegemonic media representations of themselves and their *comuna* with their own media representations.

Ciudad Comuna was created in 2006 with the support of a local community-based organization (CBO), and became an independent organization in early 2009. Its four founders ranged in age from eighteen to twenty-six at the time. The oldest and most experienced served as an informal leader, though the collective operated primarily through decision by consensus. The project grew out of a budget allocation from the 2006 local participatory budgeting process, in which residents of Comuna 8 earmarked funds for the development of community media.

Ciudad Comuna is an example of the participatory communication model. Their use of media was driven by their social purpose, rather than by a commitment to a particular technology. Ciudad Comuna described itself as a communication collective that cultivated critical consciousness and civic engagement in their community; they saw themselves serving as a "*referente* [example] of development and youth participation that supported the construction of social fabric in Comuna 8 and in the city more broadly."[47] In 2011, the collective had nine dedicated members (primarily between the ages of sixteen and twenty-two), twelve other occasional participants, and three adult advisors who periodically provided logistical, administrative, and editing support. Many more community members contributed content to their publications and participated in their workshops; the majority were under the age of twenty-five, with a roughly equal split between males and females. They published a community newspaper, *Visión 8*, and website; produced video and other multimedia investigative journalism on a number of locally relevant themes; held public film screenings and events; and offered a communication "school" consisting of popular education workshops in photography, audio and video production, and journalism. Popular education is a pedagogical philosophy, advanced by Freire (*Pedagogy of the Oppressed*), among others, to empower traditionally marginalized groups. It emphasizes horizontal processes of learning and decision making, dialogical communication, and the valuing of local knowledge.[48]

Ciudad Comuna saw their popular education-style workshops as a way to train local community members to broaden the range of contributors, and also to reach their goals of promoting critical, proactive civic engagement, particularly among youth. As one member told me, "[T]raining is fundamental, because even though [in the workshops] we're thinking about media production, it's almost like that's the pretext; because really what we're doing is a process of educating so that youth of the *comuna* find a space of participation, a space in which to propose [ideas/solutions], to speak out, to criticize, to develop their ideas. . . . If someone is able to see themselves reflected in the media they will be much more conscious of their context, of their media, of their reality, and from there can begin to be a protagonist in processes of participation that generate transformation." By 2013, more than one hundred local youth had participated in these trainings.[49] In my interviews, several youth participants felt that the process of producing locally based and locally relevant media changed their relationship to their *comuna* and city, and prompted their public participation, as they became personally invested in the issues. The experience of taking part in the creative process of storytelling about local concerns engaged them in the issues. In so doing, they gained recognition by local leaders and community members, as well as status as local journalists, which further motivated their participation.[50]

The content Ciudad Comuna published was decided upon and contributed by local citizens, with an emphasis on human rights, local planning, and development. The community newspaper *Visión 8* was circulated online, and 10,000 hard copies of each issue were distributed throughout the *comuna*. It was intended to "serve as a tool for the development of . . .

convivencia [peaceful coexistence], inclusion, integration and dialogue among the communities of Comuna 8 in the city of Medellín, and to be the principal resource for the diffusion of [information about] the Development Plan of Comuna 8 in Medellín, which . . . emerged from community initiatives, and in which there is a collective vision from all social sectors in terms of what the future development of the *comuna* should be."[51] In addition, *Visión 8* aimed to serve as an archive of the history and collective memory of the *comuna*, and to provide informed critique of local issues—particularly relating to human rights—to prompt civic mobilization and the development of community-based solutions.

Although *Visión 8* was their centerpiece, Ciudad Comuna described itself first and foremost as a communication collective with a transmedia approach that bridged multiple on- and offline platforms, determined by their social goals rather than any particular technological platform. In addition to circulating a digital version of the newspaper, the collective also published content on video-streaming websites, such as YouTube and Blip.tv, and online photo galleries, such as Flickr. They launched an online community radio station called Voces de la 8 (Voices of Comuna 8). They further disseminated their content on Facebook, the primary online social network used by the majority of their online readers. Lastly, Ciudad Comuna had an editorial board that was open to the public and included volunteers (both youth and adult) from the community who represented a variety of local organizations, associations, community leaders, and informal groups.[52]

Ciudad Comuna intentionally cultivated an ethos of participation and used horizontality, dialogue, and openness to do so. This challenged existing relations of power within the *comuna* from its inception. While the earliest edition of the newspaper included space for established local politicians to publish their own content, Ciudad Comuna rejected the perception shared by many of these power holders that *Visión 8* should serve their communication needs as public figures. They argued instead that it should serve the interests of average citizens of the *comuna* and offer in-depth, investigative coverage of issues of local concern determined by a broader range of perspectives. In other words, Ciudad Comuna wanted to make the process of creating the newspaper—a form of media traditionally associated with top-down vertical information dissemination—into a more horizontal and participatory one in which the concerns and voices of a wide array of citizens and community groups could be amplified. Some of the local leaders who had been on the editorial board of the newspaper's first edition stepped down, refusing to participate. However, by reaching out to community-based organizations and other nontraditional leaders in the community, Ciudad Comuna reestablished its community editorial board, broadened the range of participants and content contributors, and strengthened their reputation in the *comuna* as a citizens' media project.

Ciudad Comuna used horizontality and dialogic communication practices to drive its organizational decision making, promoting a culture of participation. The founding four members of the collective comprised the Junta Directiva (Board of Directors), which took legal responsibility for the association and made some of its strategic planning decisions. Yet, many decisions about programming and other operations were made by consensus in the Ciudad Comuna Assembly, composed of all of the project's approximately twenty-four participants, primarily youth under the age of twenty-five. In this way, they promoted structural participation in decision making and management through horizontal relations of power.

In another example of participatory communication, Ciudad Comuna supported the project Memoria y Territorio de la Comuna 8 (Memory and Territory of Subdistrict 8), which was carried out by local organizations and community members to develop a new map of the *comuna* that would represent the district and its needs more accurately. As its population had grown, many residents felt the *comuna* was not receiving commensurate resources and services from the local government. The new map named thirty residential neighborhoods pertaining to Comuna 8 as opposed to the eighteen recognized by the municipal government since 2000.[53]

Ciudad Comuna took a leading role in disseminating information about the map and the *comuna*'s development plan. They published the map online and in the September 2010 edition of *Visión 8* and invited local communities to reply with commentary, feedback, debate, adjustment, and approval before community organizers presented it to the municipal administration. Emphasizing dialogue and recognition, this special issue of *Visión 8* illustrated Ciudad Comuna's and their collaborators' aim of promoting what Couldry describes as a culture that values voice.[54] Ciudad Comuna's editorial argued, "To have a map of the territory in which all of its neighborhoods are included, and to know that it is the product of dialogue and recognition between the communities [of Comuna 8], and not the myopic vision of the territory of some municipal planning representatives—who, without denying their technical capacity, it is evident have never traveled across the *comuna* nor dialogued with its inhabitants—represents one of the most important achievements of the planning processes of this territory in recent years."[55] It went on to criticize the municipal government

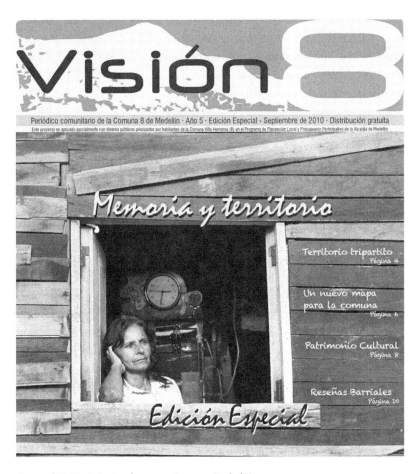

Cover of *Visión 8*, September 2010. Source: Ciudad Comuna.   **2.2**

Youth media producer for Ciudad Comuna. Source: Ciudad Comuna.   **2.3**

directly—a key source of funding for *Visión 8*—for contracting out such projects to external consultants rather than to local community organizations. It emphasized the legitimacy of the knowledge produced through this participatory dialogical process, as well as the autonomy of the project from external institutions. The updated map, subsequently recognized by local leaders, community organizations, and researchers, became a key reference for information about the *comuna*, as well as a tool for demanding recognition and services from the municipal government and for deciding on local development priorities. It inspired other neighborhoods to demand formal recognition and other *comunas* to carry out similar mapping processes, raising public awareness of the issue.[56]

In this and other instances, Ciudad Comuna strategically maintained their autonomy, and much of the content they published was highly critical of the administration—in spite of the fact that the collective received contracts from the municipal government and was funded in part by the city's annual budget through the participatory budgeting process. (Ciudad Comuna also contracted their production services to other entities to raise funds for their operations.) As they told me in a group interview, "Despite functioning with some resources from the participatory budget . . . we've maintained a very critical posture and we've had a lot of autonomy to speak out. . . . The media we create become tools through which people can denounce situations of exclusion, abandonment [by the state], marginalization. . . . This process of communication may be the only tool that the people of Comuna 8 can use to refute information that comes from the municipal administration or its development reports." The municipal government under the Fajardo and Salarzar administrations supported such autonomy by requiring community media projects that received municipal funding to raise at least 30 percent of their funding from nongovernmental sources.

Ciudad Comuna's approach included a significant degree of openness across all three levels of content, communicative architecture, and management. Decisions about thematic priorities for content were made in the open editorial board meetings to ensure direct input from a variety of community members outside of the collective. The resulting topics covered a wide range of local and more universal concerns, including information on the local development plan and participatory budgeting process; coverage of protests and other mobilizations; coverage of violence and testimonials from victims of violence; and content focusing on human rights, education, health and nutrition, gender equity, and the merits of free/open software.

Ciudad Comuna's commitment to openness extended beyond their production processes and content to the architecture and management of their communication systems, and the capacities of digitally networked technologies clearly enhanced this. In some cases, they used FLOSS, as well as open publishing and website administration.

In 2010, Ciudad Comuna launched a website to serve as a virtual community message board and mobilization tool, using open-source software designed to facilitate participatory publishing. Any local group (whether a formal organization or informal collective) with an interest in Comuna 8 could register to be an administrator and post content. There was no editing or censoring of contributions, aside from hate speech or other harmful content. Using the site was relatively simple, with low barriers to use. Ciudad Comuna offered technical and training assistance, but it did not aim to control the content posted by community groups, instead encouraging them to publish autonomously. According to Ciudad Comuna, the site received approximately 119,000 visits in a year. While the site was built by a software engineer, it was managed through what Ciudad Comuna described as *administración participativa* (participatory administration); at the time of my research, approximately twenty local groups or organizations had registered as administrators.[57] Ciudad Comuna saw the decision to use this open platform as a method of promoting local participation and autonomous content publishing, and of cultivating a sense of ownership over the platform among community groups.

Evidence that the site achieved these impacts was limited by its relatively short life-span. In August 2012, it was hacked and taken offline, drawing attention to some of the potential challenges of using open-source platforms (especially for small organizations with limited resources)—namely, security and stability. A member of Ciudad Comuna expressed concern that the attack appeared to correspond with similar attacks on other community organization websites related to human rights issues, but this had not been verified. At the time of this writing, the site remained down; Ciudad Comuna shifted the focus of their online efforts to their own multimedia website, where they continued to publish information from and about local community groups.

Ciudad Comuna won recognition for their communication initiatives from the municipal government and the University of Antioquia, including being named the best audiovisual community media producers in Medellín in the 2010 and 2011 Community Journalism Awards. At the time of this writing, Ciudad Comuna was also leading an assembly of community media projects across the city to promote participatory communication more broadly. In these various ways—ranging from content to communicative architecture to management—Ciudad Comuna created relatively horizontal and open spaces of communication with the aim of provoking critical dialogue and community engagement in local development. While not every minute decision regarding each production was made horizontally and not all of its attempts at openness proved sustainable, the collective created cultures and spaces of citizen participation. They also reduced barriers to (youth) citizen participation in public life, developed citizens' capacities to participate, and worked to amplify citizen voices—especially youth voices—to have greater influence over public policy and local decision making. These are the preconditions of participatory public culture.

Although Ciudad Comuna is an example of how participatory communication can be bolstered by digital media, and how this can promote participatory public culture, it also suggests that the communicative practices surrounding digital technologies are more determining of participation than the technologies themselves. Ciudad Comuna did not set out to cultivate digital citizens as its primary aim, but it enhanced its participatory communication practices with digital tools. In contrast to Medellín Digital's approach, which was technology driven, Ciudad Comuna's participatory communication approach was process driven. Ciudad Comuna enabled far more content-related *and* structural participation than did Medellín Digital.

Designing (Digital) Citizenship

Ciudad Comuna's and Medellín Digital's different approaches to participation—while both worthwhile in their own ways—each led to different outcomes in terms of relations of power and the quality of public participation supported by the introduction of digital tools into the civic ecology. This included differences in the kinds of digital citizenship each initiative cultivated, which literacies and skills they emphasized, and how communicative platforms/spaces were structured and managed. Thus, these cases underscore not only that our analysis of the role of digital communication in supporting participatory public culture needs to be contextually precise, but also that digital citizenship initiatives should be implemented ecologically with attention to local context.

Ciudad Comuna did not use the rhetoric of digital citizenship as explicitly as Medellín Digital, in part because they were less technologically driven and chose their communication formats (not all of which were digital) based on their broader social goals. However, their commitment to open software, user-generated content, and horizontal/participatory administration signaled that they were practicing and promoting a robust, proactive digital citizenship, along the lines of Isin and Ruppert's definition.[58] Medellín Digital's "digital citizens" were seemingly those who could use Microsoft platforms and the Internet for business and basic e-government services, while Ciudad Comuna aimed to cultivate critical, vocal, and engaged citizens willing and able to challenge the status quo using a variety of media.

Christian Fuchs argues that the notion of digital citizenship itself is part of a misplaced Web 2.0 ideology, in which too much agency is ascribed to users of user-generated content platforms while ignoring structural limitations to participation, such as proprietary software and corporate control over the architecture of participation; he refers to content-related participation in such sites as "pseudo-participation."[59] However, being entirely dismissive of the potential for content-related participation in such spaces to contribute meaningfully to social change denies users any agency and overlooks the significance of storytelling and "challenging codes"[60] to forge a more participatory and just society; in their own way, then, such critiques risk technological determinism.

Yet, drawing critical attention to the limits to structural participation in digital spaces remains crucial. Medellín Digital's initiatives tended to prioritize information delivery and technological access while maintaining the status quo in terms of relationships of power and communication between the government and citizens—ultimately promoting neither structural participation nor a more participatory public culture of any noteworthy degree. Ciudad Comuna's initiatives tended to prioritize the participation of community members in determining content priorities, and saw citizen participation as central to the process of knowledge production for community development (both problem and solution identification), challenging knowledge produced centrally by the government. Their approach included both content and structural participation, and fostered the conditions for a more participatory public culture. As with many other participatory communication initiatives historically, Ciudad Comuna's underlying conception of citizenship was counter-hegemonic and tended more toward Mouffe's theories of radical democracy, in which participation and communication are central to the project of challenging normative static conceptualizations of a more passive citizenship in favor of a proactive, critical, and self-determined one.[61]

The differences in how (digital) citizenship and participation are conceived result in distinct approaches to educating and training citizens *to participate*; this is apparent in the different kinds of trainings offered by Medellín Digital and Ciudad Comuna. María Ruth Patiño Lemos and Mercedes Vallejo Gómez found that Medellín Digital's digital literacy trainings of teachers increased their use of some computer and Internet technologies, but remained skeptical that the trainings enabled the teachers to move beyond basic instrumental adoption of these technologies in the classroom to thinking about new pedagogical approaches that digital technologies may enable.[62] For example, Henry Jenkins and colleagues have argued that "new media literacy" pedagogy should include building the capacities of networking, problem solving, performance and improvisation, simulation, remixing content, multitasking, working with distributed cognition and collective intelligence models, the ability to evaluate the sources and credibility of content, transmedia navigation (the ability to follow content across multiple platforms), and the ability to respect and negotiate with differing perspectives and norms.[63] Medellín Digital did not cultivate these forms of literacies effectively. In Patiño Lemos and Vallejo Gómez's study, less than one third of the students surveyed reported doing collaborative work in class using digital communication technologies.[64]

Interviewees from other participatory communication projects in the city suggested that Medellín Digital's training curriculum could have done far more to develop critical literacy of the technology, including an understanding of its architecture. Dorothea Kleine reached a similar conclusion in her study of Chile's national Agenda Digital initiative, arguing that people should be trained to recognize the "potential unfreedoms arising from technology use," including concerns of privacy and corporate data usage, scams, and political propaganda or fake news, as well as the biases in the design of the technology and the biases created by both English and Spanish language content.[65] Some Latin American experts emphasize that digital literacy should include the ability to use digital communication technologies to help solve problems collectively and to make or have influence over decisions that have social impact (Mitzi Vilchis, Kimberly Scott, and Courtney Besaw refer to this as "technosocial literacy").[66]

A critical digital media literacy would enable users not only to use or consume software and computer technologies, but also to analyze them in context, make proactive choices about their use, and, ideally, shape the very design of these communicative spaces. (As Ellen Middaugh and Ben Kirshner note, "The very act of design can, in and of itself, be a form of civic action.")[67] Graham Longford contends that literacy for digital citizenship should include "how code constitutes the conditions of possibility for different norms, models, and practices of online citizenship, along with the capacity to resist and reshape—to *hack*, if you will—the prevailing terms and conditions of cybercitizenship if they no longer serve our needs."[68] Medellín Digital and Ciudad Comuna had not accomplished these forms of literacy among their users/participants, though Ciudad Comuna was approaching it. This is a high standard for digital citizenship, and one that, to date, unfortunately remains accessible only to a small number of techno-elite. Yet, these perspectives help to maintain an analytical focus on the fundamental questions of power, participation, and influence that are at stake.

The technological architecture of the communicative spaces in which digital citizenship is enacted largely structure its possibilities; as Christopher Kelty reminds us, these platforms proliferate ways of "governing ourselves and others."[69] Medellín Digital's web portals used proprietary software, and its content was primarily produced centrally, while Ciudad Comuna used some open-source software and published content produced by local community members. Opting for proprietary software is frequently perceived to be a "safer" and more secure choice (depending on how safety and security is conceived), but it has significant implications for participatory culture and digital citizenship. Digital divide initiatives have often overlooked the politics behind the design of the technologies being advocated.[70] Latin American and other technology studies scholars draw attention to how the import of proprietary technology from the Global North perpetuates economic dependency and inequality, and promotes an imperialistic universalized conceptualization of the function of technology that does not match, or even value, local knowledges and innovations.[71]

Medellín Digital's partnership with Microsoft sustained the dependency of the government (and perhaps its citizens) on a global corporation, and by basing digital literacy trainings on Microsoft platforms, it limited the development of a more open digital culture. In contrast, governments and other FLOSS advocates in the Global South have used FLOSS to push back against the dominance of corporations such as Microsoft and to cultivate a more participatory digital culture (e.g., Brazil), bolster public participation in development (e.g., India), and promote cultural diversity and greater transparency in government (e.g., Peru).[72] Of course, as Anita Say Chan points out, FLOSS can become its own form of techno-fundamentalism when implemented in a traditional diffusion-centered approach.[73]

Certainly, there are limits to what technology choices and government policies alone can accomplish toward promoting more participatory public cultures. It is the *combination* of technology choices, policies (and their political economic outcomes), user practices, and cultures of production that together may or may not challenge existing inequalities. The question of what types of communicative architectures and degrees of openness best support participatory cultures and participatory communication has no singular simple answer—as exemplified by the fact that groups such as Ciudad Comuna that practice participatory communication and advocate FLOSS also make use of proprietary platforms such as Facebook and YouTube. Yet, the choice to use FLOSS carries with it broader political and cultural meaning; and Medellín Digital's choice of proprietary software signaled limitations to their commitment to participation. Given Medellín Digital's relative position of power in this ecology of participation, it is not surprising that they did not use participation as a resource for challenging the status quo and increasing the power of citizen voices as Ciudad Comuna attempted to do. The former represented a hegemonic institution promoting a minimalist, static, and largely passive form of citizenship— while the latter practiced a counter-hegemonic alternative citizenship.

Medellín Digital's portals and trainings were not being used extensively, if at all, by local community groups such as Ciudad Comuna. Members of Ciudad Comuna and other citizens' media projects in the city told me this was partly because of Medellín Digital's use of proprietary Microsoft platforms that conflicted with their groups' goals, philosophies, and practical needs. However, these groups did use other proprietary closed platforms such as Facebook and YouTube due to the size of the social networks that could be reached. Although Facebook (the most popular social networking platform in Medellín and in Colombia more broadly at the time of this research) was used ubiquitously for connecting with friends and family, it was also utilized in a very public way to share information, to publicize services and events, and to mobilize people to participate. The community groups' online content distribution took place on these more mainstream commercial platforms or on their own blogs or websites. It is important to note that neither Facebook nor YouTube are open-source or open-administration sites and therefore not participatory in the "maximalist" or structural sense described by Carpentier. (In fact, they have been criticized for being relatively closed in this sense.[74]) Yet, the widespread use of these platforms by groups that practice participatory cultures illustrates that the two are not necessarily mutually exclusive. Although limited structural participation in communication platforms may confine participatory cultures in some important ways, it does not preclude their existence, nor does it necessarily bar their content-related participation—this remains relatively open. Further, structural participation is not always of interest to or feasible for all users. This is a good example of how technology may shape—but not completely determine—participation.

State and other institutional programs such as Medellín Digital typically aim to find efficient scalable models of communication for development, but participatory communication is usually a locally specific practice—one that needs to be flexible and responsive to contextual particularities. Some participatory communication initiatives such as Ciudad Comuna have therefore been critiqued for being too localist in focus and thus unscalable.[75] Others argue against the one-size-fits-all scalable models characteristic of the modernization approaches to using ICT4D. Alfonso Gumucio Dagron has argued, "In a more reasonable framework for development, scale would have to do with linking communities with similar issues of concern and facilitating exchanges, instead of multiplying rigid models."[76] This suggests a network mentality—for example, supporting local digital communication projects such as Ciudad Comuna to network with others across the city—as opposed to a mentality of replicability and scalability.

Yet, the localism of Ciudad Comuna's approach to digital communication and participation was in fact one of its strengths; the work was firmly grounded in the particular needs of the community it served. While Ciudad Comuna may not have been scalable in the way Medellín Digital was, it was more responsive to local needs and provides an example of integrating digital tools into a particular ecology of participation. And while technology studies scholars in Latin America and elsewhere have consistently shown that even imported technological solutions go through localized translations, adaptations, or hybridization,[77] Medellín Digital's approach could have benefited from more local participation in the design and implementation of the initiative.

There are also practical organizational constraints on participatory communication. As Carpentier and others have pointed out, participatory and horizontally organized initiatives in which decision-making power is distributed have to deal with some resulting inefficiencies. The consensus-based, flexible, and horizontal nature of participatory communication is often in conflict with the timelines and expectations of funders or other stakeholders, as well as participants whose time is limited. An insistence on using participatory communication methods can itself be a form of "tyranny," such as when well-intentioned participatory methods are imposed in contexts that may not be appropriate.[78] Ciudad Comuna addressed this by having both an assembly in which decisions were made by consensus of all participants and a board of directors with the power to make some of the day-to-day decisions necessary for operation.

It is crucial to note that a number of conditions existed to make Ciudad Comuna possible, including the broader history and valorization of community media in Colombia; the willingness of participants in the *comuna*'s participatory budgeting process to allocate funds repeatedly to community media; the support of local leaders, community organizers, and established CBOs; and founders who had received leadership training and experience in other community-based projects—a condition common to all of the youth groups analyzed in this book.

Neither of the cases examined here were particularly successful at promoting public dialogue in online spaces; this underscores the fact that the introduction of digital tools alone does not lead to a more participatory public culture. Catalyzing online dialogue around issues of public concern remains a challenge in many instances. In the case of Medellín Digital, an initiative focused on enhancing public dialogue in the participatory budgeting process through digital platforms would have been one way to support a more participatory public culture in the city, perhaps even cultivating the "civic hacking" or crowdsourcing of solutions to local problems. Ciudad Comuna's communicative architectures were more explicitly designed to promote both on- and offline dialogue. Yet, a year after launching the community website, the majority of user posts were simple information sharing rather than dialogue.

Overall, Ciudad Comuna's approach clearly had greater potential to cultivate participatory public culture, but it functioned on a much smaller scale than Medellín Digital and struggled with resource constraints. Without the basic infrastructure and access that initiatives such as Medellín Digital set out to provide, Ciudad Comuna's ability to promote citizen participation and social change would be limited. Ciudad Comuna presumably benefited from citywide Internet access provided by Medellín Digital, as more people were able to access and contribute to their content online more easily. Of course, Medellín Digital's and Ciudad Comuna's approaches were not necessarily contradictory or mutually exclusive; effective public participation requires access to information, and therefore media/communication systems that promote connectivity and serve the function of information delivery remain important.

Thus, despite their differences, Medellín Digital and Ciudad Comuna (and similar citizens' or community media projects) stood to benefit from each other in a number of ways. Medellín Digital created necessary digital infrastructure (a structural contribution); Ciudad Comuna arguably cultivated digital citizens who were better prepared to engage in public life and make use of the infrastructure to amplify their voices and influence public issues (a social and political contribution). The strengths of both initiatives might have been enhanced by a closer polycultural relationship in which their contributions were intentionally more interconnected to maximize positive outcomes.

As these and the other cases throughout this book illustrate, both institutional and grass-roots efforts are necessary to promote participatory public culture. That is, top-down/transmission approaches and bottom-up/participatory approaches to communication would ideally work in a mutually beneficial way—and perhaps as networked rather than as a binary and in relative isolation.[79] The ecological approach of polycultural civics—which encourages cultivating stronger relationships between institutional actors such as Medellín Digital and grass-roots actors such as Ciudad Comuna—may also help avoid problems of technological determinism and universalizing normativity that have been observed in several digital initiatives in Latin America and elsewhere.[80] However, at the time of this research, there was little intentional cultivation of the relationship between institutional strategies of digital citizenship such as Medellín Digital's and grass-roots tactics such as Ciudad Comuna's, and the Fajardo and Salazar administrations could have done much more to develop this synergy.

In 2011, outgoing Mayor Salazar acknowledged that Medellín Digital's focus to date had been on creating utilitarian digital tools rather than on promoting local production, dialogue, or a more participatory online culture. He told me, "If we want the network to be more of a mirror of ourselves, to reflect ourselves . . . and what we want to be, then we are far [from that goal]. . . . What content will we upload to the network distinct from what we download? What content can we export? . . . If you asked me what we should do with the network, well it should also help us [develop our] identity."[81] Such a vision would merge some of the institutional and governance goals of Medellín Digital's network of portals with those of citizens' media that see participatory communication as a tool for the collective construction of society. Since the two Compromiso Ciudadano administrations that were the focus of this study, the municipal government's digital initiatives have evolved and expanded, helping to garner Medellín its status as the "most intelligent" city in Colombia.[82] This includes open data and other initiatives through which citizens can access public information as well as direct suggestions to city officials. Yet, the history of Medellín Digital highlights critical questions that remain pertinent to the design and practice of digital citizenship. And arguably, grass-roots initiatives continue to be as significant, if not more so, in cultivating participatory public culture in Medellín.

Participatory communication offers an antidote to technologically deterministic—and perhaps even neocolonial—implementations of digital technologies by maintaining a focus on the *process* of communication within a particular context. Further review of these cases—or of any other efforts to cultivate a more participatory culture—would merit an intersectional analysis of the social, cultural, and political economic constraints on the ability to have marginalized voices heard within networks of power.[83] I have addressed some of the potential constraints in the cases above (e.g., vertical or closed vs. horizontal or open practices and spaces of communication). These delimit the ways in which communication technologies may or may not encourage more inclusive, participatory practices, and whether these practices challenge inequalities in existing relations of power.

Agency after Inclusion

As part of a broader civic polyculture, digital communication technology may function as a fertilizer of public participation, potentially enhancing access, voice, and opportunity. Yet, it is now widely understood that technical inclusion does not guarantee social inclusion.[84] The practices and cultures of use surrounding the technology determine the extent to which inclusion and participation are promoted; along this dimension, Ciudad Comuna was clearly much stronger than Medellín Digital. In practice, it remains much easier to capitalize on the rhetoric of citizen participation through digital inclusion than to actually accomplish it. These cases suggest that efforts to expand participatory public culture through the digital sphere may be more effective if they are linked to communicative practices and spaces characterized by horizontality, dialogue, and openness, and implemented with attention to the local civic context.

Since 2011, global digital divide rhetoric has given way to somewhat less technologically deterministic and somewhat more nuanced discourses of digital participation, particularly as mobile communication technologies have become nearly ubiquitous, helping increase digital access across the globe. And yet, changes to policy and digital inclusion programs have been slower to come. To this day, celebratory discourses of digital communication too often collapse the agency to participate in social media platforms with the agency to participate in governing society.[85] The case of Medellín Digital offers but one example of this conflation. A key role for institutions such as Medellín Digital might be not only to help amplify a diverse range of youth/citizen voices, but also to connect these to political or other structures for influencing public decision making. Such efforts also necessitate the development of critical digital media literacies so that decisions about how to design and use these tools are not solely the purview of the techno-elite.

Jan Servaes and Rolien Hoyng argue that ICT initiatives still need to address the question of "agency *after* inclusion into information and communication networks," in terms of skills/capacities, social capital, and political efficacy.[86] What does agency after inclusion look like? It may be horizontal. It may be open and dialogical. The cases analyzed here suggest that the answer lies in an ecological understanding of how power operates through different conceptions and practices of participation, and that digital technology is but one resource within a civic ecology.

Another key question is that of the intersectional obstructions to participation—something I explore in the following chapters. While this chapter has focused primarily on communication infrastructures, platforms, and their surrounding ideologies and cultures of use, digital technologies were only one way in which participation was summoned in Medellín. The cases in this chapter make it clear that it is just as important to attend to *cultures* of participation as to *structures* of participation. The following chapter delves deeply into examples of how cultures of youth participation can be cultivated. It investigates particular tactics of participation developed by youth in precarious contexts, and why such tactics are critical to participatory public culture and polycultural civics.

Chapter Three

"We Think about the City Differently"

¿Que han oído de la 13? Que es el barrio más caliente.	What have you heard of the 13th? That it's the most violent barrio.
Mucha publicidad, nos visitó hasta el presidente.	A lot of publicity, even the president visited.
Las casitas de bla bla son llamadas invasión,	The houses of bla bla are called illegal settlements,
el barrio cambió su nombre por 'Operación Orión.'	the barrio changed its name to "Operation Orion."
¿Qué recuerdan de la 13? Plomo de arriba pa' bajo,	What do people remember of the 13th? Bullets from high and low,
no recuerdan a su gente ni el dolor que eso les trajo.	They don't remember its people or the pain that this brought them.
Pero claro! No hablan sino las cosas malas	But, of course! They only talk about the bad things,
En vez de mostrar artistas, muestran cocas en las balas. . . .	Instead of showing artists, they show cocaine and bullets. . . .
No es lo que uno quiere ver es solamente lo que le muestran	It's not what people want to see, it's only what they want to show us,
Pero para mi concepto este amarillismo apesta.	But from my perspective, this sensationalist journalism stinks.
Occidente sigue al frente por cultura no caliente	The west side still leads in nonviolent culture
Orgulloso de mi barrio en el pasado y el presente.	I'm proud of my barrio in the past and the present.

—Esk-lones (former members of
The Elite Hip Hop Network),
song lyrics from *Esta es la 13*[1]

Former Mayor Alonso Salazar once stated, "Rappers and hip hoppers are evidence of the transformation of Medellín."[2] This is in no small part because young hip-hop activists—such as JEIHHCO and El Perro, mentioned in the Introduction—were some of the most visible and noteworthy actors promoting participatory public culture in Medellín. This chapter looks at how and why this was the case. It focuses on the grass-roots tactics of La Red de Hip Hop La Elite (The Elite Hip Hop Network, referred to as "La Elite") and the Afro-Colombian youth collective Son Batá, and how they have used cultural forms to participate in public life with the effect of cultivating key conditions of participatory public culture: low barriers to participation in public life, spaces and cultures of participation, capacities to participate, and the connection of youth/citizen voices to influence over public issues.[3] I analyze four tactics of participation in particular: the reterritorialization of public space through cultural expression, popular education and mentorship, participatory decision making, and re-signification. While both youth collectives engaged in these tactics to varying degrees, the case of Son Batá illustrates how re-signification is particularly crucial for youth who have been marginalized by race/ethnicity—and shows more broadly that participation cannot be understood universally but must be analyzed in its particular historical, economic, cultural, and social context. The grass-roots tactics of La Elite, Son Batá, and similar youth groups in Medellín ultimately challenged the violence and illicit networks that otherwise dominated public space and public life in their neighborhoods in ways that were meaningful to many youth, their local communities, civil society and government organizations, and the city at large.

In late modernity, cultural production and consumption is a fundamental part of defining community or collective identity and, therefore, of public life and governance; norms and priorities are shaped in the terrain of culture. Legally or culturally barred from other forms of politics, youth often enact their politics in and through the space of culture, and the lines between the two are constantly blurred.[4] Several digital media scholars have made the case that *participatory culture*—with low barriers to entry, strong support for creating and sharing one's cultural work, informal mentorship, and social connection—can be a resource for young people's civic/political engagement.[5] Cultural participation can be a primary resource through which citizenship and relations of power between youth and institutions are negotiated. Through cultural tactics—such as those of La Elite and Son Batá—participation in public life is channeled in a way that may be meaningful to both youth and, in the Medellín model, some state institutions.

Cultural participation is also taken up as a resource by youth to challenge dynamics of armed violence.[6] In Medellín, many of the innovative, participatory initiatives led by youth have aimed, at least in part, to change the culture(s) of violence that have constrained public life. Drawing on Johan Galtung's work, Clemencia Rodríguez describes a culture of violence as "a set of relationships and discursive practices that legitimize violence or make violence seem an acceptable means of responding to conflict."[7] A culture of violence is one that symbolically and discursively legitimates the use of force in the exercise of power, and may function at the micro level (e.g., within families), at the community level (e.g., between gangs), or at more macro levels (e.g., in discourses and practices of the state). Challenging cultures of violence requires challenging discursive practices, cultural norms, and codes. I use "culture" here in the sense of "common meanings" that circulate in any society at a given moment, as described by Raymond Williams,[8] rather than suggesting any kind of intrinsic relationship between violence and Colombian or *paisa* (the colloquial name for the people of Antioquia) "culture" as a national or regional descriptor. The youth collectives of La Elite and Son Batá offer examples of discursive interventions and nonviolent physical/symbolic self-expression that not only promote participation but also challenge cultures of violence.

Angela Garcés Montoya distinguishes between youth organizations with institutional affiliations that are structured by and within an adult logic, and *colectivos juveniles* (youth collectives) that are driven by youth themselves, often as a challenge to the culture and politics of adult institutions.[9] *Colectivos* represent a more structured organizational form than a youth subculture (featuring, e.g., a shared vision or set of goals, some established form of decision making and priority setting, etc.) but one that is less structured than a formal organization. "Collectives have a defined and public group identity, imply the presence of some basic consensus and disregard unnecessary formalities. Their discourse prominently reveals the democratic-participatory character of collectives: all members think, decide, and act; there is no censorship, no bosses, representation is limited to those who want to participate; that is to say, representation is subordinate to participation."[10] *Colectivos* often use horizontal practices of self-governance in conscious contrast to hierarchical institutional practices, and their politics are expressed through cultural production and consumption, exemplifying Rossana Reguillo's notion of the culturization of politics.[11] They tend to conceive of power "not as something that one takes, but rather, associat[e] it with the positive potential of collective work. Members of these youth collectives understand power as linked to the *'hacer juntos'* ['doing together']." In other words, the focus is on power exercised by "doing together" rather than on "power over."[12] Other characteristics of youth collectives in this context often include a commitment to independent financing (as opposed to economic dependence upon the state or any one particular institution), pluralism, and a critical but proactive stance on issues of public concern. In 2007, there were approximately three hundred such youth groups documented in Medellín.[13] Many of these youth collectives are also part of larger networks organized among themselves, or in partnership with more formal (typically nonprofit) organizations. Among these collectives, art and culture (music, dance, theater, writing, etc.) are most often seen as means to social transformation rather than as ends in themselves; they commonly promote themes including nonviolent and peaceful coexistence, youth rights, civic/political participation, and gender equity.[14]

La Elite and Son Batá were two of the most widely recognized youth-run cultural *colectivos juveniles* in Medellín; both are examples of participatory cultures with a horizontal collectivist orientation but which to varying degrees (more so in the case of La Elite) also prioritized individual self-expression. That is, members tended to value both the expression of individual voices and the strength gleaned from collective action and decision making. They both had gained significant social capital across the city (and even nationally and internationally), evidenced by their relationships with government officials, sponsors, and other donors; media coverage; and public attendance at their concerts. This was particularly noteworthy because these youth hailed from one of the most marginalized, stigmatized, and violence-stricken parts of the city. In this context, they developed their own grass-roots tactics of participation in public life while at the same time negotiating their sometimes conflictual, sometimes collaborative, relationship with government strategies.[15]

La Red de Hip Hop La Elite

Vamos luchando contra el adversarios,	We continue fighting against the adversary,
haz sentir tu voz latina en los vecindarios.	make your Latino voice heard in the neighborhoods.
Nuestro itinerario en las calles,	Our itinerary in the streets,
rap que represente los barrios	rap that represents the barrios
Mas que pleito en el barrio, parce.	Instead of confrontation in the barrio, dude.
Seguimos siendo las voces de los que no tienen voz en los barrios,	We continue being the voices of those who have no voice in the barrios,
Se cuentan las historias reales se vive con sonrisas y con llantos . . .	Telling the real stories of living with smiles and tears . . .

—Zinagoga Crew, song lyrics from "Reportando Sucesos" ("Reporting Events")

"Living with smiles and tears" is an apt way to describe the contrast between the destruction of public life—and lives—and the vibrant efforts to reclaim it that characterize Comuna 13 (Subdistrict 13). Home to La Elite, "*La 13*" is comprised of twenty neighborhoods where levels of poverty and malnutrition are some of the highest in the city, while levels of education are some of the lowest.[16] Several of its neighborhoods were settled by migrants (particularly Afro-Colombians) displaced by the armed conflict in the countryside, only to land in what became one of the most contested areas of the city. This is because traffic to and from the northern coast passes through this area, rendering it crucial for both legal and illicit economies. Over the last four decades, the territory has been shaped by the presence of leftist guerrillas, networks of narcotraffickers, armed gangs of youth with varied allegiances, paramilitaries, and dramatic military interventions by the federal government—the most notorious of which was Operation Orion in 2002, mentioned in Esk-lones's rap lyrics at the beginning of this chapter.[17] During this military operation, the residents of the targeted areas were subjected to days of gunfire in their neighborhoods.

As a result of these dynamics, the *comuna* was known for having the highest rates of violence and homicides, as well as the greatest concentration of illegal armed actors in the city during the 2000s, the period in which La Elite was formed. As Pablo Emilio Angarita Cañas, Héctor Gallo, Blanca

Inés Jiménez Zuluaga, and colleagues described, "rape, killings, kidnappings, disappearances, extortions, threats, forced evictions of residents, the use of the population as a human shield and the exercise of control and surveillance by means of [forced] compliance with rules of social and individual behavior, all . . . contributed to the configuration of a climate of terror and generated trauma and fear, but also the construction of mechanisms of resistance and adaptation, of participation in the dynamics of the war and in the processes of the construction of peace."[18] These authors argue that the neglect of the *comuna*'s populace due to the relative absence of state institutions other than the military (at least until the Fajardo administration) constituted a violation of human rights and the manifestation of a second form of violence: structural violence. The relationship between the citizens of Comuna 13 and the municipal and national governments was therefore doubly fraught.

Furthermore, youth in Comuna 13 and other low-income districts of the city experienced a kind of representational violence in which media frames reified and stigmatized them as violent entities, further "ghettoizing" their social and political status in the public eye. In narrating the armed violence in the city, local and national mass media frequently used—and reinforced—the stereotype of these youth (particularly male) as delinquent, armed, and dangerous. In mass media frames, Comuna 13 itself became synonymous with Medellín's crisis of violence. This stigmatization has had material consequences for young people, "prefiguring difficulties for these shantytown inhabitants in accessing goods, services, recognition and the exercise of their rights."[19] Yet, because it was a nexus of armed violence and marginalization, Comuna 13 also became a hotspot of youth organizing as young people struggled to find alternatives to the violence and to carve out a better life.

Of the hundreds of youth groups in Medellín, some of the most prolific and widely recognized are hip-hop collectives. Hip-hop is a very popular youth subculture in Medellín, bolstered in recent years by the use of digital recording and social media technologies and by increased access to resources through the participatory budgeting process (see Chapter 4). By 2005, there were 220 documented hip-hop groups in the city, primarily in the *barrios populares* (low-income neighborhoods).[20] In a 2011 interview, a member of La Elite suggested there were more than three hundred hip-hop groups in Medellín.

Hip-hop itself first emerged in a context not entirely dissimilar to Comuna 13's, in low-income neighborhoods in the Bronx, New York, that had been shaped by large immigrant populations, an erosion or absence of public institutions, poverty, and gang violence.[21] Despite hip-hop's foreign roots, Medellín's hip-hop artists localized (or, in Nestor Garcia Canclini's term, hybridized[22]) their styles and practices as they responded to their daily contexts, reconfiguring them through symbolic form.[23] "In general what one would hear in the first local rap lyrics were responses to a society marked by urban warfare, in which narcotrafficking, insurgency, abuses by law enforcement and gangs of hit men, social inequality and the lack of opportunities" enveloped the daily lives of youth.[24] Much of these themes were still evident years later in the lyrics of members of La Elite, while at the same time the network took an explicit stance as peace activists.

The four different aesthetic elements of hip-hop—rap (MCing), DJing, graffiti, and break dancing—offer youth varied entry points and modes of self-expression that make it a relatively open cultural form, one that can be practiced by youth who may, for example, prefer physical or visual self-expressions over musical or verbal ones. In other words, the barriers to entry into hip-hop culture are relatively low. Of course, rappers need microphones, DJs need turntables (a scarce resource in Medellín, and therefore the weakest of the four elements in the city), graffiti artists need paint cans, and break-dancers need space—these barriers to entry are a key focus of fundraising efforts by hip-hop collectives across Medellín.

At the suggestion of a community worker at the local YMCA-affiliated nonprofit, the Asociación Cristiana de Jóvenes (Christian Association of Youth, ACJ), La Elite was formed in 2002 by several youth hip-hop groups who had already started using hip-hop for nonviolent social change at a time when military operations in the *comuna* had escalated. By 2011, La Elite was one of the three most established hip-hop collectives in the city; it had gained national recognition for its annual hip-hop festival Revolución Sin Muertos (Revolution without Deaths, the second-largest hip-hop festival in Colombia at the time of my research) and its cultural resistance to armed violence.

The rappers, graffiti artists, break-dancers ("bboys" and "bgirls"), and DJs of La Elite called themselves *gestores culturales juveniles* (loosely translated as "youth cultural advocates"). The goals of the network included strengthening the local hip-hop movement, offering youth new opportunities and an alternative to the culture and practice of violence, raising critical awareness among youth about their social realities, promoting civic/political engagement of youth, and positively contributing to the development of the *comuna* and the city.[25] While the ACJ supported La Elite in some ways (e.g., letting them use their office space for meetings and workshops, offering advice, and processing grants or contracts they received), the network functioned autonomously as a youth-led collective, describing itself as an "initiative for peace and nonviolence through the culture of hip-hop in the Comuna 13 of Medellín."[26] Their activities included putting on concerts and festivals to promote local hip-hop and advocate for nonviolence, offering hip-hop workshops for youth and children in a popular education "school," and participating in public events around the city that shared their aims.

La Elite was an example of cultural participation that supported the development of both individual and collective public identities, and connected these to collective action. Cultural self-expression and social status were often the initial draws for youth. Yet, in the daily activities of the collectives, they developed both their individual and collective identities and became more engaged in public and political life. As one member told me, "I started with La Elite when I was a child. Ever since I knew of La Elite Network I wanted to be a part of it because its reputation was that it had the best rappers in the *comuna*. . . . But when I had the opportunity to join La Elite, I realized that it was totally different, that these youth work for the community, and everything I thought about La Elite changed. But in the beginning, it was because I wanted to be part of the best rappers in the *comuna*."

By 2011, La Elite was comprised of twenty-three different hip-hop groups, totaling approximately eighty-five individual members. Seventy percent were between the ages of fourteen and twenty-three; nearly all were under the age of twenty-eight. Of these, approximately 80 percent were male and 20 percent female. The majority had completed secondary education but not completed higher or technical education. More than 30 percent had their own children.[27] La Elite was thus a mix of teenagers and youth in their twenties, most of whom had joined the network as teenagers and some of whom now had adult/parental responsibilities. (This resulted in positive mentoring relationships, as well as occasional tensions between the first generation of network members and those who joined later—particularly when it came to distribution of resources and paid salaries for particular projects.) Despite this age range, the collective identity of La Elite remained firmly rooted in youth culture and discourses of youth empowerment in public life. One of the ways they enacted this was through tactics of reterritorialization.

On any given day at the San Javier Park Library (where I first met JEIH-HCO and El Perro), to enter the building, you would pass by girls, boys, and young men and women using the front patio for break-dancing practice, working on their moves and developing choreography as music blasted out of a handheld stereo. In doing so, they were also performing a symbolic and physical reterritorializing of what had been contested public space, their bodies expressing the commitment they had made to a nonviolent life-style and performing a kind of public mobility that contrasted with the restrictions placed on physical mobility in their daily lives.

The limited public space that existed in Comuna 13 prior to the Fajardo administration was typically controlled and surveilled by armed gangs.[28] Residents of Comuna 13—and several other parts of the city—navigated *fronteras invisibles* (invisible borders) that were violently enforced by competing armed gangs block to block throughout the *comuna*. This heavily restricted residents' mobility and use of public space, and often threatened the lives of local youth. Several hip-hoppers (or "hoppers") have been killed in this dynamic, including four in Comuna 13 during the ten months of my field research, typically caught in a cross fire, targeted because of familial association, misidentified, or killed randomly.[29]

The Fajardo administration's institutional efforts to reclaim public spaces and forge new ones were met with the appropriation or "poaching" of these institutional spaces by the hoppers. La Elite used hip-hop culture to reterritorialize public space and re-signify it from a space controlled through armed violence (and/or the state) to one of nonviolent youth agency, community solidarity, and participation. As one member of La Elite told me:

> Until only a few months ago, we were restricted from using public space between one block and another within our neighborhood because there was an armed group for each block. So, we often used hip-hop as a shield; people would get to know us [as hoppers] and because of that, sometimes we could pass from one place to another. But as time passes, the armed actors change; one goes, another comes, including sometimes they're not even the youth of our *comuna*, but they send people from other neighborhoods to defend their interests, so there's been a big problem of restriction [of mobility].

. . . [W]e even defy some invisible borders, challenging the borders that exist—we know they are real, they're invisible but palpable—because we've unfortunately lost some members of the hip-hop community.

Youth in Comuna 13 had also been subject to government-imposed curfews that further restricted their mobility and affected the organizing of events such as hip-hop concerts. Yet, as one member of La Elite told me, "Similarly we take over the spaces, fields, high schools; we're there creating hip-hop, having events, doing 'battles' in the auditoriums . . . not just because of the slogan of the mayor's office [*"Medellín: A meeting space for citizens"*] but because it's a struggle we've been waging for a while now . . . the struggle to recover all of these spaces, precisely because they are public spaces, they are ours." The hip-hoppers tactically reterritorialized public space, playing on terrain imposed on them in the ongoing struggle between the state and conflicting armed gangs—all of whom understood public spaces as places where control is exerted.

This was perhaps most clearly illustrated by La Elite's annual two-day hip-hop festival, Revolución Sin Muertos, held in a sports field in Comuna 13. Local and national artists applied to gain a place in the lineup of performers, and a well-known hip-hop group from elsewhere in Colombia or abroad was invited to headline when the budget permitted. In 2010, Revolución Sin Muertos drew an estimated twenty to thirty thousand people from across the city and country to a *comuna* that was otherwise rarely visited by nonresidents.

Members of La Elite saw the festival as a cultural, social, and political intervention. They felt they were offering a platform for youth to develop and showcase their identities as artists, helping to create alternative life options (including earning a small income for their performances), and presenting a positive public image of youth. Members experienced the festival as something that brought them pride, respect, and public visibility: "It's a very important event and everyone wants to be there to see what the youth are creating. . . . Especially the parents come to see what the youth are doing. It's an event created by youth, so everyone's, like, I'm going to go have a look, these guys are doing something productive, I can let my child go [to the festival]." The success of the festival—evidenced by attendance, public support, and its reputation nationally—was seen by members of La Elite as proof that their work, and hip-hop culture more broadly, could help youth choose life paths that did not involve violence. Other residents of

Comuna 13 validated this perspective. As one man, aged sixty, with whom I spoke outside the 2011 festival commented, "I have seen examples. I have seen kids who were in armed gangs, they've come together in the *comuna* and they left that behind. . . . I like this festival because it brings together the youth of the *comuna* and they realize there's a lot of talent [here], and that the right path isn't drugs or arms but these festivals."

Revolución Sin Muertos had the effect of reterritorializing Comuna 13 for the two days of the festival, drawing residents of the city who otherwise might not risk traveling to the neighborhood in which the concert took place. This included residents of neighboring barrios controlled by competing gangs, and residents from less marginalized communities around the city who otherwise rarely, if ever, came to the stigmatized Comuna 13. The location of the festival was strategic on the part of La Elite to promote precisely this transcendence of invisible borders. As one member explained:

> From the last house in the uppermost neighborhood, they come down on foot without caring that they're crossing [an invisible] border. . . . There are people who normally can't come down here, but they're, like, "I can't miss this concert, Los Aldeanos [a Cuban hip-hop group that headlined in 2010], the groups from the *comuna*, or the group my friend is in who lives below, I'll risk it or go all the way around to attend the concert with my friends." . . . This concert mobilizes people. . . . Because there are times when you feel trapped, that you can't go out. I've also felt that way because everyone knows me, but just because I was from one part of the Comuna, I was associated with those *combos* [armed gangs].

In a series of audience interviews I conducted on the first day of the 2011 festival, more than half of the fifty-seven respondents had traveled from other parts of the city to attend the festival; only eight respondents (14 percent) expressed any degree of concern about their safety in traveling to or from the festival.[30] In the six years the festival had run by the time of my research, there had been no documented violent incidents with armed gangs in or around it; local gangs appeared to respect and even appreciate the concert—and the work of La Elite more broadly—sometimes attending as unarmed audience members. One elderly male audience member, who was not affiliated with La Elite, commented, "Hip-hop for the *comuna* means that we come together, people of all the different barrios, we knock down the invisible borders . . . the invisible borders stop here, we see that there are no borders."

Hip-hop festival Revolución Sin Muertos, October 2011. Source: author.　　　**3.1**

Break-dancing performance, Revolución Sin Muertos hip-hop festival, October 2011.　　**3.2**
Source: author.

Graffiti was another tactic of participation used to reterritorialize public space symbolically. Graffiti is a literal marking (through stylized spray painting) of one's artistic territory that has historically included transgressive tagging of public property, such as subway trains, bridges, and buildings. It is also a display of the artist's unique style and skill; graffiti artists typically develop their own tags (a stylized, spray-painted signature) and a particular aesthetic meant to be recognizable as their own. Reguillo describes the practice of graffiti artists as nomadic, transgressive of borders and boundaries.[31]

While graffiti started in Medellín (as elsewhere) as a clandestine activity carried out largely under cover of darkness, it has become widely accepted as a form of public art, and it adorned vast swaths of the city's walls. Graffiti and *grafiteros* (graffiti artists) went from illicit to legitimate—and even widely appreciated—in the public sphere. In a mutually reinforcing way, this acceptance brought graffiti artists financial and material support to produce more complex and larger paintings. Graffiti artists could gain some degree of cultural capital as public artists—a personally empowering experience for youth who attained it. In a small number of cases, this resulted in opportunities for economic capital through commissioned works; for example, the municipal government and some civil society organizations have hired young hip-hop graffiti artists to paint public murals. Since the time of my fieldwork, some of La Elite's graffiti artists and others have developed an additional source of income—"graffitours," in which they offer tourists a guided tour of some of Medellín's best graffiti.

Through their art, *grafiteros* in Medellín were also able to transcend some of the restrictions on mobility experienced by other youth. They did this by networking themselves such that, as one graffiti artist and member of La Elite explained:

> Almost all of the graffiti artists know each other, and they can all go to other parts of the city to paint, obviously with the help of someone from that area. Here in Medellín, invisible borders don't exist between graffiti artists. You won't clash with another graffiti artist from that area because there's like this agreement between everyone, and it's very cool because you can paint where you want— obviously, respecting the pieces of others because one has to respect the work that others do.
>
> But at times, yes, invisible borders exist between *los malos* [the bad guys].[32] It's more for other people than for graffiti artists....

Graffiti announcing "graffitour" in Comuna 13, Medellín, Colombia. Source: Palenque Tours Colombia, tripadvisor.ca. **3.3**

> People can't pass between one neighborhood and another because of the intolerance that the armed youth feel, they distrust everyone; so being a youth in a neighborhood that isn't yours makes you a target because they think you're going to harm them in some way or cause a problem. . . . If I go with someone known in the neighborhood, the [gangs] will let me paint. I've even had experiences where I'm painting, and *los malos* arrive and tell me that the piece is turning out cool and that I can paint there whenever I want. . . . Yes, being a *grafitero* has served me as a shield; being part of La Elite has also served me well.

Graffiti is not only about transcending invisible borders; members of La Elite and others used it as a symbolic intervention to challenge, and perhaps even culturally reterritorialize, spaces controlled by armed gangs. "We want people when they pass by to see that we were here, leaving positive messages. That at least a person passing by might say 'love, peace, dreams,' or some value, when they pass by the street and see this message." The *grafiteros* of La Elite emphasized that the quality of their graffiti was key to this tactic in order to appeal to youth as well as to a broader swath of the public and have the greatest impact. Some members of La Elite believed that these kinds of symbolic interventions would gradually help shift the culture of the *comuna* toward a more peaceful one in which prosocial citizen participation might become the norm. The outcome of these tactics of reterritorialization was not just a transcendence of invisible borders, but also increased participation in public life by youth who had been marginalized from it, and thus the cultivation of a richer ecology of participation.

Tactic Popular Education and Mentorship

A government representative who had worked closely with La Elite recounted, "Once I visited the hip-hop school and I saw guys who you never would have imagined having such potential and power share their knowledge with others. To see them giving workshops, transformed, with a totally different attitude than what you see in other spaces, really excited, sharing what they know—it was marvelous. I can think of a specific case of one youth, this kid who consumed drugs and wasn't in good shape, but while he was in the workshops, you should have seen how responsible he was, a total commitment to enabling others to access that knowledge." She was describing the La Escuela de Hip Hop Kolacho (the Kolacho School of Hip Hop), a popular education-style "school" run by La Elite that blended some of the principles of popular education with those of hip-hop.

Much of the scholarship in the Global North on learning in the digital age has explored the increased opportunities for peer-to-peer or horizontal learning in the digital mediascape, with studies often focusing on the learning that takes place outside of formal educational institutions and that is driven by young people's personal interests rather than by a top-down formalized curricula. Mizuko Ito and colleagues, for example, write that "peer-to-peer learning opportunities are all a click away. Through digital media, youth today have countless accessible opportunities to share, create, and expand their horizons. They can access a wealth of knowledge as well as be participants, makers, and doers engaged in active and self-directed inquiry." This network of scholars and practitioners has developed a model of "connected learning" in the digital age that "is oriented toward shared practices that emerge from youths' repertoire of practices developed in the horizontal movement and flow as youth move across everyday settings."[33] Horizontal learning may of course be greatly facilitated by the Internet as a networked communication platform. And yet, it clearly predates the digital age, and reengaging with horizontal learning models from other periods and contexts can help us to avoid technologically deterministic approaches to youth engagement in the digital age.

Popular education, for example, is a pedagogical philosophy that has been practiced in social justice movements across Latin America and elsewhere since the middle of the twentieth century. Paulo Freire helped to theorize several principles of this pedagogical approach, including horizontal processes of learning and decision making as opposed to what he called the "banking method" of traditional education, in which knowledge is "deposited" by teachers in a top-down manner for students to receive passively. Instead, Freire emphasized dialogical communication, cultural specificity, and the valuing of local or "popular" knowledge—with the goal of critical *conscientization*—to empower traditionally marginalized groups and increase their participation in decision making and social change.[34] Freire's thinking on the topic has influenced a great deal of community and youth organizing in Medellín and elsewhere throughout Latin America for decades, where popular education is most often understood as a counter-hegemonic praxis.

The Kolacho School was not the first of its kind in Medellín; popular education had flourished in the city since the 1980s in the form of hip-hop, theater, animation, and other grass-roots cultural and communication projects. By 2011, there were hip-hop "schools" in many of the low-income areas of the city.[35] Some of the members of La Elite had developed mentoring practices to pass on the four elements of hip-hop to other youth since 2005, but in 2010, the municipal government of Medellín offered to finance the piloting of a larger, more formalized mentoring process in part because they perceived La Elite and their social capital in Comuna 13 as a valuable resource for preventing future gang membership.[36] La Elite launched the Kolacho School as an initiative of "education and social outreach directed at children and youth of Comuna 13 to promote the principles of non-violence, respect for diversity, community work, and solidarity through the art of hip hop."[37]

Between ten and fifteen members of La Elite served as "popular educators" of the Kolacho School, offering daily or weekly workshops in the arts of rap, DJing, graffiti, and break dancing. The network expected approximately 150 participants, but 345 children and youth between the ages of ten and twenty attempted to enroll. They accommodated approximately 265 participants. The workshops not only taught the technical skills of each hip-hop element, but also addressed issues of gender equity, civic/political participation, local dynamics in the *comuna*, how to organize and promote events, and how to seek resources for each art form.

La Elite's approach to the Kolacho School was based on horizontal learning. As a popular educator of graffiti explained, "I don't try to teach like a professor, but rather more like a friend that can offer them some knowledge . . . so that they don't see me as the person that knows the most, but as another participant exploring different approaches. . . . [I]t's a space that belongs to everyone." One of the original founders of La Elite added, "What we want is to create a space of equality where all of the kids see each other equally. When I give a hip-hop workshop to children or youth, I go not to teach but to show a little bit of what I know and to learn a little from what the kids know."

Members of La Elite felt that their popular education school was helping them meet their goal of attracting youth away from armed gangs and into a more prosocial life-style. One member who offered classes in graffiti told me, "I've known various kids who, unfortunately, have had contact with armed gangs, and I've seen them come to my class and ask me permission to be in my class because they want to participate and learn about hip-hop and they want to be like me. . . . I can see that I'm doing positive work because they're really looking for another path."

The Kolacho School was still relatively new at the time of my research. Yet, it was clear that it had had some immediate impact—not least on the young popular educators themselves. It had helped shape their public subjectivities and leadership skills. As the director of the ACJ observed, "their lives were private but they're now becoming public because they are now public actors. And they've developed a great capacity for dialogue with the adult world." One member of La Elite also noted that public recognition of the Kolacho School made it easier for La Elite to interface with more established institutions, such as high schools, where they offered some of their workshops.

La Elite's popular educators also experienced an immediate shift in the typical youth–adult power relationship. Several of them recounted with surprise that parents of their workshop participants had come to them asking for advice about their children. One told me, "[T]hat a person older than you takes your opinions into account on such important matters such as how their child behaves at home is really gratifying; the parents are giving us their trust and believe in us." This recognition by adults was a transformative stage in the development of their public subjectivities. In tandem, the popular educators acknowledged that feeling a greater sense of responsibility was affecting their composure and daily behavior, such as how they dressed, how they spoke, and whether they chose to consume alcohol and drugs. A member of La Elite told me:

I think that La Elite has a lot of responsibility; actually, it's not that we *have* it, it's that we *want* to assume it, the responsibility of influencing more youth. We want the violence in the *comuna* to cease. If a kid doesn't have any way to help his mom or the resources to study, we try to take responsibility so that they come to us and we help. That's why we look for resources wherever they can be found, that's why we founded the school, so that kids aren't out on the street corner with nothing to do. . . . [I]f the kid has nothing to do, then they can come here and we'll teach them how to draw. . . . [M]any parents now trust us, so these are responsibilities.

This recognition by adults was a transformative stage in the development of their public subjectivities and in their capacities to engage in public life; popular education leveled the playing field and made this possible.

Much of the work on digital media and learning also theorizes engagement with cultural material (e.g., remixing music into hip-hop songs) as a gateway to or facilitator of participation in public life.[38] The case of La Elite exemplified this gateway dynamic between cultural and civic participation while also illustrating how a popular education approach may further strengthen this gateway—not just for individuals, but also for collective action or social movements. Their popular education school promoted hip-hop as an art as well as a form of civic participation and collective praxis. While few scholars substantively bridge popular education with more recent efforts to theorize participatory culture and learning in the digital age, key concepts clearly resonate across these fields: the value of horizontal, interest-driven learning and mentorship, learning through hands-on production and collaboration, and collective intelligence.[39]

Tactic Participatory Decision Making

Much of the power of participation lies in the ability to influence decisions that directly affect one's individual and community (however defined) well-being; one could argue that a participatory culture should be characterized as such based upon whether participants have a voice in, and influence over, such decisions. In this context, the *process* of decision making itself becomes central and, as the case of La Elite illustrates, can serve as a tactic of grass-roots participation.

La Elite made decisions in their weekly assembly meetings, which representatives of each hip-hop group were meant to attend per the network's rules.[40] All major decisions of the network were made during these meetings, by either consensus or voting, though members prioritized making decisions by consensus because they saw it as more truly democratic than making decisions by vote. Their assembly meetings contained moments of unity as well as tension, often fluctuating quickly between the two as debates about the network's various activities, resources, and priorities unfolded.

The identity of the collective itself was imbricated in this participatory decision-making process. While such participatory decision making is often time-consuming, members showed a remarkable degree of commitment to the process. This included sitting through several hours of meetings that frequently took most of an afternoon; some members lamented that the time they spent in meetings detracted significantly from the time they had to practice their music or art, and yet they remained committed to decision by consensus. One member who had not participated in any community or youth groups prior to joining La Elite told me, "Before, I didn't like things like organizing and meetings and such because it seemed like they weren't very important, because as a young person you think you should always be having fun, be playing . . . not be in a meeting, this wasn't my thing. But the truth is I discovered that participating in [La Elite's] meetings and all of this creates change for everyone, so I started to see that this is how change happens. I learned this in La Elite, and this motivated me to participate fully, to voice my opinion, to fight for political space." Another reported:

> Each [member] keeps growing, and you can see this reflected in their grades, in how they express themselves in a meeting . . . for example, a sister of mine joined [La Elite] because of me, and for example, at home, I already see the change, how she expresses herself, how she solves problems. I know that a lot of us here, at home, we're the ones who handle the problems, come up with solutions . . . because we've adopted a more mature consciousness . . . because all of this time spent in meetings or assemblies, each one is a different learning experience . . . these are some of the best experiences that this network has offered me.

When time-sensitive decisions were made without the input of all the groups in the network, tensions arose and were openly voiced and debated in subsequent assembly meetings, sometimes accompanied by accusations of self-interest.

Of course, horizontal decision making is never free of relations of power at the micro level. Even if the aim is to promote perfectly equal relations of power, participation in decision making happens with varying degrees of voice and influence due to the existing social configurations of power in which such processes are embedded. For example, in the case of La Elite, the low participation of women and girls in leadership positions reflected the ongoing gender disparities within the collective, as well as in much of the hip-hop movement in Medellín. The lower participation rates of females—compounded by the legacy of gender discrimination in Colombian society at large—meant that their interests and perspectives had less influence over the network's activities and over local hip-hop culture more broadly. Addressing this disparity was one of the goals of the network at the time of my research, toward which they had progressed at least at the level of discourse (according to the female members interviewed) and, in practice, among the few members of La Elite's newly formed committee on gender (four female, one male).

Participatory decision making is no panacea, but in the case of La Elite, it was both a structural and cultural practice (a system and a mind-set) through which its members experienced—and prefigured—a more participatory culture. Although La Elite developed its own internal group culture characterized by horizontality and collectivism, they also supported the development and expression of individual identity. In other words, while they were relatively communitarian in nature, they also valorized personal development and self-expression of the individual. Christopher Kelty concludes his entry on "Participation" in the collection *Digital Keywords* by writing, "we are trapped: between a participation that values the autonomy and voice of the individual, and one that values the experience of becoming-collective, of belonging. Properly speaking, participation is both of these things."[41] La Elite network exemplified the relationship between collectivism and individualism not as a binary trap but rather as a polycultural relationship in which both were nurtured.

As an outcome of La Elite's increased collaboration with such institutional bodies as the municipal government and foundations (primarily in the form of funded contracts and grants), they began to professionalize themselves as an organization. They developed a multi-year strategic plan through the participation of approximately thirty-five of the network's members and implemented a somewhat more hierarchically structured organizational form than they had had previously. For example, by 2011, there were eight "coordinators" taking on leadership roles heading up six committees but who still answered to La Elite as a whole. Institutional, adult logics, such as organizational structure and strategy, were thus being integrated into La Elite's practices of participation; their tactics were, in a sense, becoming more strategic. While the network was critiqued by other members of the hip-hop community who saw these changes as signs of becoming dependent upon or beholden to traditional authorities (such as the municipal government), I found this critique to be largely inaccurate based upon my observations of La Elite's relationship with the government, the network's daily operations, and its ongoing commitment to resistant or alternative practices of participation. Despite shifts toward somewhat more institutional, hierarchically structured practices, the vast majority of decision making within the network remained participatory.

The case of La Elite reflected the negotiation between institutional relatively hierarchical strategies, and more tactical, horizontal, networked approaches to youth participation. What emerged was not a contradiction or "mutually exclusive" binary between a hierarchy and a horizontal network,[42] but rather a productive dialectic in which power and the terms of participation were constantly being negotiated—not only between youth themselves, but also between the youth and the "adult" institutions with which they engaged. For example, within the more formalized organizing structure of La Elite's committees, some of the members reported benefitting from additional mentoring and skills building: "[I]n the fundraising committee I've learned a lot because I didn't know how to develop a project, send a letter, draw up documents and in this committee I've had the opportunity to learn who to reach out to, if I have a proposal who to address it to, what entities might support us. . . . [T]he good thing is that if you don't know something, there are others that help you, they sort of leave their legacy there." These are civic/political skills (organizing, campaign building, fundraising, proposal writing, negotiation, leadership, etc.) that are not typically learned in the traditional secondary school classroom. La Elite's committees offered a slightly more formalized space for mentorship that also projected a certain legitimacy to other institutions and the public while still maintaining a relatively open and horizontal structure as well as the pre-existing informal mentorship that had long been a part of La Elite's culture. This is an example of the potential symbiosis between grass-roots tactics and institutional strategies of participation—and between networks and hierarchies.

While the network collaborated with adult-led institutions, it carefully maintained its autonomy, and this autonomy was largely respected by its institutional partners. The support offered by the ACJ (such as assistance in administering finances and contracts) provided certain resources that enabled La Elite to remain open and relatively uninstitutionalized, while at the same time rendering it capable of engaging with formal institutions to obtain resources for their activities. This model of collaboration was one of mutual benefit; it helped to protect the autonomy of the youth collective (and its identity as a youth-run, participatory initiative) while also enabling it to interface with state and other institutions. For being allied with such a successful youth initiative, the ACJ, in turn, received a great deal of added attention, visibility, and credibility among state and donor institutions as well as the local community. This symbiotic relationship provided a model of how hierarchical and horizontal organizing structures could operate synergistically in this ecology of participation while still promoting participatory decision making that empowered members to influence the direction of the group.

In the previous chapter, I showed how the concepts of horizontality, dialogue, and openness can be used to analyze if and how particular digital communication platforms and practices can support youth agency and participatory public culture. We can extend these concepts beyond digital communication to include participatory cultural practices carried out both on- and offline. The case of La Elite illustrates horizontal, dialogical, open, and autonomous practices; it operated as a horizontally networked collective using participatory decision-making practices that sustained a relatively open system of managing the activities of the network. These attributes arguably helped ensure the popularity and success of the network.

Together, La Elite's various tactics of participation cultivated some of the preconditions of participatory public culture. They reduced barriers to and created spaces of participation. Popular education and participatory decision making promoted a culture of participation within the network that was also modeled for other local youth. Additionally, these tactics helped develop youth's capacities to participate in public life, and began to link their voices to greater influence in the public sphere. Their tactics of participation helped to challenge cultures of violence that had shaped public space and public life in their community, modeling an alternative path for youth. Promoting a more participatory public culture is, in some ways, antithetical to a culture of violence because it implies that power should be negotiated (and shared) through dialogue and self-expression rather than through force.

Using hip-hop to promote a culture of nonviolence among youth in marginalized urban neighborhoods is not new. Worldwide, alternative or independent hip-hop—commonly referred to as "underground"—often has a social justice orientation that aims at raising critical consciousness. But the case of La Elite and other similar youth collectives illustrate that certain kinds of practices and conditions enable meaningful participation in public life. Reducing barriers to participation, creating spaces and cultures of participation, developing capacities to participate, and linking voice to influence have real consequences for the quality of public life experienced by (youth) citizens. And yet each of these conditions of participatory public culture may be harder to attain for some youth than others; intersectional identity markers such as socioeconomic status, gender, sexual orientation, and race/ethnicity circumscribe opportunities for participation.

Son Batá Why "I Am Not the Same as You"

No soy igual a ustedes de eso si estoy convencido.
yo sí sé de dónde vengo y qué tierra es que me ha parido.
Más que lengua más piel, más que un color oscuro es toda una forma de ser
mi identidad, hija del mar pacifico de dioses cubanos y yo de negros palenqueros.
Mis padres chocoanos y ahora es 13.

Barrios periféricos ghettos de la ciudad
hay más desarrollo urbano, pero menos equidad. . . .

I am not the same as you, of this I am convinced.
I do know where I come from and which land birthed me.
More than language, more than skin, more than a dark color, it's a whole way of being
my identity, daughter of the Pacific Ocean, of Cuban gods, and me, of escaped Black slaves.
My parents from Chocó, and now it's the 13th.

Marginalized neighborhoods, ghettos of the city
there's more urban development but less equity. . . .

—Son Batá, song lyrics from
Mi Identidad (*My Identity*)

The Afro-Colombian music and cultural collective Son Batá is based in the uppermost reaches of Comuna 13, amidst small brick and corrugated metal houses perched precariously along the mountainsides, distanced from the developed city center both geographically and socioeconomically. To get there, you take the metro to the very last stop on the San Javier line and then the El Depósito bus to the end of its route. As the bus climbs up and

View from Son Batá's office, Comuna 13, Medellín, Colombia. Source: author.   **3.4**

Son Batá's cultural   **3.5**
center, Comuna 13,
Medellín, Colom-
bia. Source: author.

up, fewer and fewer of the buildings are painted and cleanly roofed. The narrow alleyways, raw red brick, and patchwork of corrugated metal roofs signal the hurried settlement of displaced migrants. Next to where the bus stops, there is a graffiti mural that reads: "*Comuna 13, territorio de artistas, Son Batá, My Pa13nke*" ("Comuna 13, territory of artists, Son Batá, my Palenque").[43]

Son Batá—a play on words that can be translated as both the sound of drums and "they are drums"—was created in 2004 by three male Afro-Colombian teenagers (aged fifteen, fifteen, and seventeen at the time), neighborhood friends who had their own hip-hop group. By 2011, they were running six different theater, dance, and music groups, with approximately eighty youth members who were primarily Afro-Colombian. They also ran a popular education-style school with approximately 150 children and youth participants. Like La Elite, Son Batá worked to replace membership in armed gangs with membership in a prosocial cultural group.

However, there was an important difference between Son Batá and La Elite, located at the intersection of race, identity, and citizenship. While there were Afro-Colombian members of La Elite, ethnic and racial identity were not as overtly a part of the group's collective identity as they were in the case of Son Batá. This raised different questions about the construction of youth citizenship and the dynamics of participation—such as who participates and how the barriers to participation are more significant for some than others. This case illustrates that participation cannot be defined statically or homogenously, and it cannot be experienced equally by everybody. In other words, the context in which participation is practiced, and by whom, shapes what participation looks like, as well as what it yields. The case of Son Batá is a reminder that we need to consider historical, cultural, and economic differences in an ecological approach to participation.

Peripheral Citizenship

The relationship between the Afro-Colombian population and the Colombian state has always been a troubled one. African slaves were first brought to the region in the sixteenth century, the start of a long legacy of physical as well as representational violence against Afro-descendants.[44] Even as slavery was legally abolished in the late nineteenth century, the Colombian Constitution of 1886 solidified a normatively white, Christian, Spanish-speaking citizenship, negating the country's rich diversity. While the center of Afro-Colombian culture has historically been the Pacific coast region,

Afro-descendants have also had a significant presence in the city of Medellín since at least the late nineteenth century. In the second half of the twentieth century, many Afro-Colombian residents from the Chocó region of Colombia's Pacific coast arrived in Medellín as economic migrants to fill the labor needs of Medellín's growing industrial sectors. From the 1980s onward, Afro-Colombians from various parts of the country also came to Medellín, fleeing Colombia's armed conflict, often having been forcibly and illegally displaced in land disputes.[45] The ironically named Nuevos Conquistadores (New Conquerors) neighborhood in Comuna 13, where Son Batá was based and most of its participants lived, is a shantytown settlement that resulted from these migrations. Neighborhoods such as these are commonly referred to in Medellín as *las periferias* (the urban peripheries, not just in the geographical but also in the socioeconomic and political senses of the term).

The Department of Antioquia, of which Medellín is the capital, is home to one of the largest populations of Afro-Colombians in the country.[46] There were no conclusive figures, but estimates of the total Afro-Colombian population in Medellín at the time of this research ranged from approximately 140,000 to 300,000 (approximately 6–12 percent of the population). And yet, despite hundreds of years of Afro-Colombian presence in the region, Antioquia's light-skinned elites and much of its middle class have maintained the hegemonic identity of Antioquians as strictly white. María Teresa Uribe shows how historically this has required minorities to distance themselves from their ethnic identities in order to assert their identities as *paisas*. Alternatively, some Afro-Colombian youth—including the members of Son Batá—have responded to discrimination and exclusion by asserting an outsider identity, even if they were born in Medellín. Many of the Afro-Colombian youth I spoke with in Medellín identified as *chocoanos* or *pacíficos* (people from the Chocó or Pacific coast region of Colombia) rather than as *paisas*. Yet, the fact of their being born in Medellín challenged the *paisa* identity as normatively white.

The long history of inequality and structural violence, the direct physical violence against residents of Comuna 13 by the state in the military operations of the early 2000s (see Introduction), and this entrenched outsider subjectivity experienced by Afro-Colombian youth all have direct implications for their citizenship and participation; they have lived largely apart from mechanisms, institutions, and cultures of the state and of civil society. Afro-Colombians have consistently reported higher levels of poverty and lower levels of well-being compared to other populations in the city.[47]

Historically, there have been relatively few dedicated Afro-Colombian organizations and institutions, and even fewer focused on or led by youth. Son Batá stood out for being a youth-led cultural collective with an explicit focus on Afro-Colombian identity and culture. Most other opportunities for participation in public life implied a de-racialization and homogenization of Afro-Colombian subjectivities—a process of *blanqueamiento* (whitening) for inclusion.[48]

The difference in youth's civic subjectivities in Son Batá compared to the other groups I spent time with was palpable; the distance between them and public institutions was not only geographically greater (since they lived in the uppermost reaches of Comuna 13), but also symbolically, politically, and culturally greater. The barriers to participation in public life and to a sense of empowered citizenship—even a sense of belonging *as a citizen*—were not only socioeconomic, but also cultural, political, and racial. Son Batá's youth leaders saw this as triple marginalization: first as Afro-Colombian youth, second as youth whose culture did not prepare them well for civic/political participation because of its historical marginalization, and third as youth from the stigmatized Comuna 13. In the words of one of Son Batá's founders:

> Afro-Colombians are usually located in the *periferia* of the cities, in the most hostile places, in the places where fewest institutions exist, where the fewest opportunities exist. . . . Normally in the barrios in the outskirts of the city *la ciudadanía no llega* [citizenship and civic culture do not arrive here]; exercising your rights, participating in the development of the community . . . in the Afro-Colombian population there is a reluctance to participate, and indifference in terms of the process of developing their communities. Because our parents haven't taught it to us, because they came to this city to work and that's it. . . . What we live day to day is violence, social exclusion, racial exclusion, and marginality.

Another of Son Batá's founders expressed their sense of invisibility in the public sphere: "[W]e're in a city that isn't ours, but many of us were born here; I was born here. I think that Afro-Colombian culture has contributed a lot to the construction of this city. But what happens is that the Afro-Colombian population is invisible to the local state, or rather there's an ignorance on the part of the local state; the mayor's office doesn't know how many Afro-Colombians there are in Medellín, in what conditions we're living, and how many arrive every month due to constant forced displacement."

The members of Son Batá saw this as a self-perpetuating cycle of marginality and violence that they were fighting to escape: "The only way to break this cycle is to recuperate and wake up the capacity of children to dream at an early age; that's why Son Batá focuses on the artistic process." As one of the founders of the collective explained:

> Son Batá is committed to the transformation of lives through art and music because they are tools to generate discipline; commitment; values; good practices; a commitment to development; a sense of belonging; to generate civic capacities and social and political participation. It is a process of change, [including] how to generate economic resources, how to strengthen one's capacities, one's abilities to communicate, how to establish a clear life plan, if one wants to go to university. . . . [W]e have to have a more protagonistic, more decisive role in our city. . . . We are influencing youth to study, to participate in political projects for our community; *la política* [politics and public policy] is our responsibility also.

Toward that end, Son Batá held popular education-style workshops similar to La Elite's for local youth and children in music, theater, and dance. These were meant to develop a critical consciousness among participants about their Afro-Colombian heritage, human rights, self-enfranchisement, and participation in local politics and community development. The aim was, as one of the co-founders explained, "to *concientizar* [raise critical awareness among] the public that we have to be active political agents in our city, to begin to change our cycle, to begin to change our reality . . . so that the Afro-Colombian population begins to have another status, another level of participation. . . . We [Son Batá] already have another perspective . . . not such a negative perspective but a perspective more of analysis, of understanding things to be able to propose solutions to things." As a result, Son Batá became known by some in Comuna 13 as *educadores del barrio* (neighborhood or community educators).[49]

I argue in this book that cultivating participatory public culture necessitates reducing barriers to participation, creating spaces and promoting cultures of participation, developing capacities to participate, and linking citizen voices to influence over issues that affect their well-being. Son Batá did all of these things using tactics that were often similar to those of La Elite, but because of their subjectivities as Afro-Colombians, a particular tactic became a necessary precursor to all of these: the re-signification of marginalized youth subjectivities and, ultimately, of youth citizenship.

3.6   Members of Son Batá perform for school children. Source: Son Batá.

Tactic Re-signification

In a context in which their subjectivities as low-income Afro-Colombian youth from Comuna 13 render them either invisible or criminal, participation in public life for members of Son Batá had to begin with a re-signification of their subjectivities, or what they referred to as changing *referentes* (references or representations). One of the founders of Son Batá commented that Medellín's city council lacked a single Afro-Colombian representative,[50] and generations of Afro-Colombian youth had grown up without seeing themselves represented in positions of power. In other words, they had few, if any, powerful *referentes* in the realms of political/ civic life. For some, re-signification was even seen as a matter of life and death; converting themselves into nonviolent public figures with a higher degree of positive visibility provided what one member described as a sort of shield that helped protect members of their collective from being implicated in the gang violence entrenched in their community. Despite having lost some members' lives in the violence, one member explained, "We have arrived at a conclusion and that is that the more visible [you are], the more bullet-proof you are because a person who appears in the media, in interviews, a person who is constantly working for the community and that won't just be like any other death, people will think twice before attacking you." At minimum, this "shield" served as a marker of belonging to a prominent youth collective that was known to be neutral or non-affiliated with any particular armed gang.

Son Batá became a very successful music and cultural collective—so successful that they were ultimately featured in a Red Hot Chili Peppers concert in Bogotá and appeared on Jennifer Lopez and Marc Anthony's reality television show *Q'Viva! The Chosen* in Los Angeles, California. Through their participation, members of Son Batá gained a degree of visibility, respect, and social capital unprecedented in their community and in the city at large. In doing so, they re-signified their subjectivities at numerous levels, starting in their neighborhood. One founding member explained:

> Twenty kids on a terrace at 6pm, in a city, in a *comuna* where normally you're accustomed to hearing gunshots. . . . [T]o suddenly hear the sound of musical instruments, laughter, songs; everyone comes out to their balconies, windows, to see what they're doing. From there more kids began to want to imitate this, they began to grab pots, lids, spoons, things from the kitchen, and they began to try to make the music that we were playing with the instruments. . . . So, it was no longer a process for us to learn music, but it had become a *referente* for the community. They called us *los músicos de la terraza* [the musicians from the terrace]. And more kids would want to make music, and it was a tremendous chain reaction that achieved acceptance, legitimation. . . . [K]ids are constantly seeing war . . . but if we sow *this* [Son Batá] in their mind, we are the *referente*, the role models that they will follow . . . examples of personal growth and triumph, of youth that finish high school, despite the difficulties.

The physical performance of culture is important here. Whether on a terrace or a rooftop in their neighborhood, or performing on stage in the center of the city or in the country's capital, Son Batá's bodies literally enacted their self-actualized empowerment and the commitment they had made to a more participatory culture and nonviolent life-style. Their performances were semiotic interventions aimed at disrupting the relationship between signifier (e.g., negative media representations and public stereotypes of youth from Comuna 13) and signified (the youths' own bodies and identities) by proposing new signifiers in the public sphere (e.g., Afro-Colombian youth empowered through prosocial cultural and civic/political engagement rather than gang involvement). Son Batá's performances intentionally exuded Afro-Colombian pride and communicated a strong sense of empowered physicality based on pleasure, play, and critical consciousness rather than on violence and force. Through their performance, Son Batá physically staked a claim about the change they were working to bring about, positioning themselves as role models while also living the experience of peaceful agency as they performed. Some members reported gaining both self-respect and the respect of the public, including from representatives of the municipal government.

It was against the broader backdrop of gang, paramilitary, and state violence and the stigmatization of Afro-Colobian bodies that Son Batá re-signified both individual subjectivities, as well as Afro-Colombian subjectivity in the city at large. Particularly for Afro-Colombian youth, whose bodies were so imbued with criminality by the mainstream media and in the dominant narrative of the city's recent history, the physical performances of groups such as Son Batá were acts of political and cultural resistance and re-signification. In resisting the culture of gang and other armed violence within Comuna 13, Son Batá reconfigured their public image and their opportunities for participation through a variety of cultural interventions, challenging the codes within which they had been unwillingly and detrimentally inscribed. The process of empowerment for these youth necessarily began with this struggle over the signifiers that overdetermined their public subjectivities and voices (or the lack thereof). In other words, in the context of Comuna 13, participation in public life—particularly for Afro-Colombian youth—necessitated a direct struggle over the terms of public discourse. As Arturo Escobar writes, "Power inhabits meaning, and meanings are a main source of social power; struggles over meaning are thus central to the structuring of the social and of the physical world itself."[51]

Being young, male, and from Comuna 13 implied a predetermined deficit of social capital that had very material consequences, such as difficulty obtaining employment because of one's address of residence.[52] The accomplishments and public visibility of Son Batá offered an alternative vision of success and power for local children and youth, particularly Afro-Colombian youth. Participation in a gang might be forgone for participation in a widely respected cultural practice that—importantly—might also generate income for members and their families through contracted performances. Son Batá's music, dance, and theater groups were hired to perform locally and nationally; payment was split among the performers, who in turn donated 30 percent of their earnings back to the collective to help cover administrative and supply costs. Income generation was one of several goals of the collective, which they saw as a form of community development, as well as a tool for reducing youth participation in gang violence. In this sense, the collective was also re-signifying economic possibility for local youth, intentionally aiming to replace guns with instruments as tools for income generation.

Although the tactic of re-signification was particularly essential for Afro-Colombian youth, it was also used in various ways by nearly all of the youth groups I observed. In Medellín, the history of negative media representations and stigmatization of low-income youth (see Chapter 1) necessitated the re-signification of youth subjectivities. While circumstances have changed since the 1980s, many youth still expressed a sense of being misrepresented and criminalized in public discourse; this motivated them to try to self-represent and re-signify their subjectivities through practices such as those of Son Batá's and La Elite's. Describing their work, a member and frequent spokesperson for La Elite explained, "There is a political intervention which is to change a culture through changing the *referentes* because in Medellín, we have a history in which the *referentes* are the narcotraffickers, the thug, the gangster, and to change—to provide other *referentes*—this is a great achievement." Re-signification may be crucial to enabling participation in public life in contexts of violence, where violence is also sustained through cultural meanings and signifiers and therefore must be challenged symbolically. But it may also be crucial for youth in most contexts, where traditional civic/political participation is dominated by adult perspectives and institutions that may not always value youth as agents of change on their own terms.

Artistic and cultural expression—in this case, Afro-Colombian forms—became the space in which youth could gain a sense of agency, cultural and social norms could be changed, nonviolent embodiments of power and success could be modeled, and civic engagement could be promoted among the otherwise marginalized Afro-Colombian community. Through cultural performance, Son Batá practiced nonviolent participation in the public sphere, enacting a more participatory culture and prefiguring peaceful coexistence. Like La Elite, their members gained some recognition and legitimacy in the eyes of their communities and, in some cases, government institutions; they developed a collective identity and cultivated a commitment to working for the betterment of their communities; and they acquired some of the skills necessary to do so. This helped overcome some of the particular barriers to participation in public life that for the Afro-Colombian members of Son Batá were heightened by generations of exclusion and peripheral citizenship. It is clear that historical and contextual dynamics framed their participation, and that participation cannot be understood or practiced homogenously. Son Batá's position in Medellín's civic polyculture was historically determined to be distinct from that of many other actors in the ecology of participation.

From the Periphery to Participation

The discourses and practices of La Elite and Son Batá cultivated youth cultures in which participation in collective action and in public life was the norm. Through their tactics of participation, young people reconfigured their individual and collective youth identities and asserted new/alternative modes of citizenship and participation. They also cultivated the conditions of participatory public culture (low barriers to participation, the skills and capacities to participate, spaces and cultures of participation, and a link between voice and influence). Their tactics existed in synergy and tension with state strategies within the broader ecology of participation in Medellín, suggesting certain possibilities for polycultural civics that I investigate further in the following chapter.

It is easy to romanticize youth collectives such as La Elite and Son Batá, and so far I have highlighted their contributions to participatory public culture in Medellín. It is worth noting that rhetoric of violence was exploited by these youth collectives, just as much as—if not more so than—discourses of participation. Both Son Batá and La Elite constantly referenced the violence in the *comuna* as one of their raisons d'être; they developed a sort of discursive dependency on the trope of violence that posed a challenge to changing that same culture of violence. This was in part a direct response to—and a co-optation of—the predominant rhetoric in the mainstream media. Yet, while many of their references to violence could be seen as part of their tactics to re-signify cultural codes (such as claiming that their words, drums, or paint cans are their "weapons"), they could also be understood as perpetuating the same discourse that had marginalized their subjectivities.

These cases also illustrate how discourses of participation may obfuscate and perpetuate existing hegemonies and inequalities. While Son Batá and La Elite represented an alternative to gang violence chosen by many youth, these were still only a small proportion of Comuna 13's more than eighteen thousand youth between the ages of fifteen and twenty-nine. In some ways, the power and visibility they gained created new hegemonies that—however unintentionally—left other youth overshadowed on the periphery, such as indigenous youth who remained largely invisible in Medellín. As one of the most demographically diverse *comunas* in the city, *La 13* was home to many youth who did not identify with Afro-Colombian or hip-hop culture and therefore did not experience these groups as opportunities for participation. Youth collectives such as La Elite and Son Batá were clearly not a panacea for all social inequalities, nor were they examples of perfect participation, which was further evidenced by significant gender disparities in both groups. There are, of course, no perfectly balanced relations of power and no perfectly inclusive practices of participation. The inherent imperfection of participatory practices is also evident in the case of participatory budgeting, where groups such as La Elite and Son Batá frequently interfaced with government and other institutional actors. The complex but in many ways productive tensions between these youth groups' grass-roots tactics and the institutional strategy of participatory budgeting is the focus of the following chapter.

Chapter Four

"Medellín, Governable and Participatory"

There are five *líneas estratégicas* (strategic lines) in the city of Medellín's 2004–2007 Development Plan. The first reads: "Medellín, governable and participatory." Participation was not just one of the organizing concepts of Sergio Fajardo's administration, it was the first one, and it became a central trope in the government's strategies to transform and govern the city. During this period, participation was mobilized in multiple ways; it was at once conceived by the municipal government as a tool for the integration, stabilization, and development of the city, and harnessed as a resource for resistant practices by grass-roots groups. The lines between the two were intentionally blurred when Fajardo and the Compromiso Ciudadano (Citizens' Commitment) party brought many grass-roots community organizers into government positions. One of their flagship initiatives was participatory budgeting (PB), a process that invites residents aged fourteen and up to take part in deciding on local resource allocation.

In Chapter 1, I adapted Michel de Certeau's terms to describe institutional *strategies* and grass-roots *tactics* of participation. When engaged dialectically rather than as binaries, these constructs offer a heuristic for analyzing the productive tensions between institutional and noninstitutional forms of participation. At times, strategies and tactics of participation work in synergy; at others, they exist in tension. Under the Fajardo (2004–2007) and Salazar (2008–2011) administrations, the synergies and productive tensions between the state's strategy of PB and grass-roots tactics of participation formed what I am calling a civic polyculture—a set of mutually beneficial, if imperfect and contested, relationships between institutional and noninstitutional forms of participation in a civic ecology.

PB in Medellín shows how the institutionalization of participation may serve as a form of governmentality but may *also* expand participatory public culture, particularly for youth. The case of PB therefore challenges binary claims about the institutionalization of participation being inherently good or bad (see Chapter 1) and instead foregrounds the gray area in between as a space of productive tension. Michel Foucault used the analytic of governmentality to theorize the "ensemble formed by the institutions, procedures, analyses and reflections, the calculations" of modern forms of "disciplining" citizens and exercising power.[1] Institutionalized discourses and practices of citizen participation can be understood as a form of governmentality; for example, the state may be bolstered by a cultural and political ethos of citizen participation, as citizens help to legitimize and expand the exercise of state power by participating in its institutions. This was an explicit goal of the Compromiso Ciudadano administration, which saw participation "as a privileged instrument for exercising governability and attaining legitimacy."[2] A former head of the Office of Social Development reflected in 2011, "Participation, as a strategy and public policy, is part of the stamp of Medellín today. . . . The transformation that people experience in Medellín today . . . is also a transformation in the form of governance and in the strategies and approaches that motivate community participation; greater institutional legitimacy is sought by improving the mechanisms of participation."[3]

Although the concept of governmentality is often employed in ways that are normatively negative, Foucault's use of the concept was arguably non-normative and "more or less neutral with respect to social change."[4] While participation does function as a form of governmentality, it is arguably a governing concept that has the potential to promote—though does not guarantee—more power sharing and inclusivity than most other concepts used to govern contemporary societies (e.g., exclusive discourses/policies of citizenship). This chapter investigates how these complex dynamics played out in Medellín between 2004 and 2011. It focuses on PB as an institutional strategy and youth tactics of participation within it—and how the relationship between these formed a civic polyculture.

The Turn toward Participatory Democracy in Colombia

Some of the impetus for PB in Medellín came from political discourses and policies of participation at the national level. The escalation of popular movements in the 1970s and 1980s, the armed conflict, and the crisis of legitimacy of the Colombian state prompted the country's partial turn toward participatory democracy.[5] As in other parts of Latin America at this time, a leftist discourse of participation emerged among Colombian activists and intellectuals to critique the elitist, clientelist, and increasingly authoritarian tendencies of the government, as well as the interventions of international finance and development organizations, such as the International Monetary Fund and the World Bank, which were seen as further widening socioeconomic inequalities. Social movements fomented, influenced by global trends in student, antiauthoritarian, socialist, indigenous, and feminist movements.

Faced with this pressure, the crisis of legitimacy, and ongoing conflict throughout much of the country, the national government responded by decentralizing certain mechanisms of governance to the municipalities through policies such as Law 11 of 1986, which mandated greater citizen participation in local planning and development processes. As Fabio Velásquez and Esperanza González write, "The institutionalization of spaces of citizen participation, associated with the decentralizing policies of the 1980s (Law 11 of 1986), implied a radical change in the architecture of the political system: people could intervene directly in the discussion of public policy and government programs at the local level, breaking the monopoly that the political elites (mayors and city councilmen) had over public decisions."[6] Yet, protests intensified again following the 1989 assassination of the Liberal party's presidential candidate, Luis Carlos Galán. A popular election was held to designate a national constituent assembly to revise the country's constitution, and as a result, student and other social movement actors were able to contribute to its drafting. The new constitution was ratified in 1991; it contained a political mandate for greater democratic participation and identified the promotion of citizen participation as a key function of the state.[7] It was the first time the concept of participation was constitutionally recognized in Colombia, and this further propelled discourses of participation across many spheres of public life as government and civic institutions sought ways of implementing and institutionalizing the principles of participatory democracy established in the constitution.[8] Participation thus became a key organizing concept and public policy agenda in the 1990s at both national and municipal levels.

Optimists saw the new constitution and subsequent changes in public policy as creating an opportunity, however tenuous, to better meet the needs and demands of Colombia's growing population of poor citizens. They hoped that the institutionalization of participation in governance would help to reduce clientelism, strengthen the public sphere, reestablish the credibility of the state, improve the efficacy of public planning, and modernize the political process, as well as facilitate more direct horizontal dialogue between citizens and government actors. The cynical view was that it represented simply a co-optation of popular discourse by the nation's elite—a rhetorical institutionalization of grass-roots participation and a hollow gesture to assuage the masses and maintain power.[9] And while it was remarkably progressive in its language, the 1991 Constitution has since been critiqued for lacking concrete mechanisms for citizen participation in the political system.[10]

Whether viewed optimistically or pessimistically, another way to understand Colombia's partial turn toward participatory democracy is through George Yúdice's lens of "expediency";[11] participation became reified as a political resource for both traditional power holders (responding to the crisis of legitimacy, the armed conflict, and the limited governability of much of the country) and social movement actors (responding to clientelism, elitism, and corruption, and seeking greater equality and access to power). There were thus clear parallels and relationships between the national context and Medellín's ecology of participation. In practice, processes of participation have been developed and implemented inconsistently across Colombia. At the time of its launch in 2004, Medellín's PB was considered to be a step ahead of other Colombian cities' participatory initiatives.[12]

Participatory Budgeting in Medellín

PB is a process for engaging citizens and civic associations voluntarily in decision making over part of a public budget through an annual series of meetings with government officials, thus making the allocation of resources a more localized and participatory endeavor. Ideally (though this is not always accomplished in practice), it is "a process that is open to any citizen who wants to participate, combines direct and representative democracy, involves deliberation (not merely consultation), [and] redistributes resources toward the poor."[13] According to Anwar Shah, former director of the World Bank Institute's Governance Program, PB at its best "offers citizens at large an opportunity to learn about government operations and to deliberate, debate, and influence the allocation of public resources. It is a tool for educating, engaging, and empowering citizens and strengthening demand for good governance. . . . Participatory budgeting also strengthens inclusive governance by giving marginalized and excluded groups the opportunity to have their voices heard and to influence public decision making vital to their interests."[14] PB was first attempted in Porto Alegre, Brazil, in 1989, under conditions that share some resemblance to those in Medellín. PB has since been conceived and practiced in several ways worldwide, influenced by a broad range of radical leftist, liberal, and conservative perspectives.[15] By 2013, PB had been practiced in more than 1,700 cities and towns in more than forty countries in Latin America, North America, Asia, Africa, and Europe.[16]

PB has been supported by international financial institutions such as the World Bank, prompting concerns that these institutions were using it as a tool to promote their neoliberal agenda of reducing the role of the state across the Global South by off-loading this budgeting process onto citizens and shedding partial responsibility for resolving structural inequalities. Benjamin Goldfrank estimated in 2012 that the World Bank had provided "loans or grants of at least 280 million dollars in support of PB and PB-related projects in at least fifteen countries since 2002." But he also documented that PB programs and advocates within the World Bank remained marginalized relative to the Bank's other agendas and investments. He did not find evidence that the World Bank's promotion of PB led to greater acceptance of the neoliberal agenda at the local level—or that the Bank had any significant impact on local PB outcomes.[17] While the World Bank was not involved in PB in Medellín, some scholars have argued compellingly that the city's process was in various ways amenable both to neoliberal and other elite interests, as well as to resistant or counter-hegemonic agendas.[18]

Independently of international financial institutions, PB was launched in Medellín in 2004 and written into law in 2007, localizing budgetary decisions for 5 percent of the municipal budget to each of its sixteen *comunas* (subdistricts) and five *corregimientos* (rural neighborhoods within the city's jurisdiction). Somewhat unique to Medellín, PB was linked to an existing process of participatory local development planning.[19] By doing so, the Fajardo administration aimed to make a structural change to Medellín's local development process in order "to construct a more democratic and inclusive city, with greater possibilities for the real participation of its citizens, [and] with incentives for local development starting from collective decisions."[20] Any youth over the age of fourteen was allowed to participate—by voting, proposing initiatives, and/or as a delegate (either elected by popular vote or representing a legally constituted community-based organization)—even before they reached the legal voting age of eighteen for traditional political elections. Some youth became significant actors in the process, which in turn affected youth organizing in the city in both positive and negative ways.

The government's objectives in implementing PB included cultivating civic participation; curtailing the high degree of distrust of formal politics in poorer communities; establishing the legitimacy of the municipal government and the formal economy in areas where informal markets and armed, non-state actors prevailed; reducing poverty; and developing the city. According to some analysts, PB was also implemented to improve Medellín's international image for foreign investment.[21] The introduction of PB bolstered the perceived legitimacy and effectiveness of the Fajardo administration both locally and internationally, it helped the administration earn a reputation for having recuperated public trust in public management, and it incentivized community organizing in certain ways.[22]

PB was carried out annually in stages over the course of several months. By 2011, the PB process had changed significantly from its inception and had become increasingly technical. Here, I summarize key components of the process at that time. First, neighborhood assemblies were convened for information sharing and a diagnostic process in which the public was notified of the status of the local development plan for their *comuna* (created previously through a separate participatory planning process). The public (any resident over the age of fourteen) voted on broad priorities related to that plan and elected delegates to the PB process to decide upon funding initiatives that in theory were in keeping with these broad priorities. Local civil society organizations could also send delegates to the process to represent their constituents. The PB process therefore combined both direct and representative participation; acting as a delegate (elected or representing a local organization) was a more intensive and direct form of participation. All delegates were trained on how to participate in the process and would subsequently meet in thematic working groups (on topics such as education, culture, economic development, public works, the environment, sports and recreation, and security and peaceful coexistence) to allocate funds to particular initiatives that fit those priorities. They met weekly for several weeks to present, debate, and ultimately select economic, social, cultural, educational, and infrastructural development projects for the coming year. Although meetings were open to the public and project proposals could be submitted by any formally constituted community organization, they were frequently presented by the delegates themselves, and only delegates could vote to select or reject each proposal. The municipal government reviewed the approved proposals from the working groups for viability and could suggest adjustments to them. After the working groups made any requested adjustments to the proposed initiatives, the delegates approved these in a meeting that was open to the public but in which only delegates could vote. Finally, an annual operating plan was drawn up by government authorities based on these selections, and this was submitted to the city council for approval. The government also oversaw the contracting and implementation of the approved projects. An annual evaluation of the PB process was then carried out, which informed subsequent adjustments to the process. All of the government representatives I interviewed in 2011 considered the PB process to be a system in constant need of adaptation and improvement to respond to local circumstances rather than a static system.[23]

In 2011, 110,455 people (4.7 percent of the population of Medellín) participated in the PB process, the majority through voting in the neighborhood assemblies on development priorities and electing delegates to the process.[24] The participation of women in PB was on average approximately 30 percent higher than that of men. Youth between the ages of fourteen and twenty-six comprised nearly 23 percent (24,884) of the voters, adults 41 percent, and seniors more than 36 percent. In some *comunas*, the relative proportion of youth who voted in the first stage (neighborhood assemblies) was higher than the relative proportion of adults and seniors.[25] The proportion of youth delegates year to year ranged between 9 and nearly 25 percent, reaching the higher figure in Comuna 13, one of the city's districts that has been most affected by poverty, displacement, and armed violence. In 2011, 22 percent—or 1,400—of all delegates were between the ages of fourteen and twenty-six.[26] These numbers are significant but do not adequately tell the story of youth participation in PB.[27]

Prior to the establishment of PB in Medellín, opportunities for direct citizen participation in public governance were relatively limited. This was true both structurally (formal governance was primarily practiced through elected representatives, typically the elite), and culturally (local politics were heavily shaped by clientelism). Structurally, PB created new spaces of deliberation in which decisions of public concern were made with the direct and indirect influence of local citizens;[28] these were spaces in which groups traditionally marginalized from the political process—most notably youth—had a somewhat greater chance of being heard and influencing outcomes. PB in Medellín can thus be understood as a technology for *relatively* direct, *relatively* widespread participation in public governance, and as a structure that may support (though not guarantee) a more participatory public culture.

On the other hand, PB in Medellín was established such that the government relinquished partial control over only 5 percent of its total annual operating budget to a more citizen-driven process of decision making while perhaps disproportionately increasing the political capital and perceived legitimacy of the administration. Critics argued that PB functioned as a sort of palliative treatment of the problems of poverty in the city rather than as a meaningful and expansive structural solution to a fraught economic system.[29] A cynical view of this is that PB offered a mechanism for the "responsibilization" of citizen subjects to participate dutifully in institutionalized governance while constraining this participation within particular bureaucratic systems and logics that limited challenges to hegemonic power.[30] At the same time, it partially obfuscated the responsibility that the state held for structural inequalities, shifting some of this responsibility onto civil society and community organizations at the level of the *comunas*. In his study of PB in twenty cities across different continents, Yves Cabannes concluded, "While in most cases PB improves governance and the delivery of services, it does not often fundamentally change existing power relations between local governments and citizens." Yet, he also found that PB processes "can foster the emergence of citizens' community counter-power."[31] Studies of Medellín's PB have similarly found both hegemonic and counter-hegemonic outcomes of the process.[32]

In addition to these critiques, some of my interviewees from local civil society organizations argued that there was a problematic cycle of institutionalization, bureaucratization, and in some cases corruption that was catalyzed by PB funding. For example, as described by the executive director of a local youth-focused nonprofit organization in Medellín, youth collectives that had previously functioned largely independently of adult logics "start[ed] to see that to access resources they have to institutionalize themselves. This has created many problems in the city, because many processes that are not yet mature institutionalize themselves just to participate in the use of the resources. This has created crises and ruptures of groups because there are also ethical problems in the management of these resources." So while PB in many cases increased the resources available to youth organizing, it also subjected it to the effects (both intentional and unintentional) of adult logics of institutionalization and bureaucratization—with some undesirable results. While I argue in this chapter, and more broadly across this book, that discourses and practices of participation can function either hegemonically or counter-hegemonically—and that in some cases this can create a productive tension—these are examples of its hegemonic potential.

Providing an institutionalized space of participation does not automatically change a civic culture unaccustomed to (and skeptical of) democratic transparent participation in governance. There was evidence of the replication of existing power dynamics (e.g., traditional powerholders wielding disproportionate influence) and the bleeding over of local corruption into the PB process. In some cases, paramilitary-affiliated armed groups maintained connections to and influence over local leaders, organizations, and other participants in PB; criminal activities affecting the PB process included bribes and misuse of contracted funds at local levels. Franklin Ramírez Gallegos describes how these influences impacted open dialogue and debate within the PB process in certain local contexts. While reports suggest that paramilitary influence over the PB process has increased since 2011, at the time of this research, this did not appear to occur to such a degree as to render the process dysfunctional overall.[33] My youth interviewees did not report that these dynamics significantly hindered their ability to participate in the PB process. Moreover, to dismiss the process entirely due to some instances of paramilitary influence would unnecessarily delegitimize the valid and extensive work of the majority of PB participants.

These critiques and challenges are pressing—and they are relevant not only in Medellín, but also in PB processes elsewhere. Yet, PB is not exclusively controlled by state actors; it is a space where a variety of actors and interests interface, a terrain on which power dynamics are struggled over and contested. Medellín's PB process did not overdetermine the modes of citizenship practiced within it; youth exhibited agency in their expressions of citizenship, some of which were radical or resistant. That is, PB partially shaped and constrained practices of citizenship, but it did not entirely limit the agency of its participants to express alternative conceptions of citizenship, to challenge discourses and practices of participation, or to influence the public culture being cultivated in and around it. Nor did it foreclose citizens from engaging simultaneously in more radical forms of participation. In fact, it illustrated some of the possibilities of polycultural civics and how different actors or "species" within this ecology of participation found ways to coexist and, at times, mutually benefit.

For example, from 2007 to 2011, La Red de Hip Hop La Elite (The Elite Hip Hop Network, or "La Elite"; see Chapter 3) managed to position their members as PB delegates with remarkable outcomes. Since La Elite began participating in PB in 2005, they typically placed six to nine delegates into the process each year. By 2011, the activities and goals of La Elite had been supported by the equivalent of approximately U.S.$138,000 in contracts funded through PB—a remarkable sum in this context.[34] Eight delegates (out of 378) in Comuna 13's PB process that year were members of La Elite.[35]

While initially funded through alternative (nongovernmental) sources, La Elite financed the majority of its annual hip-hop festival, Revolución Sin Muertos (Revolution without Deaths), through PB allocations. In 2010 alone, through its participation in various PB working groups, La Elite helped channel the equivalent of nearly U.S.$120,000 toward the hip-hop festival. However, due to the government's rules and regulations of contracting, these funds were not awarded directly to La Elite but rather to contractors whose proposals won the bids to provide each service needed for the festival (members of La Elite worked for free to organize the festival). Such experiences prompted critique from La Elite and other youth groups that engaged in PB but which were not legally formalized as organizations and therefore could not compete for the contracts resulting from the allocations. Many youth expressed frustration that their ideas were implemented by outside entities or contractors who might not operationalize them in the manner the youth had envisioned or be sensitive to the particularities of the local context. From this perspective, the process limited their role (and therefore their agency, as well as compensation for their labor) to one of being informants or sources of ideas but not active partners. From the perspective of government staff, such regulations mitigated abuse of the PB process for individual benefit and were required to legitimate and protect the investment of public funds. PB therefore was permeated by the distinct and often contentious logics of the state, the private and nonprofit sectors, and civil society.

The youth-led Afro-Colombian cultural collective Son Batá (Chapter 3) had the legal status to contract with the government. Yet, members still had many critiques of the PB process. One member of Son Batá explained:

> Son Batá as such doesn't [typically] participate in contracting [with the government on projects resulting from PB funding] because of

the dynamics of the Mayor's Office. Like, a project that was going to be carried out over eight months you have to execute in three months, so you and your organization end up looking bad, you do the work poorly, not in the way you had planned. So, Son Batá doesn't engage in contracting with the Mayor's Office, but we do engage in political spaces [such as PB] because that is where important decisions are made in terms of the direction of the city.

This is just one example of tensions between institutional and grass-roots approaches to participation. Son Batá took a more resistant stance toward the municipal government than La Elite did, but they still saw PB as an important space where they could influence decisions that affected their well-being and that of their *comuna.*

La Elite operated within—and in some ways embraced—the procedures established by the municipal government for PB, but they also took advantage of the opportunities it afforded, playing within its institutional terrain and "poaching" (to use de Certeau's term[36]) this space of participation in the service of youth and hip-hop culture. La Elite's more experienced delegates fanned out across nearly all of the working groups of the PB process— including education, culture, youth programs, and *convivencia* (peaceful coexistence)—taking their younger delegates with them to learn how to participate effectively, and to add their vote to each thematic working group. In La Elite's own weekly assemblies, members reached a consensus in advance on which initiatives their delegates would propose in the budgeting process, so that delegates across each working group were working to secure resources for the same initiatives. Often, the network would also coordinate with other youth groups who participated in PB, or with other leaders sympathetic to youth concerns, to mobilize as many delegate votes in support of youth-focused initiatives as possible. As one former delegate from La Elite told me, "Obviously, since it's all by vote, it depends on the alliances that you make within each working group." Such alliances were partly responsible for the fact that at the time of this research, the greatest allocation of PB funds was to arts and culture initiatives.

The strong presence of youth delegates in the PB process, and their use of such tactics, posed a challenge to existing relations of power in their *comuna* and to hegemonic conceptions of community development. As one La Elite member explained:

We go there to *pelear* (argue or fight), so to speak, with the traditional political community of this *comuna,* who are older adults;

men of forty years or older who were the *dueños* (owners) and the presidents of the Juntas de Acción Comunal (Comuna Action Councils), the Juntas Administradoras Locales (Local Administrative Councils). They keep a certain distance from us because the problem with them is that they don't see development if there isn't cement. . . . If there isn't a new street supposedly there isn't development. . . . For them, the only form of development of the *comuna* and of community participation is building a new street and putting the community to work there. . . . Because of this we scatter various youth across different working groups and there they make the argument for giving more resources to culture, health, education—finding resources wherever we can to try to be self-sustaining.

The Juntas de Acción Comunal (JACs) are elected citizens' committees for each *comuna* that were established in 1958 to involve community members in local development decisions. The Juntas Administradoras Locales (JALs) were later established by the Colombian constitution to improve public services and municipal development through citizen participation in oversight. In some cases, the JACs and JALs in Medellín had become entities shaped by dominant power holders in the *comunas* and subject to corruption and clientelism, rather than entities that promoted diverse and transparent participation. By the time of my research, these structures of participation were seen by several of my youth interviewees as representing the old school or as dominated by traditional power holders, while groups such as La Elite and Son Batá represented the latest generation of activists trying to forge new cultures of participation and propose new visions for local development.

The tactics of youth groups such as La Elite and Son Batá received significant criticism and pushback by adult participants in the PB process—particularly those whose traditional hold on power in the *comuna* was threatened. According to some youth delegates, traditional power holders intentionally blocked the influence of youth in Comuna 13's PB process for 2010. Some youth were prevented from assuming their delegate roles through charges of absenteeism, incorrectly filed paperwork, or representing community organizations that did not fully meet the criteria for participation. According to one youth delegate, "all of the important [youth] leaders were pulled out of the process, [including] some members of [La Elite and] Son Batá, for reasons of supposedly not having enough signatures or the signatures never arrived, things like that. . . . This was in 2010. In 2009, the majority of the budget was allocated to youth programs, culture, and education. So, seeing that they were losing the wall for the neighborhood, the stairs, all of that . . . they tried to take us out [of the process] the next year." This claim was not verifiable, but it reflected intergenerational tensions and struggles between youth organizers and traditional power holders in the *comuna* that played out in this space of institutionalized participation as these different actors interacted within the civic polyculture.

On the other hand, many adult delegates appeared to respect the youth's contributions and visions for development. In a July 2011 meeting of the working group on culture, several delegates (primarily adults not affiliated with La Elite) repeatedly referenced Revolución Sin Muertos (Chapter 3); the event appeared to be widely viewed as a well-established and valuable annual activity for the *comuna*. A former technical director of PB for the city also saw the youth's tactics in a positive light: "They have successfully converted themselves into political strategists of their own development. . . . And this was difficult, there was confrontation [with] older adults . . . [but] the youth have succeeded in getting themselves into working groups that are different than those that naturally correspond to youth." So, while a clear outcome of youth participation in PB was an increase in budget allocation toward cultural initiatives, youth delegates also engaged in other topics of debate in order to influence local development in ways that were not solely self-interested. Of the more than ten youth PB delegates I interviewed in Comuna 13, all emphasized that serving the interest of the *comuna* (and not just their own group) was a goal they shared. The concept and terms of community development were debated and contested in the PB process. For these youth, PB was seen as an imperfect improvement in the governance system and a space where they had greater success in participating in political life. It was a hegemonic space of participation to which they brought their counter-hegemonic tactics, and the result was multivalent—and in some ways mutually beneficial.

One evening in July, I attended a meeting of the Economic Development working group for Comuna 13's PB process. Four members of Son Batá were present as delegates; the one female delegate (aged twenty-four) was acting as the secretary of the working group, and another male delegate (also aged twenty-four) was sitting in as the temporary chair of the meeting. Traditional gender roles aside, it was remarkable that the two most significant positions within the meeting were held by Afro-Colombian youth, a group that has historically been profoundly marginalized in Medellín (see Chapter 3).

Co-founder of Son Batá, Jhon Fredy Asprilla Jave, in a participatory budgeting meeting in Comuna 13, Medellín, Colombia, 2011. Source: author.

4.1 &
4.2

Indeed, for those youth who participated in the PB process, significant outcomes of the experience included developing leadership skills and learning how to navigate institutional political processes and local power relations. All the youth delegates I interviewed reported learning various civic, political, and leadership skills.[37] One of the most active and publicly recognized members of La Elite reflected:

> For me personally, the majority of my training was because of participatory budgeting. Learning to speak, to justify why hip-hop is important, learning how to create initiatives, do projects, learning about the laws, statutes, decrees, learning to tolerate others and how diversity works. If you go and listen to the elderly wanting to do a dance project—wow, what a beautiful thing! So, they should get some funding, it doesn't matter if less is left for the rest of us; so this also gets us to support the *comuna*. We also learn about bad behavior and what not to do . . . we learn to recognize and anticipate the corrupt leaders.

A younger member reported:

> It's been really important because obviously you learn to defend yourself and defend what you want and you realize how things work within participatory budgeting, how you have to argue . . . [and] gather contacts; often people from the mayor's office or from many important places go. You make alliances so you know who you can count on and who you can't. So, for me, this experience has been very important. . . . By the second year, you already know how things go in participatory budgeting . . . already you start to make yourself noticed as a leader, people begin to recognize you, you learn to reason more, to know how and when you have to say things.

PB often appealed to youth who were not drawn to other more traditional political participation. In La Elite's case, their members consistently expressed disinterest in participating in the Consejo Municipal de Juventud (Municipal Youth Council, established to serve as an intermediary between Medellín's youth and the state) but proactively engaged in PB. While all the youth delegates I interviewed remained critical of several aspects of the PB process, they also expressed a sense of agency, influence, and accomplishment through their participation. As a delegate from La Elite argued, "Youth have a lot of influence [in Comuna 13's PB], we've empowered ourselves in this process over time and in reality we're the ones pushing the process."

They perceived positive outcomes of their participation at the individual, group (organizational/collective), and community (*comuna*) levels. In addition to developing leadership skills, this included attaining resources and public support for youth initiatives and influencing the development of the *comuna* through budgetary allocations. In the process, they were learning how to perform as subjects within an institutional apparatus of participation, but at the same time, they retained a critical or counter-hegemonic perspective—an alternative vision of citizenship—and attempted to work the apparatus in favor of their goals for their group and their broader visions for the *comuna*.

PB can be understood as having helped to create spaces and structures for more horizontal decision making and open dialogic communication around issues of local development in Medellín—key characteristics of participatory public culture. The PB process also became a space for civic education that helped develop participants' capacities to participate in public life. In addition to my own findings, several studies have documented that Medellín's PB during this period cultivated nontraditional leaders.[38] It had comparatively lower barriers to participation for non-hegemonic groups than other forms of governance in the city—for example, for Afro-Colombians, who were otherwise scarcely represented in city governance.[39] Certain groups that had been historically underrepresented in processes of governance (e.g., youth, women, and lower-income citizens) participated in disproportionately high numbers and, to varying degrees, directly benefited from this participation.[40] Participation rates of both youth and adults were often higher in districts with lower socioeconomic averages.[41] In PB's first four years, more than 30 percent of the total PB was allocated to initiatives that benefited youth; young people clearly influenced the outcomes of these budgetary decisions. A member of the municipal administration reported that PB had also familiarized government authorities with more of the city's community groups and organizations, particularly youth groups, than they had previously been aware of, and appeared to have increased communication between these groups and the government. The participation of marginalized youth was generally valued and encouraged by the municipal government, motivated in part by the need to stabilize the areas in which these youth resided.

Yet, PB is an inevitably flawed process of participation in that different citizens face different barriers to participation. For example, even though the proportion of women participating in PB during this period was relatively high, women with demanding household and employment responsibilities, particularly single mothers, found it difficult to participate; some women reported that participation in PB became another burden on their already demanding days.[42] At the time of my research, only one female member of the youth collectives I studied in Comuna 13 was participating in the PB process. Participants' preexisting social capital and the level of their skill in articulating and lobbying for their desired outcomes can be further barriers or enablers to their effective participation in PB.[43] Youth living in *comunas* with high rates of violence and *fronteras invisibles* (invisible borders patrolled by competing gangs) at times could not attend PB meetings, which were often held at night, without putting themselves in danger. Indeed, Medellín's PB must be understood as particularly shaped by its context of violence and could never be completely isolated from it; it affected who participated, when, and how.

The promotion of self-interest in the PB process was another commonly cited criticism among both youth and adult interviewees, as in this comment from a former government advisor to the PB process and a co-founder of a community-based organization: "There is a problem when local organizations think about the PB as the only way to fund their work. Because instead of participating in PB for local development, they are fighting for the survival of their organization." Of the youth delegates interviewed for this study, however, all expressed both an interest in lobbying for their own groups' agendas and a commitment to participating in decisions for the betterment of their *comuna* as a whole. Son Batá was one example of a youth-driven organization whose participation in PB tended to be oriented more toward the well-being of the *comuna*—and especially that of the Afro-Colombian community—rather than the interests of their organization alone.

The dialectic nature of PB was evident in how tensions and problems in the process spawned public discussion over what it means to participate in local governance, what constitutes direct participation in the public sphere, and even what constitutes development. From youth activists to academics to civic organization leaders to municipal government representatives, the strengths and weaknesses of the PB process were widely debated, and it was often criticized as much as it was celebrated—if not more so. For example, in 2004, when PB was first implemented in Medellín, the municipal government offered a menu of options from which each local PB process would choose certain predetermined initiatives. These options were based on the municipal government's development plan and significantly restricted the decision-making power of the local communities. In response to public criticism, the municipal government changed the procedure in 2009 so that it would be based on the local development plans for each of the *comunas*—plans that had been decided upon through a previous participatory planning process with local citizens. A former government advisor to the PB process and a co-founder of a community-based organization in Medellín recounted, "When we started listening to [the local communities], the whole thing changed because they were proposing strategies that worked. . . . The challenge in participatory budgeting was about the idea of participation that the municipality had versus the idea that the community had."[44] Both ceded and gained ground in an ongoing negotiation—and reinvention—of participation.

The fact that PB sparked debate about the terms of citizen participation offered early evidence of its impact on Medellín's public culture.[45] One interviewee with experience in both the local government and a youth-focused civil society organization, and who was in many ways critical of PB, nonetheless felt that it had contributed to

> the transformation of the mentality of the city, to allow people to be more engaged in the decision-making process, even though it's not happening all of the time. . . . It could be improved a lot, but it's doing a great job of posing a problem to the city about citizens' participation, and encourages people to think about "What if I can make the decisions myself?" and by inviting them to that position of decision making, it's increasing the levels of self-awareness of the local situation, and thinking about solutions. Even if they can't be achieved, thinking about local strategies and solutions to local problems is a good way to increase the awareness of our context and encourage people to get more involved.

These were important steps toward a more participatory public culture, and they arguably helped to establish an expectation of participation among youth and other citizens who might not have access to more formalized or centralized forms of political decision making.

Further, the broader discourse of participatory democracy on which PB in Medellín was based is one that can be—and was being—appropriated by citizens outside of institutionalized spaces of participation. As Juan Fernando Londoño writes, "In many cases citizens have appropriated this concept to reconfigure their relation to the State and redefine in practice the way in which democracy is understood" through noninstitutionalized forms of political participation such as marches and strikes.[46] In other words, PB may have helped proliferate an ethos of participatory democracy that fueled other expressions of participation.

PB in Medellín between 2004 and 2011 can therefore be understood as both a technology of governmentality *and* an imperfect but productive mechanism for encouraging a more participatory public culture. Yet there were limits to this institutional strategy, which was—importantly—supplemented by grass-roots tactics. The work of groups such as La Elite and Son Batá, which practiced cultures of participation aimed at reconfiguring how young people related to and interacted with their communities, was a crucial complement to the macro-level structural change that PB represented. Such groups cultivated a cultural ethos of participation, as well as some of the skills needed to participate. Without such cultural work, the effectiveness of PB would be limited. While some structural changes may occur more quickly (such as implementing a PB process, allocating more resources to public education, providing Internet access, or other measures to address economic inequality), the ultimate efficacy of such strategies rests upon the extent of cultural change occurring in society in tandem. Creating institutionalized spaces of public participation in decision making about local development alters the terrain on which different actors struggle to exert agency, but it does not necessarily change the underlying culture in which existing relations of power are entrenched and maintained. In other words, structural change through public policy initiatives alone cannot cultivate a participatory public culture; social/cultural meanings and practices must also change, and this is where grass-roots tactics become particularly important.

Participatory Budgeting as Civic Polyculture

We can understand PB as a polycultural relationship between an institutionalized form (or strategy) of participation and the alternative relatively uninstitutionalized participatory cultures (or tactics) of youth collectives such as La Elite and Son Batá. As in agriculture, where polyculture refers to the mutual benefit of planting multiple different crops together, even if they may sometimes compete for the same resources, the relationship was characterized by both tension (e.g., between hierarchical institutional bureaucracies and more horizontal autonomous youth practices) and symbiosis (e.g., between the benefits youth attained through participating and the increase in legitimacy gained by the government in otherwise hostile neighborhoods).[47] In many instances, PB increased the resources available for youth organizing. However, it also brought an institutional adult logic and bureaucracy to the ecology of youth organizing in Medellín. At the same time as PB influenced youth organizing, youth organizing influenced the outcomes of the PB process by contributing new ideas—including ways to help reduce gang membership—and helping ensure its legitimacy in the eyes of the public. Understanding this as a civic polyculture draws attention to the potential of institutional strategies and grass-roots tactics to be mutually beneficial and, in some cases, interdependent. Some strategies of participation were informed by grass-roots tactics, and some tactics were shaped by institutional strategies; this was central to the construction of participatory public culture in Medellín.

Youth collectives such as La Elite and Son Batá had complex relationships with the municipal government that included both collaboration and contestation. As the director of the YMCA-affiliated Asociación Cristiana de Jóvenes (Christian Youth Association, ACJ) explained, "La Elite has disagreements with the state and they express these. But they also negotiate agreements with the state. La Elite assumes a political posture that in the construction of democracy, you have to speak with an actor that's different from you. So, you'll see that all of the members have their cell phones with their [government] contacts." At times, La Elite's tactics not only resisted the culture of violence perpetuated by illicit networks but also challenged the state and the ways in which the government was directly or indirectly involved in the violence in Comuna 13. For example, funding for their Kolacho School of Hip Hop was first offered by the Secretaría de Gobierno (Office or Department of Government), which ran a controversial initiative called Fuerza Joven (Youth Power) targeting at-risk youth and offering incentives for gang members to disarm. The youth I interviewed in Medellín were widely critical of this initiative because they saw it as ineffective at keeping young people out of gangs. They argued that many simply turned in a gun, received the incentives, and then returned to gang life; the initiative might, in fact, have provided greater incentives to own a gun than to join a nonviolent youth group. They felt that the culture and practices of violence (as well as the economy that fueled it) remained essentially unchanged.

Four members of La Elite between the ages of eighteen and twenty-five attended meetings with the municipal government to negotiate the terms of the collaboration for the launch of the Kolacho School. As one of them recounted:

We had to go to the mayor's office with proposals of what we wanted to do. . . . They sent us to Fuerza Joven, which is a process for high-risk youth, but obviously we said, "But we're not high risk youth, we don't want to be involved in any gang, we are very clear about what we want." An intense discussion began because we didn't want to participate in any way with Fuerza Joven—in other words, the money had to come from somewhere else because we wouldn't touch that because we're not in agreement and because the kids that are involved in [Fuerza Joven] are those that have guns and are in gangs but we're very clear that that's not our thing, our thing is music and art. . . . We fought with them over this and said no. So, they decided to send the money to the Department of Civic Culture. So, we calmed down and started talking to [the Deputy Director of Metrojuventud, the office in charge of youth programs in the Department of Civic Culture].

This negotiation illustrates a moment in which institutional strategies and grass-roots tactics clashed in the process of trying to institutionalize youth participation. In this case, it was largely a productive tension in which youth leaders asserted a position of power—to which the government ceded in the negotiation—strengthening their public voice and learning more about navigating institutional systems in the process. It illustrates the conflictual and symbiotic relationship that may exist between institutional and noninstitutional efforts to promote participation. Reflecting on the relationship from the government's perspective, a representative from the Department of Civic Culture told me, "Sometimes it's hard to understand why at times there's so much clashing [with La Elite], if there's such a close relationship, why is there so much questioning [by La Elite]. Obviously there are things to change, but what these last administrations [of Fajardo and Salazar] have created—and I know this, I've been there—is the relationship with citizens is totally different. It's about creating together, thinking together."

Not only were the Fajardo and Salazar administrations politically invested in citizen participation and the PB process in particular, but both were composed largely of community organizers, academics, and activists who were less predisposed to clientelist relationships and corruption than previous administrations of traditional political party elites. However, subsequent administrations placed less emphasis on community-based practices of citizen participation. In 2016, the mayoral administration of Federico Gutiérrez Zuluaga instituted a reform to the PB process on grounds that some of the PB funds were being misused. However, by several accounts, the reform placed greater constraints on public participation and limited that of noninstitutionalized groups, delegitimizing the process and leading to a significant decline in participation in PB; by the time of this writing; some of the youth groups I'd followed in the process had decided not to participate.[48] The municipal government's stance toward youth/citizen participation under Fajardo and Salazar was unique in the history of the city and illustrates the precarity of PB—and its dependence upon the political culture and actors of the state.[49]

There has been a debate in both media studies and development studies about whether participation is hegemonic or counter-hegemonic (see Chapter 1)—are you participating *in* hegemonic relations of power, or are you challenging these *through* participation? Of course, the answer lies in the particular circumstances. But the cases of PB, La Elite, and Son Batá—and of Medellín more broadly—trouble the very premise of this binary construction. The episteme of participation can be simultaneously wielded by state actors to stabilize and govern (i.e., governmentality) and by grass-roots groups (including youth groups) to challenge hegemonic relations of power and exert greater agency. The answer can thus be both, and we should instead think ecologically about participation as a resource that can be wielded differently by various actors (sometimes in synergy, sometimes in conflict). Participation in PB during this time period was not simply empowering or exploitative, authentic or co-opted; it was part of a polycultural civics. This offers a way to think about the possible mutual benefit of both institutional strategies and grass-roots tactics of participation in relation to each other, even if they sometimes compete for or clash over the same resources in the ecology.

The use of digital communication technologies to "fertilize" participatory democracy initiatives in Medellín was still minimal in 2011. Yet, the possibilities were numerous and have only grown. Hollie Russon Gilman's *Democracy Reinvented* reviews several cases of PB worldwide, including in Latin America, where digital tools have enhanced the process. This includes increasing participation by enabling online idea generation and submission of proposals; online debate and voting; using text messaging to mobilize people to participate in person; and measuring the impact of PB-funded projects. She concludes that digital tools have enhanced the process in several instances. At the same time, face-to-face participation remains crucial to the effectiveness of PB, given the centrality of dialogue to this model of participation.[50]

In sum, PB in Medellín under the Fajardo and Salazar administrations created an institutionalized space for participation with lower barriers than most traditional government institutions. It became a terrain in which some youth (and other citizens) engaged in dialogue, decision making, and the construction of a somewhat more participatory public culture—albeit one that remained contested and fraught with obstacles to participation. Despite its shortcomings, PB was a key part of a productive civic poly-culture during this time period. PB catalyzed public debate over the logic and terms of participation and citizenship, changing the discourse through which public culture was constructed.

This shift toward more participatory governance through PB was one that was relatively more empowering to marginalized groups and other nontraditional power holders than traditional political spaces, even as the limitations of, and obstacles to, participation remained significant. By ne-gotiating the relationship between tactics and strategies in this ecology of participation, youth in Comuna 13 and elsewhere across the city articu-lated alternative forms of what Evelina Dagnino and others have called "citizenship 'from below'"[51]—in this case, citizenship based on the notions of participation, horizontality, and cultural/social change rather than on traditional politics and dominant notions of development. These and other insights that can be adapted from Medellín's civic polyculture and applied in other contexts are the focus of the final chapter.

Chapter Five

Polycultural Civics
in the Digital Age

A lthough many have called its transformation from an epicenter of narcotrafficking and urban warfare to a trendy hub of innovative urban
planning, tourism, and youth organizing "the Miracle of Medellín,"[1] this is
partial hyperbole. The media, the private sector, and government officials in
and beyond Medellín produced and marketed the idea of the city's transformation, largely through rhetorics of citizen participation and connectivity.
Yet, Medellín remains a city that is challenged by multiple forms of criminality, armed violence, and inequality. And the progress made (in citizen
participation, infrastructure development, education, etc.) has not been a
"miracle," but rather the hard-won outcome of extensive efforts of many
people, including government officials, local business people, community-
based organizations, and youth activists. While the overly simplistic international narrative of Medellín's transformation tends to credit the city's
gains to the administration of Mayor Sergio Fajardo (2004–2007),[2] in this
book, I have focused on the crucial role that youth cultures, activists, and
networks also played.

These chapters have explored how an ethos of citizen participation was
intentionally cultivated to help organize and govern society in Medellín
between 2004 and 2011, and the productive tensions between state strategies and grass-roots tactics of participation. Youth participation in Medellín challenged and reconfigured the boundaries of these categories; it was
enacted and defined at the messy intersections of power and counterpower,

where narratives of institutionalized and noninstitutionalized participation crossed and were mutually shaping. For this reason, I have advocated in this book for the concept of polycultural civics as a way to understand and cultivate the complex but potentially mutually beneficial relationships between these different forms of participation in public life.

Grass-roots and, to a lesser degree, institutional actors pursued tactics and strategies of participation before and after the two Compromiso Ciudadano administrations (2004–2011), but during this particular period, participation was a central organizing concept in state strategies to an unprecedented degree, under the banner of social urbanism. This yielded mixed results, but on balance, it resulted in a noteworthy period of polycultural civics that helped promote a more participatory public culture. Structurally speaking, infrastructure such as impressive public libraries, computer labs, and transportation systems helped connect communities at the periphery with resources and the city center both digitally and geographically. Thousands of young people who engaged in the participatory budgeting (PB) process received a new kind of civic/political education while at the same time influencing decisions about local development. Culturally speaking, youth collectives such as Ciudad Comuna, La Elite, and Son Batá were helping establish prosocial public participation as a norm for young people in low-income neighborhoods and as a way to access power and build social capital without joining an armed gang.

Among the youth I interviewed, perceptions about Medellín's "transformation" were mixed. They generally expressed a sense that the city had moved toward a more participatory public culture with greater opportunities for prosocial youth empowerment, but they still saw many areas for improvement. By way of example, I will quote at length from an interview with an Afro-Colombian member of Son Batá. It demonstrates sentiments repeated by many of my youth interviewees, who had all experienced some positive outcomes, including greater ability to participate in public life and to improve their own well-being:

> Undeniably, this city has transformed from the state not reaching the citizens, from armed groups having control of the *comunas* [referring here to the poorer subdistricts of the city], from youth in the *comunas* not having access to higher education, from not having support if you had an idea to launch a small business, from art and culture being seen as distant things—now they play a protagonist role in the city . . . megaprojects like the Medellín metro, the Metrocables

[gondolas], the Park Libraries, the gardens; projects that are arriving directly to the heart of [poorer] communities, to that corner there, to the periphery, that are generating real impact in the city. And further, they come from a couple of transparent administrations, which are constantly telling the city how they are investing their resources . . . which has given the community the power to decide over part of the resources as well. . . . Participatory budgeting is a great strategy that they put in the service of the communities. I believe that, with all of this, today Medellín is a model city, although there are still things lacking, there are still many things to improve—*many* things to improve, many things to do—but that's because all of the bad of many decades can't be resolved in two administrations, in eight or nine years, it's little by little. But it has begun to be resolved in a transcendental way. In the *comunas*, there are still hit men, there is still death, there are still kids with arms, but they do not have control of the *comunas*. Now, the kids of the *comunas* can go to university, can go to other parts of the city, there are big Park Libraries, quality high schools that are changing education, changing how the state is viewed, [and] the community is influencing their budget. There are many things that are changing radically in this city . . . because in addition to the state, community organizations like Son Batá are working for transformation, to take youth away from the negative things and add them to the positive things. . . . I do believe in this transformation because I have seen it and I have lived it. Before, private business and public administration *no llegaba hasta aquí* [didn't arrive here], but now their plans, their programs, their projects, their budgets arrive. Education, culture, art arrives. . . . It's getting much better.

Certainly, prosocial youth participation in Medellín's public culture was both a contributor to and a beneficiary of these changes.

Yet, several factors continued to limit participation in public life in Medellín, most notably the ongoing neo-paramilitary and narcotrafficking violence at both local and national levels. As a former senior government official in Medellín's Office of Social Development told me in July 2011:

There is a factor that is always disrupting the opportunities for the people, which is narcotrafficking. . . . It is like a disease, that is to say it's festering like a cancer. It is a cancer that is very difficult to kill and that metastasizes. So, a community might organize itself, and when you least expect it a gang of *narcos* [narcos or drug traffickers] appears and damages the life of the people. . . . I believe it is the great enemy of this society, of the entire country, and of the world.

While homicide rates fell significantly during the majority of Fajardo's time as mayor, the violence escalated once again during Alonso Salazar's mayorship (2008–2011) due to the extradition of top narco-paramilitary commanders to the United States in 2008 and subsequent struggles for territorial control. The reintegration program for paramilitaries that had been mandated by the national government also fell short of its intended benefits. Clearly, central government policies and the national context influence a city's public culture. By 2017, however, homicide rates had continued to decline overall. Medellín had remained off the list of the world's fifty most violent cities for three consecutive years, and it had been ranked highest among Colombia's cities in terms of residents' perceptions of quality of life.[3]

Mass displacement also continued to weigh heavily on Medellín's development as those fleeing the conflict in the rural countryside settled in informal neighborhoods and elsewhere throughout the city, adding to the demand for public services. Moreover, corruption and clientelism remained significant challenges to the city's public culture, although roughly a third of citizens in 2011 believed that civic participation was changing that. In 2011, a citywide survey of public opinion regarding life in Medellín among those aged eighteen and older found that three in every ten respondents felt that civic participation had helped to reduce clientelism, *politiquería* (politicking, in a manipulative or otherwise negative sense), and corruption. Four in ten believed that participation offered a way to influence the decisions of local authorities and to speak as equals with them.[4]

While many residents, including many of my youth interviewees, did experience a positive transformation, some analysts conclude that this aided the elite business and political classes as much as, if not more so than, average citizens. They argue that despite social urbanism's redistributive initiatives that focused development in the poorest parts of the city, the branding and relative stabilizing of the city bolstered foreign investment and local corporations in ways that more substantially benefitted elites. Foreign direct investment increased tenfold in Medellín between 2002 and 2009, and while levels of poverty were reduced, income disparities increased.[5] These are important qualifiers, but they do not negate the lived reality—and impactful efforts—of youth who experienced transformation within the city but also within their communities and themselves as a result of their acts of participation.

In 2011, Aníbal Gaviria, a former governor of the Department of Antioquia and a member of the Colombian Liberal Party—one of the country's two traditional parties—was elected mayor, bringing an end to this unprecedented period of nontraditional leadership by the independent coalition Compromiso Ciudadano (Citizens' Commitment). Echoing Mayor Fajardo's sentiments at the end of his term, outgoing Mayor Salazar worried that the sustainability of the innovations and accomplishments of the two Compromiso Ciudadano administrations were precarious.[6] For example, even though PB had become legally mandated, subsequent administrations weakened the process by limiting the degree of citizen participation possible within it.

Indeed, some of the government's initiatives from 2004 to 2011 have had a lasting impact, others less so. Yet, the insights we can gain from this noteworthy period in the city's recent history can make a lasting contribution to the study of participatory public culture and can inform research, policy, and practice well beyond Medellín. These include the concepts of:

- *participatory public culture*, and its preconditions (reduced barriers to participation, spaces/structures and cultures of participation, capacities to participate, and participant voices linked to influence over decisions that affect their well-being);
- *polycultural civics*, as a way to understand the potentially productive relationships between institutionalized and noninstitutionalized forms of participation; and
- *horizontality*, *dialogue*, and *openness* as lenses through which to analyze digital communication in relation to participatory public culture.

This study was not intended to present the case of Medellín as an ideal model of youth engagement; while certain aspects are replicable, each context and ecology of participation is particular. Instead, in the spirit of Gilles Deleuze's reflection that "A theory is exactly like a box of tools," I have offered this set of concepts to inform research and practices of youth participation in the contemporary moment.[7] My hope is that these concepts advance critical but productive analysis—and practices—of participation; I have used them here to help identify the relations of power in which youth participation is embedded; the kinds or degrees of participation being offered or enacted, whether structural or content-related; the barriers to participation, particularly for historically marginalized groups; and where and how institutionalized and noninstitutionalized civic participation might be mutually beneficial (i.e., polycultural). All of these considerations must be taken into account in efforts to cultivate youth engagement and participatory public culture.

Digital Communication in the Civic Polyculture

At the time of my research, most youth in lower-income neighborhoods in the city accessed the Internet in schools, public libraries, or Internet cafés at minimal or no cost, thanks in part to efforts by the municipal government such as Medellín Digital to provide Internet access throughout the city (Chapter 2). The participatory cultures of La Elite and Son Batá emerged before the widespread adoption of social media platforms in the late 2000s/early 2010s in Colombia. However, the networked capacities for sharing information and user-generated content that characterize social media platforms significantly reduced these collectives' costs of communicating, networking, and mobilizing, and amplified their reach.

Many youth (including nearly all of those I interviewed) used Facebook as a primary interpersonal communication tool in addition to cellular phones.[8] Yet, they also used Facebook as a semi-public sphere; I say "semi-" because the architecture of the site is such that users can only access the content of their Facebook "friends" (or public Facebook groups), but in many instances, users would "friend" other users whom they'd never met but found through mutual Facebook friends. While few of La Elite and Son Batá's members owned a personal computer or a smartphone with private Internet access in 2011, nearly all of the members I interviewed each had more than 1,500 Facebook friends, and many had several thousand. As a point of comparison, in 2012 the typical (median) teen Facebook user in the United States had three hundred friends.[9]

Youth organizers, activists, and artists in Medellín saw Facebook—along with YouTube and, to a lesser extent, Twitter—as a key resource for making their work more visible, marketing it, and mobilizing their audiences. Facebook status updates[10] had largely replaced the need for printing flyers and posters to engage the public in their activities; members of La Elite and Son Batá used them to circulate announcements, links to a new hip-hop song, and schedules of concerts and festivals, as well as to recruit participants for their popular education-style schools (Chapter 3), or solicit input from fans. For example, when La Elite members invited suggestions from their Facebook publics about which hip-hop groups to recruit to headline the

Revolución Sin Muertos (Revolution without Deaths) hip-hop festival, extensive online discussion ensued among members and fans. Their members also used Facebook and Twitter to express political opinions and prompt public dialogue, and they regularly conversed directly with government officials. In one tragic example from March, 2011, following the homicide of a young hip-hop artist from Comuna 13, a Facebook exchange took place via status updates and comments between several youth activists and two municipal government officials. Youth activists directly pressured representatives of the municipal government through a semi-public conversation on Facebook to take some "big, strong, impactful" action in response to the homicide. Several thousand people potentially had access to this conversation.[11]

Shortly after this Facebook dialogue, youth and community leaders (including members of La Elite and Son Batá) organized a march protesting the violence, largely using status updates and Facebook groups to mobilize participants. Subsequent Facebook status updates requested transportation and other forms of support from the mayor's office to enable more youth to participate in the march. Ultimately, the municipal government (specifically, the Office of Civic Culture, to which the two previously mentioned government officials belonged) supported the march by providing logistical resources for the concert following it. Between one and two thousand people participated.[12] It is highly unlikely that the mobilization—organized within a couple of days—would have reached the same scale and drawn such rapid attention from the local government (and, subsequently, the media), without the use of these digital tools. They enabled horizontal, open, and dialogic communication between youth activists and government officials, and amplified the outcome; digital communication technologies thus served as a sort of fertilizer of this polycultural relationship.

In a related example, a member of La Elite posted a commentary criticizing the seemingly more tokenistic deployment of youth participation by a subsequent mayoral administration. The semi-public visibility of such exchanges was important; Facebook served as a digital public sphere, predominantly of youth, but also—crucially—including government administrators. It was one in which youth attempted not only to dialogue with but also to openly criticize the government.

Digital technologies did not determine the participatory cultures of Ciudad Comuna, La Elite, Son Batá, and other youth collectives, but they did strengthen and amplify them, in some cases reducing the costs of organizing and enabling what Sidney Tarrow calls "scale shifts" in their visibility and mobilizations (e.g., from localized to citywide and beyond).[13] The way these collectives used digital communication tools helped reduce barriers to participation, bolster young people's capacity to participate in public life, and link their voices to centers of influence. And yet, the culture of youth organizing in Medellín and the culture of the municipal government from 2004 to 2011 explain why social media tools were wielded with significant impact. In other words, digital communication tools may—like fertilizer—enhance but do not entirely determine grass-roots tactics of participation. Digital communication technologies can act as a fertilizer in a civic polyculture because they can help promote horizontal, open, and dialogic communication in ways that may be more accessible to citizens than some traditional media, given their networked, mobile, and relatively low-cost characteristics. And yet, this is clearly not guaranteed; it depends greatly on the available digital infrastructure, the surrounding cultures and practices of use (including digital literacies), and the structure and management of the digital communication platforms. When digital tools are not implemented in contextually specific ways that take into account the local civic ecology, their impact falls short of their potential (see Chapter 2).

While both Medellín Digital and Ciudad Comuna attempted to promote public participation and social inclusion using digital communication tools, the stark differences in their respectively top-down and bottom-up approaches revealed distinct ideologies and practices of digital inclusion, citizenship, and participation. These differences have fundamental implications for how we understand and cultivate participatory public cultures. Bridging insights from participatory communication, digital media studies, and Latin American science and technology studies, I have argued that analyzing practices and platforms of digital citizenship through the lenses of horizontality, dialogue, and openness can help us distinguish between different communicative approaches to participation in public life and their various merits and drawbacks. A participatory communication perspective maintains a focus on relations of power and on the communicative process versus just its product or outcome, and it helps avoid technologically deterministic approaches to digital media policy, design, and research. It also prompts critical questioning of the kind of citizenship being enacted through the communicative process.

Medellín Digital's choices of communicative architecture (e.g., proprietary rather than open software and centrally controlled rather than open publishing) and its relatively narrowly conceived approaches to digital literacy and digital citizenship did not match its stated goals for participation and inclusion. Here, Nico Carpentier's distinction between structural participation and content participation offered a useful analytic for understanding the extent to which (digital) communication platforms may or may not be participatory.[14] Medellín Digital afforded very few opportunities for structural participation and some limited opportunities for content-related participation. In contrast, Ciudad Comuna did both, including developing an open publishing platform using open-source software for local social organizations and citizen groups.

However, the widespread use of proprietary social media platforms such as Facebook (which offer limited opportunities for structural participation) by groups that practice participatory culture (such as Ciudad Comuna, La Elite, and Son Batá) illustrated that proprietary software and participatory cultures are not necessarily mutually exclusive. Limited structural participation in communication platforms may constrain participatory cultures in some important ways, but it does not preclude their existence or ability to flourish. As these cases showed, important tactics of participation (e.g., reterritorialization and re-signification) may be performed through or bolstered by the production and circulation of content, even on platforms with limited structural participation. Facebook and other proprietary social media platforms are not a panacea for youth engagement, but they can be (and are) significant resources, if highly flawed, within contemporary ecologies of youth participation. What's more, while structural participation allows users to help shape their communication platforms, it is not always of interest to (or feasible for) all users; it is often only the well-resourced techno-elite who experience this level of structural participation in digital communication. And yet, the case of Medellín Digital illustrated that digital citizenship initiatives would do well to expand the opportunities for young people to be involved in the design of digital communication technologies; this is particularly pressing, as their social and economic realities (including education, employment, medical care, etc.) are increasingly shaped by algorithms that tend to reflect the values of designers and dominant groups. The United Nations Children's Fund (UNICEF) and other youth-oriented organizations are rightly calling for greater involvement of youth in technology development.[15] This may necessitate a deeper commitment to cultivating critical (digital) media literacy among young people, and raising public awareness about the less visible forms of governmentality that operate through digital algorithms.[16]

Content-related participation also has its limits. The online explosion of user-generated content does not necessarily mean that more voices are being heard; and when they are heard, the questions as to who hears and with what impact are still of concern. Nor does it mean that meaningful, engaged dialogue (rather than individual expression alone) is taking place. Additionally, most of the largest existing user-generated content platforms for digital communication were designed primarily for individual rather than collective expression and, in some ways, may hinder the latter.[17] Yet, as concerns persist about the seeming individualization of social and political participation online,[18] La Elite serves as an interesting exemplar in that it functioned as a network of hip-hop groups that promoted both individual expression and collective action.

There are ample reasons to hold a more pessimistic view of participation in the current moment, in which concerns about surveillance, privacy, and misuse or exploitation of user data dominate international discussions about digital communication. Participation in/through the digital mediascape can no longer be romanticized, and offline participation once again appears all the more relevant. For all of these reasons, content-related participation must be analyzed in context on a case-by-case basis, rather than making sweeping conflations of digital modes of expression with participation and the empowerment of citizen voices. Andrea Cornwall rightly pushes back against the conflation of voice and participation when she argues that "translating voice into influence requires more than simply effective ways of capturing what people want to say."[19] A participatory public culture is one that values individual and collective political agency, participation, and the contributions of diverse viewpoints in the social construction of society; it is one in which listening and responding becomes as important as speaking. As the previous chapters have shown, some officials in the two Compromiso Ciudadano administrations in Medellín arguably made some important efforts to cultivate a political culture of listening. It is not difficult to imagine the potential societal benefits of doing so in contexts elsewhere across the globe. More work needs to be done, however, to critically theorize listening in relation to the many contemporary modalities of expressing voice and the algorithmic architectures that shape these.

Learning from Medellín

Analyzing participation ecologically helps us understand it as more than a buzzword and as dependent upon far more than digital media platforms. The case of Medellín illustrates that there is no pure or perfect form of participation—rather, participation is an episteme through which relations of power are enacted and contested. It is a powerful episteme that can become a key resource in a civic ecology, wielded as both a technology of governmentality (e.g., to stabilize and govern) and as a tool for grass-roots resistance and agency. In this sense, participation is not normatively good or bad; it is nuanced and shaped by context. Some institutional strategies of participation are informed by grass-roots tactics, and some tactics are shaped by institutional strategies—and none of these may be sufficient on their own. The concept of polycultural civics offers a way out of binary thinking that pits "authentic" grass-roots participation against institutionalized participation, and emphasizes that the relationship between the two is central to the construction of participatory public cultures. Medellín's polycultural ecology of participation shifted the expectation of many youth and other citizens toward a norm of participatory public culture, however imperfect the experience of participation was in practice.

Three factors in particular enabled polycultural civics in Medellín. The first was a youth movement fueled by collectives that promoted proactive citizenship and often engaged with the local government while maintaining a critical stance. The second was the existence of some institutional entities that facilitated youth participation in public life but did not overly control it or appropriate it. The third was that there were two municipal administrations sympathetic to community-based organizing that implemented initiatives aimed at engaging a wider and more diverse array of citizens (including youth) than had been the case historically. These three factors were mutually reinforcing.

There is a widely held view, backed by several studies, that today's younger generations are disengaged from and often dismissive of public institutions, rendering these institutions less relevant (see Chapter 1). As cyberoptimist Clay Shirky has argued, "We are living in the middle of a remarkable increase in our ability to share, to cooperate with one another, and to take collective action, all outside the framework of traditional institutions and organizations."[20] Such perspectives tend to understate the ongoing role of institutions in shaping public and political culture and even in supporting youth participation. Clearly, institutions (from government agencies to civil society organizations to commercial enterprises) are still scrambling to adapt to cultural and political shifts enabled by rapidly evolving digital networks, and expectations of responsiveness to the public have increased. But instead of seeing institutions and the state as irrelevant to contemporary youth engagement, we would do well to think about how all can adapt and play a role in developing a polycultural civics that cultivates mutual benefits between informal youth networks and public/civic institutions. Doing so requires that we understand how different actors or "species" within a civic polyculture enact—and struggle over—participation as a resource and as a form of power.

The grass-roots-friendly stance of certain government representatives and offices between 2004 and 2011 was crucial to the development of Medellín's civic polyculture in favor of a more participatory public culture. The Compromiso Ciudadano administrations advanced positions such as the following, which was part of a 2009 citywide report on youth groups co-published by the municipal government and an association of civil society organizations:

> Institutions are obligated to detach themselves from their omnipotent roles, and instead to create conditions that favor intergenerational interaction and integration, through the valorizing of these [youth] forms of expression, of the creation of symbols and meanings that are ever renewed, through which youth name and remake life. . . . Public institutions have a responsibility to continue supporting the strengthening of youth group processes in accordance with social and political participation. Nonetheless, it is recommended that special attention be given to the tendency to institutionalize the youth processes, which is almost always a result of state intervention.[21]

This research-based policy recommendation underscores what we can learn from Medellín about the complex but potentially productive polycultural relationship between institutional and noninstitutional approaches to public participation, particularly when it comes to youth engagement.

Similarly, Mizuko Ito et al.'s analysis of "connected civics" found that bridging noninstitutional youth-driven activities and networks with formal institutions holds the greatest potential for positive impact—that is, if adults serve mentoring and connective roles "on young people's terms" while not constraining youth-driven "affinity networks." They note that "research indicates that these connections between participatory culture and politics don't necessarily form automatically and can be actively brokered by peers and adults, and through organizational infrastructures. . . . When young people are able to connect *both* flexibly networked as well as more formalized and capitalized kinds of infrastructures and institutions, we see the largest impacts, both personal and societal."[22] Bridging studies of digital media activism and development communication, Jan Servaes and Rolien Hoyng likewise conclude that "possibilities for progressive politics lie at the intersections of institutions and extra-institutional networks."[23] Medellín shows us that there are important roles to be played by youth/grass-roots and adult/institutional modes of participation if the relationship between these can be cultivated in a mutually beneficial polycultural manner.

Of course, certain youth face greater obstacles to participation in public life than others, as the case of Son Batá illustrated. For these Afro-Colombian youth, grass-roots tactics did, in some cases, serve as a bridge to institutional participation that otherwise seemed out of reach. Yet, institutional participation remained a fraught terrain for them, given the history of marginalization and exclusion of their communities from spaces of public participation and governance. In his multidisciplinary review of youth participation, Barry Checkoway concludes, "Participation is affected by race, gender, age, income, education, national origin, family and community context, rural or urban residence, residential segregation, religious tradition, cultural beliefs, mass media, television watching, social science, professional practice, civic knowledge, extracurricular activities, community service, public policies, legal constraints, institutional barriers, school disparities, parental and teacher encouragement, adult attitudes, and other factors."[24] Indeed, as these chapters have relayed, many factors mediate youth participation in intersectional ways, necessitating an ecological approach to understanding and supporting it.

Ciudad Comuna, La Elite, and Son Batá illustrated actions that I proposed are also crucial to the development of participatory public culture, namely reducing barriers to participation, creating spaces or structures of participation (on- and offline), cultivating cultures of participation, developing capacities to participate, and linking the expression of voice to influence over decisions that affect participants' (and their community's) well-being. Their tactics created modes and spaces of participation in which youth could be recognized, respected, and even heard by centers of power—prompting historian and former municipal government official Gloria Patricia Uribe Neira to comment, "Today it is clear that the youth of the city are effective protagonists in creating their own symbols of resistance, counter-cultural proposals and critique—in many cases proposing solutions."[25] While these accomplishments are quite significant and overwhelmingly positive, in Chapter 3, I also noted the ways in which youth collectives can inadvertently perpetuate existing social (e.g., gender or racial) inequalities.

Youth groups are relatively transient and heavily determined by the personalities of their participants (especially those in leadership positions) whose interests and commitment levels may change. From a policy and planning perspective, supporting the work of youth groups may seem a high-risk investment of time and resources, but it is one of great importance to the cultivation of engaged youth citizenship, polycultural civics, and participatory public culture. What is clear is that the resources in the surrounding civic ecology influence youth organizing. Several youth leaders I interviewed had received leadership training and capacity building in both formal and informal educational settings, and these significantly impacted youth organizing in the city. Part of encouraging a civic polyculture is providing such resources, which can act as fertilizers without limiting the "organic" growth of youth engagement on its own terms.

PB was another important part of Medellín's civic polyculture from 2004 to 2011. It illustrated how the institutionalization of participation can, in some instances, help to expand participatory public culture, particularly for youth and other non-hegemonic groups, by putting in place a (somewhat) more accessible structure for political participation. The imperfections and tensions within the PB process in Medellín catalyzed critical public debate over the very terms of participation, what it means to participate in local governance, and what constitutes direct participation in the public sphere, further contributing to the city's ethos—and citizens' expectations—of participation.

It is worth noting that while PB especially aims to enable citizens who are typically underrepresented in government to influence development in their communities directly, such opportunities for participation are not necessarily to the exclusion of professionals with expert knowledge. Both the PB process and all the youth collectives studied here had benefited from input by professionals and established organizations with relevant expertise—another sign of the importance of cultivating synergies or polycultural relationships between institutional and grass-roots/noninstitutional forms of participation. As Carpentier notes, "the models that support stronger forms of participation (even the most maximalist versions) do not aim for the (symbolic) annihilation of elite roles, but try to transform these roles in order to allow for power-sharing between privileged and non-privileged (or elite and non-elite) actors."[26] Moreover, while participatory projects are characterized as being relatively horizontal in their organization, certain participants invariably take on leadership roles, or function as more influential nodes in a network, and their presence or absence affects a project's trajectory and often its sustainability. In its focus on horizontality, scholarship has mostly overlooked the question of leadership within participatory cultures—a topic that merits further study.[27]

As the case of Medellín illustrates, it is also vital to think about how to cultivate cultures of participation, not just impose structures for it. The municipal administration's strategies for participation were inevitably more structural, such as providing free Internet access or implementing a PB process. While such structural changes may occur relatively quickly, the ultimate efficacy of their strategies rests on the extent of cultural change happening in tandem, but this often occurs more slowly. Much of the groundwork for cultural change in Medellín was being laid by youth collectives such as La Elite and Son Batá. Medellín's Secretary of Civic Culture, Lina Botero Villa, put it this way: "The hip-hop culture in Medellín has been a key piece in the construction of the city's collective imagination." Thousands of young people have attended hip-hop schools such as La Elite's across the city over the past two decades, and similar models exist from Venezuela to South Africa.[28]

Indeed, the hip-hop movement in Medellín, while locally focused in terms of its intended social impact, reflects an international youth culture that cannot be understood outside of globalization—and while young people in the Global South have suffered in numerous ways under the conditions of globalization, global connectivity also brings additional possibilities for youth citizenship. Rossana Reguillo sees a "new political cosmopolitanism" emerging from the youth-led international protest movements of the twenty-first century.[29] If this is indeed the case, this cosmopolitanism is enhanced by digital communication technologies but may depend equally on interest-driven youth culture networks. (And of course, digital technologies' global connectivity can equally be used by anti-cosmopolitan, exclusionary networks.)

If cultivating a more participatory public culture occurs through a variety of means, then it also occurs at different rates. Researchers of participatory communication and communication for social change have repeatedly pointed out the incompatibility of such practices with the short-term agendas and fiscal cycles of the development and state institutions that often fund them.[30] The impacts of a youth collective or other participatory culture are not easily measured and may not become evident until later in the lives of their participants. Setting short-term, strictly defined measures of evaluation of participatory practices confines our ability to understand the myriad and nuanced ways in which individuals and communities may change through these practices, and how this affects public life in the years and decades following—for example, if a member of a youth collective goes on to become a community organizer for a civil society organization and ultimately becomes a government official able to direct changes in public policy and resource allocation (as was the case with one of my interviewees in Medellín).

Participation is a form of labor—typically unpaid—that produces both stability and instability, governance and resistance. Most of the people I encountered in Medellín viewed participation as inherently positive. Similarly, the vast majority of the literature on participatory culture makes an implicit normative assumption that participatory cultures are intrinsically positive for society, although it is increasingly obvious that some examples of participatory culture may have negative consequences, such as those that promote hate speech or intolerance of difference.[31]

Economics clearly also plays a role in participatory public culture, as I have touched upon briefly across the cases in this book. However, I intentionally subsumed it to an emphasis on cultural, political/civic, and communicative participation. I did so as a sort of counter-rationality to neoliberal logic, which heavily privileges economic rationality over any other in public policy. Economic status affects youth participation in public life in numerous and complex ways; analyzing this properly requires investigating not only the local economic contexts, but also the impacts of globalized markets on youth participation. Tobias Franz, for example, argues that despite Medellín's "social urbanism," globalized neoliberal development agendas have continued to dominate the city's development.[32] A related factor that is crucial to the future of Medellín and several other cities but which was beyond the scope of this study is the role that countries with major markets for illegal drugs, such as the United States, play in perpetuating the narcotrafficking violence that threatens the sustainability of Medellín's transformation. Local forms of public participation are circumscribed by global dynamics.

The case of Medellín and its particular history of violence may strike some readers as too exceptional and contextually specific to inform more broadly applicable analytical concepts such as participatory public culture and polycultural civics. All my youth interviewees had experienced the direct impacts of armed violence, including the loss of friends or family—this certainly factors into their levels of motivation and commitment to engaging in civic/political life. However, by no means does this imply that the myriad forms of youth organizing in Medellín were solely a product of the violence, or that they could not exist without it. Lessons from Medellín can be applied to other contexts of youth participation, including those that are less affected by armed violence. Unfortunately, gang, narco-, and structural violence, stark socioeconomic inequality, displacement, the delegitimization of government institutions, concerns about the disengagement of youth from traditional political institutions, and the frustrated desires of many youth for greater agency are all too familiar problems for societies worldwide.

Participatory projects such as Ciudad Comuna, La Elite, and Son Batá are constantly evolving and changing, particularly as their strongest leaders, visionaries, and advocates come and go. To my great sadness, some of the youth involved in these collectives lost their lives to the armed violence. This includes one of the founding members of La Elite, whose murder by a young gang member in 2012 shook the network to its core, ultimately contributing to a change of course. Some members split off to start a different collective that continued to offer a hip-hop school, while others decided their work should be less politically engaged and therefore less likely to position them as potential targets—although it continued to be debated whether their public participation was putting them at risk or protecting them (see Chapter 3).

Although I did not explicitly frame this book as an exploration of how participatory practices may contribute to peace building, these cases can clearly inform our understanding of this relationship. The tactics of participation used by Ciudad Comuna, La Elite, and Son Batá also served as tactics of peace building, such as the reterritorialization of public spaces controlled by their armed counterparts for performances of nonviolence, the acts of negotiation and consensus building through participatory decision making, and the popular education-style schools that help children and youth forge a life path that does not depend on engaging in armed violence. These tactics helped establish not just a more participatory public culture but also a more peaceful one. They can inform approaches to peace building that focus not only on armed actors but also, crucially, on the unarmed.

At a time of rapid change and uncertainty it is tempting to fall back on familiar binaries that conflate digital participation with democracy and equity, or to dismiss these as forms of exploitation in a culture of increasing surveillance and algorithm-mediated life. Instead, we need to historicize and evolve the paradigm of participation and look beyond the digital technologies to the ideologies, discourses, practices, and material contexts that shape their uses and their potentials. The findings of the previous chapters make clear that discourses and practices of participation cannot yield purely or perfectly participatory public cultures; as a terrain of struggle over relations of power, participation is always imperfect and contested. Yet, in these precarious times, as we witness unprecedented levels of both grass-roots activism and political attacks on public institutions, it is my hope that the concepts of participatory public culture and polycultural civics may serve as orienting goals for those working toward more equitable societies.

Transmitiendo Desde Los Angeles (Broadcasting from Los Angeles)

One afternoon in January 2012, after I had returned to my home in southern California, I received a message from a member of Son Batá that read: "*transmitiendo desde Los Angeles California. esta* [sic] *brutal!!!*" ("broadcasting from Los Angeles, California. it's awesome!!!"). The next day, I met him and several other members of the group in the lobby of a large hotel downtown. Son Batá had come for the filming of pop stars Jennifer Lopez and Marc Anthony's reality TV show Q'Viva! The Chosen.

Q'Viva! The Chosen followed the iconic Latino celebrity couple—newly separated at the time—in their search to cast a live music and performance spectacle in Las Vegas that represented the "spirit of Latin American culture."[33] To do so, Lopez and Anthony, along with choreographer/producer Jamie King, selected artists from twenty-one Latin American countries to come to Los Angeles to compete in the reality TV series for a spot in the live show. Q'Viva! The Chosen was broadcast in the United States on Univision and Fox, as well as networks across Latin America and Canada starting later that January. As the first bilingual reality TV show to be broadcast on a major U.S. network, it became a landmark in the mainstreaming of Latin-focused, bilingual entertainment in North America. In the first episode, Lopez celebrated this by (rather narcissistically) exclaiming, "This is like me being able to really, really go: *I am Latina, and this is who we are!*"[34] The way she and the show's producers framed it suggested that the show offered commercial and cultural empowerment to the Latin American artists who participated, and greater visibility and appreciation for their cultures more broadly—even as Lopez's rhetoric homogenized the continent's diverse cultures.

When Marc Anthony travelled to the outskirts of Medellín to "discover" Son Batá, he remarked on camera, "[W]hen you do something artistic to survive, it just comes from a totally different place. This is what it's all about . . . we have to come to these *barrios* [low-income neighborhoods] to find talent like Son Batá."[35] As the cameras rolled, Anthony handed the group airline tickets to Los Angeles. Unfortunately, this marked the first of several ways in which Son Batá's participation in the show was compromised. These imitation tickets were soon to be replaced with real airline tickets for the smaller number of members whose travel visas were actually approved (visas for Colombians to visit the United States are frequently denied). For those members of Son Batá who were able to make the trip, it was both their first time in an airplane and their first time leaving Colombia.

A young musician known as Bomby had joined Son Batá at the age of ten and was sixteen by the time he came to Los Angeles. While quiet and shy offstage, by the age of fourteen, he was the star of the group, playing his clarinet and animating audiences in Medellín and across Colombia. Shortly before Anthony "discovered" them, Bomby and others from Son Batá had opened for the American rock band the Red Hot Chili Peppers in Bogotá.

In Los Angeles, Bomby became the protagonist of one of *Q'Viva's* dramatic subplots. In Episode 4, he was offered a place in the Las Vegas show, but the other members of Son Batá were cut and sent home. The obvious tension for Son Batá was that they operate as a collective, seeing their unified strength as greater than the sum of their individual members, and their success as tied to the accomplishments of the group. Their cultural practices were defined by an ethos of participation. Prior to coming to Los Angeles, they had agreed among themselves to compete in the show as a collective, not as individual artists. Bomby was thus faced with a difficult choice: whether to trade his identity as part of Son Batá (which he called *mi familia* [my family]) and the bonds of this participatory culture for the potential fame promised by Anthony if he went solo. Ironically, this storyline was being exploited within a television genre that itself has been marketed as a form of participatory culture.[36]

Bomby initially agreed to accept Anthony's offer. Some of his peers were disappointed in the decision, while others felt he had made the right choice for both himself and the collective. Some time later, on camera, Bomby met with Anthony to explain that he had changed his mind and would not accept the offer. "I am leaving the show because, [even] if I want to be an artist, I want to be a good person first—that is what I want to be. I am returning to Colombia to finish becoming [that person]."[37]

This clash of cultures—one of individual fame and commercial success, the other of creative collective action for both individual and social transformation—offered an unforeseen but apt bookend to my time with

Son Batá. It was yet another illustration of the expediency of participation as a resource for very different actors, in this instance, commercial television producers, Latinx celebrities in the United States, and Son Batá. Both *Q'Viva!* and Son Batá were premised, at least in part, on the offer of cultural participation as a form of empowerment. Of course, applying the preconditions of participatory public culture discussed in this book to analyze *Q'Viva!* quickly reveals the limits of the participation the show offered, particularly in contrast to Son Batá. The show did not notably reduce barriers to sustained participation, create spaces or cultures of participation in which participants had a significant say in decision making, develop capacities to participate, or link participants' voices to influence. The show offered another example of how discourses of participation may serve as resources for commerce as well as for prosocial counter-rationalities. Members of Son Batá were certainly interested in commercial success, and rightly so, given their limited means and socioeconomic status. They worked hard to brand themselves and provide a source of income to their participants. They continually navigated between commercial and participatory logics, which at times were contradictory and at other times overlapped—as has become increasingly common in the contemporary moment. It is clear that "participation" is partly to credit for their commercial successes; it was part of their mission, their origin story, and their social capital. Yet, Son Batá was only briefly among *The Chosen* in Hollywood, where participation is excessively determined by commercial logics. The group returned to Medellín to help more youth choose a clarinet instead of a gun, and cultivate a more participatory public culture.

NOTES

Introduction

1 Tim O'Reilly, "The Architecture of Participation," O'Reilly Media, June 2004, http://archive.oreilly.com/pub/a/oreilly/tim/articles/architecture_of _participation.html.
2 Kelty, "From Participation to Power," 227.
3 Kelty, "From Participation to Power," 229.
4 Cornwall, "Historical Perspectives."
5 Allagui and Kuebler, "The Arab Spring"; Gladwell, "Small Change."
6 Castells, *Networks of Outrage and Hope*, 15.
7 See, e.g., Brough et al., "Mobile Voices." On free/libre and open-source software, see Chapter 2.
8 Eubanks, *Automating Inequality*; Noble, *Algorithms of Oppression*; Srinivasan and Fish, *After the Internet*; "Once Considered a Boon to Democracy, Social Media Have Started to Look Like Its Nemesis," *The Economist*, November 11, 2017; Amanda Taub and Max Fisher, "Where Countries Are Tinderboxes and Facebook Is a Match," *New York Times*, April 21, 2018; "Cambridge Analytica CEO Claims Influence on US Election, Facebook Questioned," Reuters, March 20, 2018; Negroponte, *Being Digital*; Rheingold, *Smart Mobs* and "Using Participatory Media"; Shirky, *Here Comes Everybody*.
9 See Allen et al., "Participations."
10 ITU, "ICT Facts and Figures 2017," accessed June 6, 2018, https://www.itu.int /en/ITU-D/Statistics/Documents/facts/ICTFactsFigures2017.pdf.
11 Ito et al., *Hanging Out*; Third et al., "Children's Rights."
12 I use the terms "Global North" and "Global South" with some reservations because they are at once hard to define and an overly simplistic binary categorization. Yet, they are slightly less deterministic than the designations "developed" and "developing" countries, which they have generally come to replace. All of these terms are grounded in a Western-centric paradigm that

fails to account for shifts in global geopolitics such as the People's Republic of China emerging as a new hegemon with its own vibrant digital technology sector. Similarly, while I reference Latin America as a whole throughout this book, I do not mean to homogenize a large and diverse region. A notable amount of the research and practice of participatory communication has been developed in various parts of Latin America (see Barranquero, "Latinoamérica"; Gumucio Dagron, *Making Waves*; Gumucio Dagron and Tufte, *Communication for Social Change Anthology*; Huesca, "Tracing the History"; Rodríguez, *Citizens' Media*). However, a detailed analysis of the differences across Latin American contexts is not within the scope of this book.

13 Throughout this book, I use the terms "polycultural civics" and "civic polyculture" (described in Chapter 1) interchangeably.

14 Urban Land Institute, "City of the Year: Statement from Urban Land Institute," accessed November 1, 2013, http://online.wsj.com/ad/cityoftheyear.

15 Coryat, "Challenging the Silences"; Gumucio Dagron, *Making Waves*; Martín Barbero, *De los Medios*; Riaño, *Women in Grassroots Communication*; Rodríguez, *Citizens' Media*.

16 Unless otherwise noted, all translations are mine.

17 I anonymized all youth interviewees in this study with the exception of these two highly visible youth activists, who preferred I use their actual stage names in the recounting of this meeting.

18 Departments are country subdivisions or administrative regions in Colombia.

19 DANE, "Estimaciones de población 1985–2005 y Proyecciones de Población 2005–2020," accessed November 2017, http://www.dane.gov.co/files /investigaciones/poblacion/proyepoblao6_20/Municipal_area_1985-2020 .xls; DANE and Municipio de Medellín, "Proyecciones de Población"; Bernal, "Contexto," 28.

20 The Colombian government uses six strata to describe socioeconomic status, where *estrato 1* is considered very low, *estrato 2* is low, and so on.

21 Martha Arias Sandoval, "Medellín Vive en Estratos 1, 2 y 3," El Colombiano, September 15, 2012, http://www.elcolombiano.com/BancoConocimiento/M /medellin_vive_en_estratos_1_2_y_3/medellin_vive_en_estratos_1_2_y_3.asp; Lowenthal and Rojas Mejía, "Medellín"; Roldán, "Wounded Medellín."

22 Villa Martínez, "Medellín"; see also Naranjo Giraldo, "Medellín en Zonas" and *Entre Luces y Sombras*.

23 Roldán, "Wounded Medellín," 129.

24 Uribe, "La Territorialidad."

25 Roldán, "Wounded Medellín."

26 Salazar and Jaramillo, *Medellín*. The authors point out that these gangs were not formed by narcotraffickers, but rather emerged out of social and familial associations in the context of increasing economic hardship and the failure of civic and political institutions. They took on new forms as they adapted to and became key players in the narcotrafficking and other illicit economies. See also Bernal, *Contexto*; Martin, *Medellín Tragedia y Resurrección*.

27 Amnesty International, "Colombia: The Paramilitaries in Medellín: Demobilization or Legalization?," August 31, 2005, http://www.amnesty.org/en/library/info/AMR23/019/2005; Vanda Felbab-Brown, "Reducing Urban Violence: Lessons from Medellín, Colombia," The Brookings Institution, February 14, 2011, http://www.brookings.edu/research/opinions/2011/02/14-colombia-crime-felbabbrown.

28 As Gerard Martin writes, "Every national and international newspaper of repute sent a war correspondent to Medellín" (Martin, *Medellín Tragedia y Resurrección*, 266). Hollywood examples include the HBO series *Entourage* (2004–2011), in which the protagonist endeavors to make a dramatic film about the Medellín cartel, and Netflix's web drama *Narcos*, based on the story of Pablo Escobar and the U.S. Drug Enforcement Administration's activities in Colombia. Visitors to Medellín can take Pablo Escobar tours, although these are frowned upon by the tourism bureau for the obvious reason that they perpetuate a negative portrayal of the city. Karen Catchpole, "Selling Pablo," *Slate*, October 18, 2013, http://www.slate.com/articles/news_and_politics/roads/2013/10/pablo_escobar_tours_are_drawing_tourists_to_colombia_the_south_american.2.html.

29 During La Violencia, the warring Liberal and Conservative parties (the two traditional parties of Colombia) attempted to consolidate power, carrying out armed violence primarily in the countryside. For discussions of the ways in which Colombia's history of narcotrafficking may be traced back to La Violencia, see Chernick, *Acuerdo Possible*; Pécaut, *Crónica de Cuatro Décadas*; Castells, *End of Millennium*.

30 The United Nations High Commissioner for Refugees (UNHCR) reports that there are approximately 7.6 million internally displaced people in Colombia, and that internal displacement continues, despite the 2016 formal ceasefire and peace agreement. UNHCR, "Forced Displacement Growing in Colombia Despite Peace Agreement," March 10, 2017, http://www.unhcr.org/afr/news/briefing/2017/3/58c26e114/forced-displacement-growing-colombia-despite-peace-agreement.html; UNHCR, "Colombia," accessed May 28, 2019, http://www.unhcr.org/en-us/colombia.html.

31 Castells, *End of Millennium*; Salazar and Jaramillo, *Medellín*. In 1986, some forty of the sixty tons of cocaine entering the United States came from Colombia (Pécaut, *Crónica de Cuatro Décadas*).

32 As Castells explains, the extradition of drug traffickers to the United States was just one of the various ways in which the U.S. war on drugs played a determining role in the history of narcotrafficking, its criminalization, and the response of the Colombian state (*End of Millennium*). See also Salazar and Jaramillo, *Medellín*.

33 Salazar and Jaramillo, *Medellín*.

34 For more on the history of paramilitarism in Medellín, see Martin, *Medellín Tragedia y Resurrección*; Salazar and Jaramillo, *Medellín*; Amnesty International, "Colombia"; see also Riaño-Alcalá, *Dwellers of Memory*.

35 Amnesty International, "Colombia"; Tubb, "Narratives of Citizenship."

36 Riaño-Alcalá, *Dwellers of Memory*; Martin, *Medellín Tragedia y Resurrección*; Roldán, "Wounded Medellín," 144. At the national level, the conflict between the government, leftist guerrilla groups (most prominently the FARC), and paramilitaries also became imbricated in narcotrafficking. Both guerrilla and paramilitary groups used it to finance their campaigns, and international aid (primarily from the United States) flowed heavily to Colombia's military to fight the so-called war on drugs.

37 Martin, *Medellín Tragedia y Resurrección*, 137, original emphasis.

38 Salazar and Jaramillo, *Medellín*, 92.

39 Martin and Ceballos, *Bogotá, Anatomía de una Transformación*, 104.

40 Doyle, "Explaining Patterns of Urban Violence"; Martin, *Medellín Tragedia y Resurrección*; Roldán, "Wounded Medellín."

41 Riaño-Alcalá, *Dwellers of Memory*; Villa Martínez et al., *Rostros del Miedo*.

42 Vélez Rinón in Amnesty International, "Colombia." According to a survey of demobilized paramilitary fighters published by the Mayor's Office, the primary reasons youth joined paramilitary groups were economic necessity, threats against their lives, and personal vengeances. Alcaldía de Medellín, *Programa Paz y Reconciliación*.

43 This includes not only the Colombian state, but also the U.S. government. The U.S. military aid program Plan Colombia, launched in 2000 to help the Colombian government combat narcotrafficking and guerrilla activity, contributed to the intensification of the war on drugs and the resulting displacement of people from surrounding rural areas to the urban shantytowns of Medellín.

44 Eleven military operations were carried out in Comuna 13 in 2002. Grupo de Memoria Histórica, *La Huella Invisible de la Guerra*, 76; Cañas et al., *Dinámicas de Guerra*; various interviews in Medellín, 2010–2011.

45 Riaño-Alcalá, *Dwellers of Memory*, 181. Most paramilitary groups in Medellín at this time belonged to the narco-paramilitary network the Autodefensas Unidas de Colombia (Self-Defense Forces of Colombia, AUC). Former members of the AUC later testified to having collaborated with military and police forces during some of these operations, including Operation Orion. Cañas et al., *Dinámicas de Guerra*, 56; Grupo de Memoria Histórica, *La Huella Invisible de la Guerra*, 78. See also Amnesty International, "Colombia."

46 While homicide rates fell by nearly 50 percent between 2002 and 2007 (Francis Fukuyama and Seth Colby, "Half a Miracle," *Foreign Policy*, accessed October 10, 2011, http://www.foreignpolicy.com/articles/2011/04/25/half_a_miracle), the demobilization process—an initiative of the central government—has been widely criticized by observers in and outside of Colombia for being ineffective at reintegrating former paramilitary soldiers, and for continuing to mask relationships between Colombian elite and paramilitary actors. See Amnesty International, "Colombia"; BBC, "Fuego Cruzado en Medellín," October 17, 2002, news.bbc.co.uk/hi/spanish/latin_america/newsid_2337000/2337667.stm; Arthur Bright, "Report: Colombian Army Head Collaborated with 'Terrorist' Paramilitaries," *Christian Science Monitor*,

March 26, 2007, http://www.csmonitor.com/2007/0326/p99s01-duts.html; Fukuyama and Colby, "Half a Miracle"; Paul Richter and Greg Miller, "Colombia Army Chief Linked to Outlaw Militias," *Los Angeles Times*, March 25, 2007, https://www.latimes.com/archives/la-xpm-2007-mar-25-fg-colombia25 -story.html.

47 Hugh Bronstein, "Colombia's Medellín Hit by New Wave of Drug Violence," Reuters, October 20, 2009, https://www.reuters.com/article /idUSN20434908.

48 Velásquez and González, *¿Qué Ha Pasado?*, 89, 93; Botero, *Medellín 1890– 1950*; Franco, *Poder Regional*.

49 Moncada, "Urban Violence, Political Economy," 230.

50 Alcaldía de Medellín, *Plan de Desarrollo 2004–2007*. *Compromiso* translates as "agreement," "commitment," or "engagement." *Ciudadano* as a noun translates to "citizen," but as an adjective, it often refers to "civic." Compromiso Ciudadano can therefore also be translated as "Civic Engagement" or "Citizens' Commitment." The rise of Compromiso Ciudadano and other nontraditional political parties elsewhere in Colombia was facilitated by national reforms in the late 1980s and the 1991 Constitution, which helped to deinstitutionalize the traditional Colombian party system and devolve certain powers from the central state to local governments (Moncada, "Urban Violence, Political Economy," 228; Tubb, "Narratives of Citizenship," 634). Compromiso Ciudadano's platform was also inspired by approaches to urban transformation in Bogotá; see Martin and Ceballos, *Bogotá, Anatomía de una Transformación*; Tubb, "Narratives of Citizenship."

51 See, most notably, Salazar, *No Nacimos pa' Semilla*.

52 "The Trouble with Miracles," *The Economist*, June 7, 2014, https://www .economist.com/the-americas/2014/06/07/the-trouble-with-miracles. Medellín had a history of local business elites engaging in urban planning and development, and in some of the efforts in the 1990s to combat the violence. See Moncada, "Urban Violence, Political Economy"; Maclean, *Social Urbanism*.

53 Fajardo, "Medellín, la Más Educada." Much of this was financed by the locally based *Empresas Públicas de Medellín* (Public Companies of Medellín, EPM), a publicly owned utility company and one of the region's wealthiest, in addition to other public–private partnerships.

54 Maclean, *Social Urbanism*. For further discussion of the role that Medellín's business elites have played in the city's transformation, see Moncada, "Urban Violence, Political Economy," and "The Trouble with Miracles," *The Economist*.

55 Moncada, "Urban Violence, Political Economy"; Tubb, "Narratives of Citizenship."

56 Alcaldía de Medellín, *Del Miedo a la Esperanza*.

57 Various interviews, Medellín, 2010–2011; personal correspondence with Pilar Riaño-Alcalá, February 9, 2014; Doyle, "Explaining Patterns of Urban Violence"; Amnesty International, "Colombia"; Human Rights Watch,

Smoke and Mirrors; Tubb, "Narratives of Citizenship." Gerard Martin argues, however, that Don Berna's power has been exaggerated (Martin, *Medellín, Tragedia y Resurrección*; personal correspondence with the author, January 15, 2014).

58 For relevant examples in Mexico, see Reguillo, *Culturas Juveniles*, and danah boyd's study of teens' online activities in the United States, which found that gang dynamics were similarly shaping the mobility of youth of color in Los Angeles, as well as their on- and offline participation in social/public life (boyd, *It's Complicated*).

59 See, e.g., Rheingold, "Using Participatory Media."

60 See the Chiapas Media Project (accessed January 28, 2020, https://chiapasmediaproject.org).

61 YouTube, "YouTube Unveils New Advertising Concepts," August 22, 2006, http://www.marketwired.com/press-release/youtube-unveils-new-advertising-concepts-697771.htm.

62 Enghel and Becerra, "Here and There," 113.

63 Researchers have taken an ecological approach to studying cities since at least the early twentieth century, e.g., the Chicago School sociologists. More recently, scholars in communication studies such as Sandra Ball-Rokeach and associates, and Lewis Friedland, have developed frameworks for analyzing communication ecologies (Ball-Rokeach et al., "Storytelling Neighborhood"; Kim and Ball-Rokeach, "Community Storytelling Network"; Friedland, "Communication, Community, and Democracy"); see also Mercea et al., "Protest Communication Ecologies," and Treré, "Social Movements as Information Ecologies." On media ecologies, see Postman, "The Humanism of Media Ecology," and Clark, "Theories."

64 Rose et al., "Governmentality"; see also Chapter 4.

65 All interviews were anonymized to protect participants' identities, except in cases when interviewees were highly visible public figures. The majority of my interviewees were between the ages of eighteen and twenty-six. This enabled me to capture their reflections on several years of their adolescence and youth.

66 These collective memory-based participatory research workshops were designed to reach a greater balance of power in the research process, improve validity, and avoid extractive research. For details, see Acosta Valencia and Garcés Montoya, *Proyecto Comunicación*; and *Colectivos de Comunicacion*.

67 I am particularly indebted to Clemencia Rodríguez and Camilo Pérez for reviewing many of my translations.

68 Clifford, "On Ethnographic Authority."

69 Giroux, *Border Crossings*, 2, 6. See also Leonard and McLaren, *Paulo Freire*; Rosaldo, *Culture and Truth*.

70 Haraway, "Situated Knowledges."

71 See Chapter 3. See also Brough et al., "Mobile Voices"; Chambers, "Participatory Rural Appraisal"; Cornwall and Jewkes, "What Is Participatory

Research?"; Fals-Borda and Rahman, *Action and Knowledge*; Freire, *Pedagogy of the Oppressed*.

72 Mouffe, "Feminism, Citizenship," 376, 378.

73 This book draws inspiration from others who have done the same, such as Anita Say Chan's study of Peru in *Networking Peripheries*. See also Medina et al., *Beyond Imported Magic*, and Takhteyev, *Coding Places*.

74 See, e.g., Maclean, *Social Urbanism*; Moncada, "Urban Violence, Political Economy"; Doyle, "Explaining Patterns of Urban Violence"; Tubb, "Narratives of Citizenship."

Chapter One

1 Mark Zuckerberg, Video address to Facebook users, Mark Zuckerberg, Founder and CEO of Facebook, April 20, 2009, https://www.facebook.com /video/video.php?v=186119950483.

2 Interestingly, Facebook chose Colombia as the first Latin American country to launch its free internet.org service, an initiative that drew criticism internationally for violating net neutrality. Helen Murphy and Luis Jaime Acosta, "Facebook's Zuckerberg brings free Internet to Colombia, mute on China," Reuters, January 14, 2015, https://www.reuters.com/article/us-facebook-colombia /facebooks-zuckerberg-brings-free-internet-to-colombia-mute-on-china -idUSKBN0KO0BS20150115. Facebook, Inc. "Second Quarter 2018 Results Conference Call," July 25, 2018, https://s21.q4cdn.com/399680738/files/doc_financials /2018/Q2/Q218-earnings-call-transcript.pdf; Kelty et al., "Seven Dimensions."

3 "Cambridge Analytica CEO Claims Influence on U.S. Election, Facebook Questioned," Reuters, March 20, 2018, https://www.reuters.com/article/us -facebook-cambridge-analytica/cambridge-analytica-ceo-claims-influence -on-u-s-election-facebook-questioned-idUSKBN1GW1SG.

4 Flock Associates Ltd., "Flock Associates—Mountain Dew: DewMocracy Integrated Campaign by BBDO Worldwide," September 10, 2013, https://youtu .be/1K779wr5994.

5 For more on the conflation of participation and interactivity, see Jenkins and Carpentier, "Theorizing Participatory Intensities."

6 Andrejevic, *iSpy*; Staples, *Everyday Surveillance*.

7 Laurie Ouellette and James Hay argue, for example, that rhetoric of participation has been conflated with consumer empowerment, naturalizing the latter as a mode of citizenship; Ouellette and Hay, *Better Living through Reality TV*. Yúdice, *The Expediency of Culture*, 215.

8 Cornwall, "Historical Perspectives"; Dagnino, "Citizenship"; Banet-Weiser and Lapsansky, "RED Is the New Black"; Ouellette and Hay, *Better Living through Reality TV*.

9 Shifman, "Meme," 200.

10 Barber, "Participatory Democracy."

11 Bishop, *Participation*; Brough, "Participatory Culture"; Carpentier, *Media and Participation*; Kelty, "From Participation to Power"; Velásquez and

González, *¿Qué Ha Pasado?* Participation was also part of the utopian imaginaries of early visionaries and devotees of computer and digital culture, who were influenced by some of the countercultural movements of this period. See Delwiche, "The New Left"; Turner, *From Counterculture to Cyberculture.*

12 Andrejevic, *iSpy*; Harvey, *A Brief History of Neoliberalism*; Youniss et al., "Youth Civic Engagement."

13 Office of the Secretary-General's Envoy on Youth, "#YouthStats," accessed June 6, 2018, https://www.un.org/youthenvoy/youth-statistics/.

14 Kelty, "From Participation to Power," 29; see also Quodling, "Platforms are Eating Society," 131.

15 De Certeau, *The Practice of Everyday Life*, 37. Similarly, James Scott reminds us that "the binary division between resistance and non-resistance is an unreal one" (Scott, *Weapons of the Weak*, vii). See also García Canclini, "El Malestar en los Estudios Culturales."

16 The irony of using terms that originate from military planning to analyze efforts to counter armed violence in the Colombian context gives me pause. Still, I find it analytically useful to join many others, including activists of various stripes, who have utilized these terms in numerous ways and contexts to think about social change. See, e.g., Boyd and Mitchell, *Beautiful Trouble*; Fine, "Choose Tactics that Support Your Strategy"; Quodling, "Platforms Are Eating Society."

17 This understanding of public culture is informed by the work of Antonio Gramsci, Michel Foucault, Nancy Fraser, Raymond Williams, and Chantal Mouffe, among others.

18 Bennett, "Changing Citizenship," 13. See also Third and Collin, "Rethinking (Children's and Young People's) Citizenship," 47.

19 Bennett, "Changing Citizenship"; Bennett et al., "Changing Citizen Identity"; Brough and Shresthova, "Fandom Meets Activism"; Burgess et al., "Everyday Creativity"; Cohen and Kahne, *Participatory Politics*; Ito et al., *Hanging Out*; Jenkins, *Convergence Culture*; Jenkins et al., *Confronting the Challenges*; Kahne et al., "Youth, New Media"; Kassimir and Flanagan, "Youth Civic Engagement"; Levine, "A Public Voice"; Livingstone, *Children and the Internet*; Loader, *Young Citizens*; Middaugh, "Service and Activism"; Middaugh and Kirshner, *#youthaction*; Pettingill, "Engagement 2.0"; Reguillo, *Culturas Juveniles*; Zuckerman, "New Media"; Zukin et al., *A New Engagement?*

20 See Herrera et al., *La Construcción*; Restrepo, "Los Jóvenes"; Torney-Purta and Amadeo, *Fortalecimiento de la Democracia*; Torney-Purta et al., "Trust in Government-Related Institutions"; Vega Casanova and Escalante Orozco, "Organizaciones Juveniles." While there are some general similarities in the trends in youth engagement in the Global North and South—such as apathy toward traditional political institutions, and low rates of voting— there are also crucial differences, often determined by the particular power dynamics shaping the contexts of these youths' lives. Large numbers of youth in the Global North (disproportionately youth of color) experience poverty, problems of racial/ethnic/social inequality, limited opportunities,

and various types of discrimination, but these conditions are the norm for the vast majority of youth in the Global South who make up approximately 90 percent of the global youth population (Kassimir and Flanagan, "Youth Civic Engagement").

21 Alcaldía de Medellín, "La Participación"; Cañas et al., *Dinámicas de Guerra*. Many of my interviewees in Medellín confirmed this perception. See Introduction.

22 Freire, "Education and Community Involvement," 88.

23 Freire, *Pedagogy of the Oppressed*; Mefalopulos, "Theory and Practice"; Servaes, "Participatory Communication"; Gumucio Dagron, *Making Waves*; Tufte et al., *Trazos de Una Otra Comunicación*.

24 Development communication—driven primarily by U.S. and European institutions—has historically entailed one-way, transmission models of information delivery, in which information was instrumentally transmitted in order to reach predetermined aims for modernization, often at the expense of local knowledge and priorities. Among others, Colombian intellectuals and activists such as Orlando Fals Borda contributed to a transnational critique of the modernist development paradigm, exemplified in the New World Information and Communication Order debates of the late 1970s and 1980s. They developed and advocated bottom-up, participatory practices in communication, the arts, and research. See Barranquero, "Latinoamérica"; Carlsson, "The Rise and Fall"; Escobar, *Encountering Development*; Fals-Borda, "Grietas de la Democracia" and "The Application of Participatory-Action Research"; Fals-Borda and Rahman, *Action and Knowledge*; Gumucio Dagron, *Making Waves*; Huesca, "Tracing the History"; Servaes, *Communication for Development*.

25 Bordenave, "Participative Communication," 43, 44, original emphases.

26 Huesca, "Tracing the History."

27 See Barranquero, "Latinoámerica"; Beltrán, "Adeus a Aristóteles"; Carpentier, *Media and Participation*; Gumucio Dagron, *Making Waves*; Huesca, "Tracing the History"; Servaes, *Communication for Development*; Servaes and Malikhao, "Participatory Communication"; Sáez and Manuel, "El Enfoque de la Comunicación Participativa."

28 Couldry, *Why Voice Matters*. See also Gumucio Dagron, *Making Waves*; Riaño, *Women in Grassroots Communication*; Rodríguez, *Citizens' Media*.

29 Couldry, *Why Voice Matters*, 1; Servaes and Hoyng, "The Tools of Social Change," 259.

30 Butler, "Giving an Account." See also Chow, "Gender and Representation"; Fanon, *Black Skin*; Spivak, "Can the Subaltern Speak?"

31 Carpentier, *Media and Participation*.

32 Arnstein, "A Ladder of Citizen Participation."

33 Cornwall, "Unpacking 'Participation'" and "Whose Voices." See also Carpentier, *Media and Participation*.

34 Carpentier, *Media and Participation*; Cornwall, "Unpacking 'Participation'"; Farrington and Bebbington, *Reluctant Partners*; White, "Depoliticizing Development."

35 For example, Christopher Kelty and associates' study in 2015 of more than
    one hundred cases of online participation proposed seven analytical dimen-
    sions, each along a weak/strong spectrum. While useful, these are heavily
    geared toward online platforms, rather than thinking about participation
    within a broader ecology of social relations both on- and offline. Kelty
    et al., "Seven Dimensions," 476. See Literat et al., "Analyzing Youth Digital
    Participation," for a model that incorporates but also moves beyond binary
    categories of analysis.

36 In one study, youth who participate in interest-driven online activities
    reported engaging in nearly four times as many political acts as youth who
    infrequently participate in such activities (Kahne et al., "The Civic and Po-
    litical Significance"). See also Cohen and Kahne, "Participatory Politics"; Ito
    et al., "Learning Connected Civics"; Jenkins et al., *By Any Media Necessary*;
    Kahne et al., "Youth, New Media."

37 Jenkins, *Convergence Culture*.

38 Jenkins, *Convergence Culture*; Jenkins et al., *Confronting the Challenges*. See
    also Jenkins and Shresthova, "Transformative Works and Fan Fiction."

39 Jenkins et al., *Confronting the Challenges*. See also Brough, "Participatory
    Culture."

40 "Participatory politics" is a term that has been used differently in other mo-
    ments in history, e.g., in the student and other social movements in the 1960s
    and 1970s (see Delwiche, "The New Left"). On this contemporary usage of the
    term "participatory politics," see Cohen and Kahne, "Participatory Politics";
    Jenkins et al., *By Any Media Necessary*; Kahne et al., "Youth, New Media." On
    participatory civics, see Ito et al., "Learning Connected Civics," and Ethan
    Zuckerman, "What Ancient Greek Rhetoric Might Teach Us about New Civ-
    ics," November 19, 2012, http://www.ethanzuckerman.com/blog/2012/11/19
    /what-ancient-greek-rhetoric-might-teach-us-about-new-civics/.

41 Kahne and Bowyer, "The Political Significance of Social Media."

42 See Connor et al., *Crop Ecology*; Altieri, *Agroecology* (especially "Polyculture
    Cropping Systems" by Matt Liebman).

43 Scholars, game designers, and others have begun using the term "ecology of
    participation" to describe a particular media or entertainment platform, or even
    the Internet as a whole (see Fish et al., "Birds of the Internet"; Benkler, *Wealth of
    Networks*). Drawing on Marshall McLuhan's work, Tobias Olsson used the term
    "ecology of participation" to theorize the Web 2.0 mediascape as different from
    what he calls the pre-Internet "ecology of broadcasting" or the "ecology of inter-
    activity" that characterized Web 1.0 (Olsson, "From the Ecology"). All of these
    uses of the phrase attribute the qualities and agency of participation to the tech-
    nologies themselves. Some scholarship conceives of a broader communication
    ecology but is not focused specifically on the question of (youth) participation
    in public life. With some exceptions, this work still tends to focus on individuals
    and their microecologies, rather than considering entire communities, cities,
    or publics. An important exception is Sandra Ball-Rokeach and her associates'
    work on communication ecologies, which provides an ecological framework

for studying communication processes within a neighborhood context. For a list of relevant publications, see http://www.metamorph.org/research_areas /communication_ecology_and_icts/ (accessed January 19, 2020). See Introduction for further discussion of ecological approaches.

44 Kassimir and Flanagan, "Youth Civic Engagement."

45 Concejo de Medellín, "Acuerdo Municipal 076 de 2006, por el cual se adopta el Plan Estratégico Municipal de Desarrollo Juvenil de Medellín 2007–2015." More colloquially, in Medellín, "youth" often refers to the age range fourteen to twenty-nine.

46 Jesús Martín Barbero describes the social construction of youth as paradigmatic of modernity and yet "a nomadic object, of diffuse contours." Martín Barbero, "Jóvenes," 22.

47 Gilbert, *A Cycle of Outrage*; Frank, *The Conquest of Cool*; Kwon, *Uncivil Youth*; Light, "Putting Our Conversation in Context"; Youniss et al., "Youth Civic Engagement."

48 As Kwon (*Uncivil Youth*) found in the United States, Rossana Reguillo (in *Culturas Juveniles*) notes that Latin American youth have frequently been criminalized as well as inscribed (willingly or unwillingly, visibly or invisibly) as strategic actors for development.

49 Rose, "Government and Control."

50 Reguillo, *Culturas Juveniles*. Reguillo's ethnography of youth cultures in Mexico finds potential in the particular disenchantment youth feel about adult institutions; she traces how "active disenchantment" becomes agency when it fuels collective action.

51 In a Tocquevillian vein, Robert Putnam argued that civic engagement increases social capital, which leads to a "more efficient" and healthy society; Putnam, *Bowling Alone*, 21; Verba et al., *Voice and Equality*; Youniss et al., "What We Know."

52 Ginwright and Cammarota, "Introduction"; Kwon, *Uncivil Youth*.

53 See Youniss et al., "Youth Civic Engagement," 133; Checkoway, "What Is Youth Participation?"; Coleman and Hendry, in Livingstone, *Children and the Internet*; Middaugh, "Service and Activism"; Shah et al., "Civic Norms and Communication Competence."

54 Levine, "A Public Voice for Youth"; Sherrod et al., "Dimensions of Citizenship"; Youniss et al., "What We Know" and "Youth Civic Engagement." Of course, correlation does not necessarily imply causation.

55 Kassimir and Flanagan, "Youth Civic Engagement." There are approximately 1.8 billion young people between the ages of ten and twenty-four globally, 90 percent of whom live in the developing world (UNFPA, "Adolescent and Youth Demographics: A Brief Overview," accessed June 29, 2018, https://www .unfpa.org/resources/adolescent-and-youth-demographicsa-brief-overview ?page=8%2C0%2C5; data from 2010).

56 Velásquez and González, *¿Qué Ha Pasado?*

57 Constitución Política de Colombia 1991, accessed July 10, 2019, http://www .alcaldiabogota.gov.co/sisjur/normas/Norma1.jsp?i=4125.

58 Leyva Botero, "El Proceso de Construcción."

59 Martin, *Medellín, Tragedia y Resurrección*, 141.While fifteen to nineteen is a widely cited age range, Gerard Martin describes the majority of gang members as being youth between twelve (or younger) and twenty-six.

60 Salazar and Jaramillo, *Medellín*.

61 Riaño-Alcalá, *Dwellers of Memory*, 1.

62 Riaño-Alcalá, *Dwellers of Memory*.

63 Roldán, "Wounded Medellín."

64 Salazar and Jaramillo, *Medellín*.

65 For more information on this participatory communication project, see Vega Casanova et al., "Pasolini en Medellín" (Pasolini in Medellín) and http://pasolinienmedellin.org (accessed July 10, 2019).

66 Consejo de Medellín, "Acuerdo 02." This accord was based on national policy adopted in 1997.

67 A 1995 study by the Red Paisa Joven (Paisa Youth Network) identified 570 active youth organizations across the city. A similar number were registered by the municipal Oficina de la Juventud (Office of Youth) in 2003. In "De Organizaciones a Colectivos," Angela Garcés Montoya, one of the foremost researchers of youth culture in Medellín, published data from 2007 showing just under 300 documented youth groups in the city, 55.5 percent of which had a cultural focus (art, music, performance, etc.). A 2009 study published by the municipal government in collaboration with the Federación Antioqueña de ONG (Antioquian Federation of Non-Governmental Organizations) found that 93 percent of the thirty youth networks they studied across the city had some degree of a cultural/artistic focus (Uribe Neira, *Jóvenes y Acción Colectiva*).

68 Uribe Neira, *Jóvenes y Acción Colectiva*; Garcés Montoya, "De Organizaciones a Colectivos."

69 And while the leftist guerrilla movements in Colombia changed over time and became increasingly characterized by violence and narcotrafficking rather than a collectivist political agenda, nonviolent collective projects continued to thrive in other sectors of civil society.

70 See, e.g., an extensive interview excerpt to this effect in Chapter 5.

71 Cooke and Kothari, *Participation*.

72 Cornwall, "Historical Perspectives." For example, in 2009, the World Bank published *Participatory Communication*, illustrating the trend among international finance and development agencies to appropriate and institutionalize participatory practices (Tufte and Mefalopulos, *Participatory Communication*). See also Leal, "Participation"; Stiefel and Wolfe, *A Voice for the Excluded*. There is in fact a long history of the institutionalization of participation in the development sector, dating back at least as far as colonial practices in the early twentieth century. Andrea Cornwall has traced it back to the United Kingdom's Colonial Development Act of 1929 and various other ways in which participation was used as a discursive trope to justify and structure colonial relations of power. She provides historical evidence of

nearly a century of the West's use of participation as a technology of governmentality (Cornwall, "Historical Perspectives").

73 Hickey and Mohan, *Participation*, 4, 5. This is a suggestion that Cooke and Kothari themselves make, albeit more skeptically. See also Cornwall, "Historical Perspectives"; Guijt et al., "Tracking Change"; Leal, "Participation."

74 Hickey and Mohan, *Participation*, 62–63, 66, 69.

75 See, e.g., Cornwall, *The Participation Reader* and "Historical Perspectives"; Singhal and Devi, "Visual Voices in Participatory Communication."

76 Brough and Shresthova, "Fandom Meets Activism." See, e.g., Cohen and Kahne, "Participatory Politics"; Gladwell, "Small Change"; Ito et al., *Hanging Out*; Morozov, *The Net Delusion*; Zuckerman, "What Ancient Greek Rhetoric"; Ross, "In Search"; Terranova, "Free Labor"; Zuboff, "Big Other."

77 See Fenton and Barassi, "Alternative Media"; Morozov, *Net Delusion*; Srinavasan and Fish, *After the Internet*.

78 Amanda Taub and Max Fisher, "Where Countries Are Tinderboxes and Facebook Is a Match," *New York Times*, April 21, 2018; "Once Considered a Boon to Democracy, Social Media Have Started to Look Like Its Nemesis," *The Economist*, November 11, 2017.

79 Relevant research includes: boyd, "White Flight"; Couldry, *Why Voice Matters*; Everett, *Learning Race and Ethnicity*; Hargittai, "Digital Na(t)ives?"; Hargittai and Walejko, "The Participation Divide"; Jenkins, "Why Mitt Romney Won't Debate a Snowman"; Juhasz, "Learning the Five Lessons of YouTube"; Seiter, "Practicing at Home"; Watkins, *The Young and the Digital*. Engin Isin and Evelyn Ruppert's review of existing research finds little evidence that the participation of marginalized groups increases when politics is conducted online (Isin and Ruppert, *Being Digital Citizens*, 84).

80 Castells, *Networks of Outrage and Hope*; see also Isin and Ruppert, *Being Digital Citizens*.

Chapter Two

1 The concept of a "digital city" was popularized in the mid-1990s, becoming a buzz phrase for certain commercial ICT systems and municipal e-government initiatives. Rhetoric subsequently shifted toward the nominally less technologically deterministic term "smart," rather than "digital" cities. An earlier version of this chapter was published as Melissa Brough, "Analytical Antidotes to Technological Determinism."

2 Agencia Efe, "Medellín to Build LatAm's Largest Technology District," GlobalPost, 2013, accessed November 11, 2013, http://www.globalpost .com/dispatch/news/agencia-efe/130710/Medellín-build-latams-largest -technology-district; Anthony Ha, "Co-Working Space Espacio Launches to Turn Medellín into a Startup Hub," TechCrunch, October 11, 2012, http:// techcrunch.com/2012/10/11/espacio-medellin/; Harriet Alexander, "Inside Medellín: How Pablo Escobar's Hometown Hopes to Become South America's 'Silicon Valley,'" *The Telegraph*, May 17, 2014, https://www.telegraph.co.uk

/finance/10836478/Inside-Medellin-How-Pablo-Escobars-hometown-hopes
-to-become-South-Americas-Silicon-Valley.html.

3 Third and Collin, "Rethinking (Children's and Young People's) Citizenship," 56.
4 Ribble et al., "Digital Citizenship," 7; Vivienne et al., "Digital Citizenship
   as Fluid Interface"; Third and Collin, "Rethinking (Children's and Young
   People's) Citizenship," 41–60.
5 Mossberger et al., *Digital Citizenship*, 2.
6 Isin and Ruppert, *Being Digital Citizens*, 10.
7 Mouffe, "Feminism, Citizenship." See also Vivienne et al., "Digital Citizenship
   as Fluid Interface," 1–18.
8 Article 20, in Rodríguez, *Citizens' Media*, 30, 287.
9 For a useful overview, see Carpentier, *Media and Participation*. See also
   Chapter 1.
10 See Riaño, *Women in Grassroots Communication*; Gumucio Dagron and
   Tufte, *Communication for Social Change Anthology*; Vega, "Tecnologías de
   la Información."
11 Gumucio Dagron, *Making Waves*; Huesca, "A Procedural View."
12 Boal, *Theater of the Oppressed*.
13 Castells, "Communication, Power and Counter-Power" and *Communication
   Power*.
14 Benkler, "Practical Anarchism," 214.
15 Wikipedia is a collaboratively produced free encyclopedia based on a model
   of openness; see https://www.wikipedia.org/. FLOSS is collaboratively
   produced computer software that users are free to use, copy, and adapt,
   and the program coding is open and accessible rather than proprietary. It is
   typically "free" in two senses of the term, hence the addition of "libre" to the
   title. It may be used free of a licensing fee, and it enables greater freedom
   in how it is used. Graham Longford describes the open-source software
   movement as defined by collaborative and inclusive design, openness and
   transparency of source code for modification, universal access to software,
   and non-restrictive licensing, all of which are in direct response to monopo-
   listic software firms, particularly Microsoft (Longford, "Pedagogies of Digital
   Citizenship," 89). For a discussion of the FLOSS movement in Peru, see Chan,
   Networking Peripheries.
16 Both Kelty (*Two Bits*) and Isin and Ruppert (*Being Digital Citizens*) point out
   that "openness" is a social imaginary that operates in variable ways.
17 For a useful summary of relevant research and further discussion of this
   Internet myth, see Srinivasan and Fish, *After the Internet*.
18 Beyer and McKelvey, "You Are Not Welcome Among Us"; Castells, *Communication Power* and *Networks of Outrage and Hope*; Sierra Caballero and
   Gravante, "Ciudadanía Digital."
19 Ames, "Learning Consumption."
20 Medina et al., *Beyond Imported Magic*; Firmino et al., eds., "Surveillance in
   Latin America"; Andrejevic, *iSpy*; Morozov, *The Net Delusion*; Williams, *Television*; Winner, "Do Artifacts Have Politics?"

21 These case studies focus on the first five years of each initiative, spanning approximately from 2006–2007 to 2011–2012. My analysis is based on twenty-five in-depth interviews with Ciudad Comuna participants, Medellín Digital staff, municipal and national government officials, and representatives from other relevant organizations; observation and a participatory research workshop carried out with Ciudad Comuna in collaboration with researchers at the University of Medellín (see Acosta Valencia and Garcés Montoya, *Proyecto Comunicación* and *Colectivos de Comunicacion*); a review of documents, websites, and other content produced by each initiative; and existing research by local scholars.

22 The initiative was launched with the support of various public and private institutions, including the foundation of the public utility company Empresas Públicas de Medellín (EPM), the public, regional telecommunications company UNE EPM, the national ministries of ICTs and Education, and a private university. To my knowledge, community-based organizations were not significantly involved in the design of the initiative—a fact that some of my interviewees criticized.

23 Escobar Arango, "Medellín Digital," 34, emphasis added.

24 DANE and Municipio de Medellín, "Proyecciones de Población."

25 Convergencia Research, *Ranking Motorola.*

26 Sey et al., *Connecting People for Development.*

27 www.Medellíndigital.gov.co, accessed August 4, 2012, site no longer available.

28 Medellín Digital, "El Circular Medellín Recorre Medellín," accessed August 4, 2012, www.Medellíndigital.gov.co, site no longer available.

29 See Robins, "Are African Women Online Just ICT Consumers?"; Jandrić and Kuzmanić, "Digital Postcolonialism."

30 XII Encuentro Iberoamericano de Ciudades Digitales, "Qué es," accessed September 14, 2012, http://www.ciudadesdigitales2011.com/que_es.html.

31 See de la Peña, "Slow and Low Progress"; Vaidhyanathan, *The Googlization of Everything*; Chan, *Networking Peripheries*, 178.

32 Convergencia Research, *Ranking Motorola*, 21.

33 www.Medellíndigital.gov.co/ciudadanodigital/Paginas/default.aspx, accessed August 7, 2012, site no longer available.

34 Carpentier, *Media and Participation.*

35 www.Medellíndigital.gov.co/nuestraestrategia/Paginas/contenidos.aspx, accessed August 7, 2012, site no longer available.

36 Facebook, Twitter, and cellular phones were seemingly more significant tools for dialogue between government officials and the public; see Chapters 3 and 5.

37 See Peixoto, "Beyond Theory"; Gilman, *Democracy Reinvented*. In 2017, Medellín's residents had the option to vote online in part of the participatory budgeting process.

38 In 2011, Medellín Digital reported approximately 140,000 registered users for all of their portals, though it is unclear how many were repeat users and what uses they made of the sites. Since simply accessing the portals required

potential users to register, there were likely fewer regular/repeat users. The portals received a total of approximately nine million cumulative visits per year. Medellín Digital's portal for government services accounted for only approximately 240,000 (about 3 percent) of those visits; the education portal accounted for the vast majority of visits (more than seven million, cumulatively). (Figures provided by Medellín Digital in September 2012.) These figures tell us little about the actual usage of the portals.

39 Axel Bruns (*Blogs, Wikipedia*) coined the term "produsage" to refer to the increasingly interconnected practices of user-led production and consumption (usage) of online content. In 2011, there were an estimated seventy to one hundred community media projects in Medellín.

40 "Proyecto Medellín 'Va Viento en Popa,'" *El Tiempo*, March 21, 2011, http://www.eltiempo.com/colombia/medellin/proyecto-medellin-digital-va-viento-en-popa-con-la-promocion-de-las-_9048660-4; Grupo de Trabajo de Medellín Digital, "Medellín Digital," 2; G. Marulanda, "Medellín Crece en Conectividad," TeleMedellín, May 17, 2012, http://www.youtube.com/watch?v=yZTRxLU57x0.

41 Interview with researchers in the *Educación en Ambientes Virtuales* (Education in Virtual Environments, EAV) research group at the Universidad Pontificia Bolivariana, Medellín, January 25, 2011; Patiño Lemos and Vallejo Gómez, "Caracterización de Prácticas con TIC."

42 Patiño Lemos and Vallejo Gómez, "Caracterización de Prácticas con TIC."

43 In 2011, 54.3 percent of people aged five and older in Medellín used the Internet, up from 31.6 percent in 2007. Of course, this rise in use cannot be exclusively attributed to Medellín Digital (DANE, "Indicadores Básicos de Tecnologías de Información y Comunicaciones (TIC)," September 2, 2008, http://www.dane.gov.co).

44 A study of Medellín Digital's impact carried out between 2009 and 2011 by Patiño Lemos and Vallejo Gómez ("Caracterización de Prácticas con TIC") found that 26 percent of student respondents were able to publish their own content online independently using social media platforms. Only 12 percent of small business people surveyed reported having skills to produce and publish content online.

45 Carpentier, *Media and Participation*, chapter 1.

46 *La Sierra*, directed by Scott Dalton and Margarita Martinez (2005; Brooklyn, NY: Icarus Films).

47 Ciudad Comuna, *Proyectos Comunicativos*, 2.

48 For more on popular education, see Chapter 3.

49 Ciudad Comuna, "Impacto Social," ciudadcomuna.org, 2010, accessed September 2013, http://www.ciudadcomuna.org/impacto-social.html.

50 Researchers (and my collaborators) at the University of Medellín produced similar findings about Ciudad Comuna; see Acosta Valencia and Garcés Montoya, "Prácticas de Comunicación."

51 Ciudad Comuna, *Proyectos Comunicativos*, 8. At the time of this writing, *Visión 8* was available online at http://issuu.com/ciudadcomuna and

http://www.ciudadcomuna.org/ciudadcomuna/vision8.html (accessed January 2020).

52 According to Ciudad Comuna, approximately thirty people participated in editorial board meetings in 2011. In 2012, after multimedia efforts to recruit more residents, approximately 130 participated, fifty of whom then contributed content to Ciudad Comuna's subsequent publications.

53 Ciudad Comuna, "Un Nuevo Mapa Para la Comuna," 7.

54 Couldry, *Why Voice Matters.*

55 Ciudad Comuna, "Un Nuevo Mapa Para la Comuna," 6.

56 Personal correspondence with local CBO representative and facilitator of the Memoria y Territorio project, November 2012.

57 In 2011, groups posting to the website included the Mesa Interbarrial (a network of neighborhood organizations), the Red Juvenil (Youth Network), and committees of the Plan de Desarrollo Local (Local Development Plan), among others.

58 Isin and Ruppert, *Being Digital Citizens,* 85.

59 Fuchs, *Foundations of Critical Media,* 279.

60 Melucci, *Challenging Codes.*

61 Mouffe, "Feminism, Citizenship." For relevant historical examples of participatory communication see Gumucio Dagron, *Making Waves*; Rodríguez, *Fissures in the Mediascape* and *Citizens' Media against Armed Conflict.*

62 Patiño Lemos and Vallejo Gómez, "Caracterización de Prácticas con TIC."

63 Jenkins et al., *Confronting the Challenges.*

64 Patiño Lemos and Vallejo Gómez, "Caracterización de Prácticas con TIC."

65 Kleine, *Technologies of Choice,* 213.

66 Vilchis et al., "COMPUGIRLS Speak," 61. Galindo Cuesta, "Ciudadanía Digital." See also Garcia Ávila, "Alfabetización Digital"; Guillén-Rascón et al., "Alfabetización Digital."

67 Middaugh and Kirshner, *#youthaction,* 210.

68 Longford, "Pedagogies of Digital Citizenship," 69, original emphasis.

69 Kelty, "From Participation to Power," 29.

70 Longford, "Pedagogies of Digital Citizenship," 70.

71 Medina et al., *Beyond Imported Magic.* See also Chan, *Networking Peripheries*; Srinivasan and Fish, *After the Internet,* 8.

72 Horst, "Free, Social, and Inclusive"; Thomas, *Digital India*; Chan, *Networking Peripheries.*

73 Chan, "Balancing Design."

74 Kelty et al., "Seven Dimensions."

75 Carpentier, *Media and Participation*; Gumucio Dagron, *Making Waves*; Heeks, "The Tyranny of Participation"; Quarry and Ramirez, *Communication for Another Development*; Servaes and Malikhao, "Participatory Communication"; Tufte and Mefalopulos, *Participatory Communication.*

76 Gumucio Dagron, *Making Waves,* 11; see also Kleine, *Technologies of Choice.*

77 Bar et al., "Mobile Technology Appropriation"; García Canclini, *Hybrid Cultures*; Medina et al., *Beyond Imported Magic*; Kleine, *Technologies of Choice,* 52.

78 Carpentier, *Media and Participation*, 102; see also Cooke and Kothari, *Participation*; Heeks, "The Tyranny of Participation."

79 See also Kelty, "From Participation to Power."

80 Chan, *Networking Peripheries*; Medina et al., *Beyond Imported Magic*.

81 Interview, Alonso Salazar, Medellín, July 11, 2011.

82 Heidi Tamayo Ortiz, "Lo que hace de Medellín la ciudad más inteligente de Colombia," *El Tiempo*, July 17, 2017, https://www.eltiempo.com/colombia/medellin/medellin-es-la-ciudad-mas-inteligente-de-colombia-109826.

83 Some of these dynamics are further explored in the discussion of Son Batá and Afro-Colombian youth citizenship in Chapter 3.

84 Servaes and Hoyng, "The Tools of Social Change."

85 Kelty, "From Participation to Power."

86 Servaes and Hoyng, "The Tools of Social Change," 263, original emphasis.

Chapter Three

1 I am grateful to Clemencia Rodríguez for her assistance with all song translations.

2 Medina Holguín et al., *Somos Hip Hop*, 4.

3 The analysis in this chapter is based on approximately forty in-depth interviews with participants, as well as advisors or mentors to the groups; observation of meetings, events, and other activities over the course of more than six months; and a review of documents produced by the collectives (including online publications, songs, and videos), as well as existing research by local scholars. In the case of La Elite, data are also drawn from audience interviews at their 2011 annual hip-hop festival Revolución Sin Muertos (Revolution without Deaths), and from a collective memory-based, participatory research workshop, the details of which are included in Acosta Valencia and Garcés Montoya, *Proyecto Comunicación* and "Prácticas de Comunicación."

4 Reguillo, *Culturas Juveniles.*

5 Ito et al., "Learning Connected Civics"; Jenkins, "Why Mitt Romney Won't Debate a Snowman"; Jenkins et al., *Confronting the Challenges*; Kahne et al., "The Civic and Political Significance"; and Kahne et al., "Youth, New Media."

6 See, e.g., Yúdice, "Afro Reggae."

7 Rodríguez, *Citizens' Media*, 254. See also Martín Barbero, "Jóvenes"; Salazar, *No Nacimos Pa' Semilla.*

8 Williams, "Culture Is Ordinary."

9 However, G. P. Uribe Neira notes that of thirty youth networks she studied in Medellín, adult-led civil society organizations played some kind of supporting role in the formation of 40 percent of these (Uribe Neira, *Jóvenes y Acción Colectiva*, 194).

10 Garcés Montoya, "De Organizaciones a Colectivos Juveniles," 5. See also Reguillo, *Culturas Juveniles*, 43.

11 Reguillo, "Ciudadanías Juveniles."

12 Garcés Montoya, "De Organizaciones a Colectivos Juveniles," 5.

13 Garcés Montoya, "De Organizaciones a Colectivos Juveniles," 5.

14 Uribe Neira et al.'s study of youth collectives and networks in Medellín found that 60 percent have a community development or political agenda, with the latter broadly conceived as the intention of provoking change in "youth's social, cultural, political, environmental, economic, and personal realities" (Uribe Neira, *Jóvenes y Acción Colectiva*, 191).

15 For a discussion of how I adapt Michel de Certeau's use of the terms "tactics" and "strategies" to describe grass-roots and institutional forms of participation, see Chapter 1.

16 The population of Comuna 13 in 2011 was approximately 135,000 (DANE and Municipio de Medellín, "Perfil Sociodemográfico 2005–2015"). Approximately 75 percent of the residents were classified as living in the two lowest socioeconomic strata, and some 40 percent of homes had single-mother heads of household (Departamento Administrativo de Planeación [Administrative Office of Planning, Mayor's Office of Medellín]). Approximately 60 percent of children under the age of five suffered from malnutrition (Cañas et al., *Dinámicas de Guerra*, 36).

17 Operation Orion was one in a series of military operations carried out in 2002 in Medellín under then-President Alvaro Uribe to eliminate guerrilla groups from the city. See Introduction.

18 Cañas et al., *Dinámicas de Guerra*, 5.

19 Cañas et al., *Dinámicas de Guerra*, 64.

20 Garcés Montoya notes that this number of hip-hop groups is remarkable, given the limited amount of support and spaces (both public spaces and concert venues) in which to feature hip-hop artists in the city at the time (Garcés Montoya, *Nos-otros los Jóvenes*, 210).

21 Rose, *Black Noise*; García Guzmán and Giraldo Obando, "HipHop y Educación."

22 García Canclini, *Hybrid Cultures*.

23 Garcés Montoya, *Nos-otros los Jóvenes*.

24 Medina Holguín et al., *Somos Hip Hop*, 15.

25 La Red de Hip Hop La Elite, "Resumen del plan Estratégico de la Red de Hip Hop la Elite" (Medellín, Colombia: La Red de Hip Hop La Elite, 2010); La Red de Hip Hop La Elite, "Manual Operativo" (Medellín, Colombia: La Red de Hip Hop La Elite, 2010).

26 La Elite project document (Medellín, Colombia: La Red de Hip Hop La Elite, n.d.).

27 Proyecto Gestores Culturales Comuna 13, "Caracterización de los y las Jóvenes Gestores Culturales de la Escuela de Hip Hop Kolacho." These data are from a 2010 survey of fifty of the network's most active members carried out by Metrojuventud (the municipal department of youth programs) in the Secretaría de Cultura Ciudadana (Office of Civic Culture).

28 By the time of my research, the density of Comuna 13 averaged 0.38 m² per inhabitant compared to the 2.95 m² of public space per inhabitant averaged in the city as a whole, despite advances made by the Fajardo administration

(Departamento administrativo de Planeación, Alcaldía de Medellín, "Encuesta de Calidad de Vida 2011").

29 This led some hip-hoppers and their supporters to speculate about whether
hip-hop activists were being targeted by armed gangs because of their
nonviolent agenda. Views on the matter differed. However, the predominant
opinion at the time was that the only difference between hip-hop activists
and other youth caught in the cross fire of gang warfare is that their deaths
received more publicity in the media due to their public profiles.

30 I carried out audience interviews during the first day of the 2011 Revolución
Sin Muertos festival with the help of volunteer assistants who were both local
and foreign. We interviewed a total of fifty-seven audience members (thirty
female and twenty-seven male), with a mean age of twenty-two. Approximately 70 percent of interviewees identified themselves as associated with
hip-hop culture, as either hip-hop artists or fans.

31 Reguillo, *Culturas Juveniles*, 94, 122.

32 *Los malos* (the bad guys) is used to refer to illegal armed actors without having to name any in particular. For further discussion of the cautious use of
language among youth in Medellín to discuss the dynamics of the conflict,
see Riaño-Alcalá, *Dwellers of Memory*.

33 Ito et al., *Connected Learning*, 6, 47.

34 Freire, *Pedagogy of the Oppressed*, 72. *Conscientization*, or *conscientizaçao*,
refers to "learning to perceive social, political and economic contradictions,
and to take action against the oppressive elements of reality" (35). For Freire,
the importance of *conscientization* was that people need to perceive the
causes of their reality in order to bring about change (131).

35 García Guzmán and Giraldo Obando, "HipHop y Educación."

36 The Fajardo administration (whose staff included several former community
organizers with experience in popular education) financed popular education
schools for sports, music, cultural centers, and community media across the
city. The Secretaría de Cultura Ciudadana (Office of Civic Culture) funded three
months of workshops with modest salaries for La Elite's popular educators.

37 La Elite project document (Medellín, Colombia: La Red de Hip Hop La Elite,
n.d.).

38 See, e.g., Ito et al., *Hanging Out*; Ito et al., "Learning Connected Civics";
Jenkins, *Convergence Culture*; Kahne et al., "The Civic and Political Significance"; Kahne et al., "Youth, New Media"; Neta Kligler-Vilenchik, "De-
creasing World Suck: Fan Communities, Mechanisms of Translation, and
Participatory Politics," 2013, accessed January 2014, http://henryjenkins.org
/blog/2013/06/decreasing-world-suck-fan-communities-mechanisms-of
-translation-and-participatory-politics.html.

39 For some relevant scholarship, including López, "Circling the Cross," see
Digital Media and Learning Research Hub, accessed January 2020, http://
dmlhub.net/. See also Carpentier, *Media and Participation*; Jenkins and
Carpentier, "Theorizing Participatory Intensities"; Jenkins et al., *Confronting
the Challenges*; Lankshear and Knobel, "From 'Reading' to 'New' Literacies,"

in *New Literacies*, 7–28. On collective intelligence, see Lévy, *Collective Intelligence*.

40 Attendance fluctuated, but there were typically twenty to twenty-five participants at each assembly for the twenty-three groups of the network.

41 Kelty, "From Participation to Power," 238.

42 Kelty, "From Participation to Power,"23.

43 The sign incorporates the number 13 to reference Comuna 13. Palenque is an
Afro-Colombian town near Cartagena that was founded by escaped slaves
in the seventeenth century. As one of the earliest independent communities
of Afro-descendants in the Americas, it serves as an important cultural and
historical referent among Afro-Colombians.

44 Rojas, *Civilización y Violencia*.

45 Colombia's rural ethnic communities were disproportionately affected by the
war. See García Sánchez and Montoya Arango, *Jóvenes Afrocolombianos*.

46 García Sánchez and Montoya Arango, *Jóvenes Afrocolombianos*, 24. Departments are country subdivisions, or administrative regions in Colombia.

47 García Sánchez and Montoya Arango, *Jóvenes Afrocolombianos*, 25.

48 García Sánchez and Montoya Arango, *Jóvenes Afrocolombianos*, 40.

49 J. Saldarriaga, "Entre Disparos, Se Oye un Clarinete," *El Colombiano*, July 3,
2011, http://www.elcolombiano.com/BancoConocimiento/E/entre_disparos
_se_oye_un_clarinete/entre_disparos_se_oye_un_clarinete.asp.

50 A separate Consejo Municipal para Asuntos y Políticas Públicas de las
Comunidades Afrodescendientes (Council on Afro-Colombian Affairs and
Public Policy) was created in 2006, during the Fajardo administration. However, it remained relatively marginalized and its powers limited; the center of
power and decision making in the city resides with the general City Council
and the Mayor's Office.

51 Escobar, *Territories of Difference*, 14.

52 Cañas et al., *Dinámicas de Guerra*, 251.

Chapter Four

1 Foucault, "Governmentality," 20. See also Rose et al., "Governmentality," 86;
Lemke, "Foucault, Governmentality and Critique." On participation as a form
of governmentality in mainstream development discourse, see Cornwall,
"Historical Perspectives," 79.

2 Alcaldía de Medellín, *La Participación en Medellín*, 231.

3 Jorge Melguizo, "Participación para la Transformación de Medellín," 2011,
accessed December 2012, http://www.campuseuroamericano.org/pdf
/es/Participacion%20para%20la%20transformacion%20de%20Medellin
_Melguizo.pdf.

4 Yúdice, *The Expediency of Culture*, 107. In a similar vein, in her study of youth
of color activism in the United States, Soo Ah Kwon used the term "affirmative governmentality" to analyze youth participation and empowerment as a
relationship of government (Kwon, *Uncivil Youth*).

5 Pécaut, *Crónica de Cuatro Décadas* and "From the Banality of Violence"; Velásquez and González, *¿Qué Ha Pasado?*

6 Velásquez and González, *¿Qué Ha Pasado?*, 50.

7 See especially Articles 2, 40, 95, and 103, accessed April 5, 2013, http://pdba .georgetown.edu/constitutions/colombia/col91.html#mozTocId792303; Observatorio Legislativo del Instituto de Ciencia Política, "Ley Estatutaria de Participación Ciudadana"; Velásquez and González, *¿Qué Ha Pasado?*

8 On participatory democracy in modern societies, see Barber, "Participatory Democracy"; Fuchs, "Participatory Democracy"; Pateman, *Participation and Democratic Theory* and "Participatory Democracy Revisited"; Velásquez and González, *¿Qué Ha Pasado?*

9 Bernal, "Contexto"; Fals Borda, "Grietas de la Democracia"; Londoño, "Aproximación a la Democracia Participativa"; Velásquez and González, *¿Qué Ha Pasado?*

10 Bernal, "Contexto"; Velásquez and González, *¿Qué Ha Pasado?*

11 Yúdice, *The Expediency of Culture.*

12 León Gutiérrez et al., "Potencial Social y Político"; Velásquez and González, *¿Qué Ha Pasado?* Some analysts feel that the implementation of processes of participation (mandated by the 1991 constitution and other policy reforms) have largely failed for reasons including lack of public awareness, bureaucratic obstacles to participation, and ineffective structures of participation. See Observatorio Legislativo del Instituto de Ciencia Política, "Ley Estatutaria de Participación Ciudadana."

13 Goldfrank, "Lessons from Latin American Experience," 92.

14 Shah, *Participatory Budgeting*, 1.

15 See Goldfrank, "Lessons from Latin American Experience" and "The World Bank."

16 Cabannes, "The Impact of Participatory Budgeting"; see also Participatory Budgeting Project, "PB Map & Process List," accessed June 18, 2018, https:// www.participatorybudgeting.org/pb-map/.

17 Goldfrank, "Lessons from Latin American Experience" and "The World Bank," 3; see also Cabannes, "Participatory Budgeting."

18 León Gutiérrez et al., "Potencial Social y Político"; Pimienta Betancur, "La 'Ciudad Educadora.'"

19 León Gutiérrez et al., "Potencial Social y Político." Initial but limited steps toward PB and other forms of citizen participation were made by previous administrations to comply with national policy, but none to the degree taken by the Fajardo and Salazar administrations. See Veeduría Plan de Desarrollo de Medellín, "Balance de la Gestión de los Planes de Desarrollo," 69; Castañeda Osorio and Botero Valencia, "Caracterización de la Participación Ciudadana."

20 Restrepo Mesa, "El Presupuesto Participativo"; see also Foronda Cano, "Hacia una Estrategia de Desarollo Participativo," 3.

21 See Pimienta Betancur, "Escenarios de Educación Informal"; Gómez Hernández, "El Presupuesto Participativo."

22 Veeduría Plan de Desarrollo de Medellín, "Balance de la Gestión de los Planes de Desarrollo"; Restrepo Mesa, "El Presupuesto Participativo."

23 For further details of how the PB process was structured in 2011, see Alcaldía de Medellín, *ABC de Planeación Local.*

24 DANE and Municipio de Medellín, "Proyecciones de Población."

25 In Comuna 1 in 2012, for example, 7.22 percent of youth in the *comuna* participated, while 5.7 percent of adults and 5.3 percent of seniors participated. Personal correspondence, Secretaría de Participación Ciudadana de la Alcaldía de Medellín (Office of Civic Participation in the Medellín Mayor's Office), May 14, 2013.

26 While the overall percentage of youth delegates was proportionately lower than adults, it was more or less proportionate to the population of youth in the city at large (approximately 21 percent). Personal correspondence, Secretaría de Participación Ciudadana de la Alcaldía de Medellín (Office of Civic Participation in the Medellín Mayor's Office), May 14, 2013.

27 Analyzing youth engagement in PB strictly by number of participants offers a very limited understanding of youth participation. Such a metric may serve the interests of the government (when numbers are favorable), providing a simple and relatively superficial indicator of youth engagement in local development. Yet, it does not serve the interests of the youth participants, for whom the quality and outcome of their experiences of participation are far more significant. The literature on participation in the field of development has extensively debated how best to measure participation. See Gumucio Dagron, *Making Waves*; Gumucio Dagron, "Playing with Fire"; Huesca, "Tracing the History"; Tufte and Mefalopulos, *Participatory Communication*.

28 Pimienta Betancur, "Escenarios de Educación Informal" and "La 'Ciudad Educadora.'"

29 Fierst, "Jóvenes y Su Participación en la Política de Medellín"; Gómez Hernández, "El Presupuesto Participativo"; Pimienta Betancur, "Escenarios de Educación Informal," 9.

30 On responsibilization, see Rose, "Government and Control." See also Cornwall, "Historical Perspectives."

31 Cabannes, "The Impact of Participatory Budgeting," 257, 273.

32 See, e.g., León Gutiérrez et al., "Potencial Social y Político"; Pimienta Betancur, "La 'Ciudad Educadora.'"

33 C. M. Cano R., "Recursos del Presupuesto Participativo de Medellín Fueron Desviados," *El Tiempo*, accessed September 2013, http://m.eltiempo.com /colombia/medellin/recursos-del-presupuesto-participativo-de-medelln -fueron-desviados/11952341, link no longer active; Doyle, "Explaining Patterns of Urban Violence," 11; Germán Jiménez Morales, "Así 'Vacuna' la Delincuencia los Sagrados Dineros Públicos," *El Colombiano*, August 13, 2013, http://www.elcolombiano.com/BancoConocimiento/A/asi_vacuna_la _delincuencia_los_sagrados_dineros_publicos/asi_vacuna_la_delincuencia _los_sagrados_dineros_publicos.asp; Hajdarowicz, "Does Participation Empower?"; Moncada, "Urban Violence, Political Economy," 241–242; Ramírez

Gallegos, "El Espacio Público," 69–70; Universidad de EAFIT and Universidad de Medellín, "Reporte Breve." This, of course, is not unique to Medellín. Shah, a key advocate of PB in his former position at the World Bank, noted that PB processes are shaped by the preexisting relations of power and can be "captured by interest groups," thus "giving the appearance of broader participation and inclusive governance, while using public funds to advance the interests of powerful elites" (Shah, *Participatory Budgeting*, 1).

34 This estimate is based on figures provided by La Elite and Metrojuventud, the department of youth programs in the municipal government.

35 Personal correspondence, Subsecretaría de Planeación y Presupuesto Participativo (Sub-Department of Planning and Participatory Budgeting); Secretaría de Participación Ciudadana (Office of Civic Participation), July 2012.

36 De Certeau, *The Practice of Everyday Life*, 37.

37 Gilman reports similar findings in her study of PB in the United States (Gilman, *Democracy Reinvented*); see also Hajdarowicz, "Does Participation Empower?"

38 Fierst, "El Presupuesto Participativo"; Gómez Hernández, "El Presupuesto Participativo"; Hajdarowicz, "Does Participation Empower?"; Pimienta Betancur, "Escenarios de Educación informal" and "La 'Ciudad Educadora.'"

39 Precise data on the rate of participation of Afro-Colombians in PB were not available in 2011. This statement is based on observation and several interviews with PB participants and government administrators.

40 Andreas Novy and Bernard Leubolt found similar results in Porto Alegre's PB process (Novy and Leubolt, "Participatory Budgeting").

41 Personal correspondence, Secretaría de Participación Ciudadana de la Alcaldía de Medellín (Office of Civic Participation in the Medellín Mayor's Office), May 14, 2013.

42 Hajdarowicz, "Does Participation Empower?" 12.

43 Pimienta Betancur, "La 'Ciudad Educadora,'" 45.

44 For an example of popular mobilization to change the PB process of a particular *comuna*, see Urán, "Participación Ciudadana," 37.

45 Some survey data suggested that 20–30 percent of Medellín's citizens were aware of the PB process [Medellín Como Vamos, *Encuesta de Percepción Ciudadana*; Subsecretaría de Metrojuventud (the municipal department of youth programs), "Resultados Encuesta Juvenil 2009," Alcaldía de Medellín, 20090. So, debates about participation in and around PB probably did not circulate beyond that percentage of the public. Nonetheless, this was still a significant swath of the population who could be directly engaged in or influenced by these conversations.

46 Londoño, "Aproximación a la Democracia Participativa," 22.

47 For further details on my use of the term "polyculture," see Chapter 1.

48 Alejandro Arboleda Hoyos, "Cambios al Presupuesto Participativo, en Debate," *El Colombiano*, March 29, 2017, http://www.elcolombiano.com/antioquia/cambios-al-presupuesto-participativo-en-debate-YB6232441; "Editorial: Reforma al Sistema de Planeación Municipal de Medellín, ¡en

Deuda con la Participación Ciudadana!" Corporación Región, May 2, 2017, http://www.region.org.co/index.php/opinamos/item/195-editorial-reforma -sistema-planeacion-municipal-medellin-en-deuda-con-la-participacion -ciudadana; Luisa Fernanda Sierra García, "Presupuesto Participativo no Tomó en Cuenta a Comunidades," *El Mundo*, November 28, 2017, http:// www.elmundo.com/noticia/Presupuesto-Participativo-no-tomo-en-cuenta -a-comunidades/363435; Víctor Vargas, "El Presupuesto Participativo Vive Entre el Desencanto y las Críticas," *El Tiempo*, May 24, 2018, http://www .eltiempo.com/colombia/medellin/el-presupuesto-participativo-vive-entre-el -desencanto-y-las-criticas-en-medellin-221550.

49 Uran, "Medellín Participatory Creativity," 152.

50 Gilman, *Democracy Reinvented*, 124. See also Peixoto, "Beyond Theory." By 2017, residents of Medellín were able to vote online in the PB process.

51 See Dagnino, "Citizenship: A Perverse Confluence," 103.

Chapter Five

1 See Michael O'Hanion and Elizabeth Pearce, "Once a Drug Den, Medellín is on a New Path," Brookings, August 13, 2016, https://www.brookings.edu/blog /order-from-chaos/2016/08/13/once-a-drug-den-medellin-is-on-a-new-path/; Francis Fukuyama and Seth Colby, "Half a Miracle," *Foreign Policy*, accessed October 10, 2011, http://www.foreignpolicy.com/articles/2011/04/25/half_a _miracle; Maclean, *Social Urbanism*.

2 See, e.g., Simon Romero, "Medellín's Nonconformist Mayor Turns Blight to Beauty," *The New York Times*, July 15, 2007, http://www.nytimes.com/2007 /07/15/world/americas/15medellin.html?pagewanted=all; Christopher Bagley, "Medellín Sheds Cocaine Image to Become Cultural Hot Spot," Bloomberg, November 21, 2013, http://www.bloomberg.com/news/2013-11-21/medellin -sheds-cocaine-image-to-become-cultural-hot-spot.html.

3 Medellín Cómo Vamos, "Informe de Calidad de Vida de Medellín."

4 Medellín Cómo Vamos, "Encuesta de Percepción Ciudadana, Medellín."

5 Doyle, "Explaining Patterns of Urban Violence"; Franz, "Urban Governance and Economic Development"; Moncada, "Urban Violence, Political Econ- omy," 239; see also Maclean, *Social Urbanism*.

6 Interview with Alonso Salazar, Medellín, July 11, 2011; Alcaldía de Medellín, *Del Miedo a la Esperanza*.

7 Deleuze and Foucault, "Les Intellectuels et le Pouvoir," 8.

8 Approximately 37 percent of all Colombians used Facebook in 2011 (Internet World Stats, "Colombia"). Nearly all the youth interviewed for this study used the social networking platform.

9 Madden et al., "Teens, Social Media, and Privacy," May 21, 2013, http:// assets.pewresearch.org/wp-content/uploads/sites/14/2013/05/PIP _TeensSocialMediaandPrivacy_PDF.pdf.

10 Status updates allow users to post messages to their network of "friends" on Facebook. Friends may respond with a comment (and/or by clicking "like,"

"love," or other emoticon buttons). In many instances, status updates prompt online conversations between multiple users.

11   The participants in the dialogue averaged approximately 2,800 Facebook friends each, and there were eighteen different users who had commented or liked this dialogue, meaning at least eighteen users made the dialogue potentially visible to their own networks of thousands of Facebook friends. However, it is likely that many of these networks overlapped significantly and that Facebook algorithms limited the number of actual views.

12   Reports of the size of the march vary ("Capturan a Dos Presunto Asesinos de Rapero de la Comuna 13," *El Tiempo*, accessed April 2011, http://m.eltiempo .com/colombia/medellin/capturan-a-dos-presuntos-asesinos-de-rapero-de -la-comuna-13/9141925; Juan Carlos Monroy Giraldo and Juan Guillermo Duque, "Sí a la Vida a Ritmo de Rap," *El Colombiano*, March 30, 2011, http:// www.elcolombiano.com/BancoConocimiento/S/si_a_la_vida_a_ritmo_de _rap/si_a_la_vida_a_ritmo_de_rap.asp).

13   Tarrow, *The New Transnational Activism*.

14   Carpentier, *Media and Participation*.

15   UNICEF, "Adolescent and Youth Engagement," 19; see also Middaugh and Kirshner, *#youthaction*, 210. On the impacts of digital communication platform design on youth and other non-dominant groups, see Literat and Brough, "From Ethical to Equitable Social Media"; Bivens and Haimson, "Baking Gender"; boyd et al., "The Networked Nature of Algorithmic Discrimination"; Burgess et al., "Making Digital Cultures"; Eubanks, *Automating Inequality*; Hersh, "Science, Technology and Values"; Massanari, "#Gamergate and the Fappening"; Noble, *Algorithms of Oppression*; Vodanovich et al., "Cultural Values Inherent in the Design of Social Media Platforms."

16   See Andrejevic, *iSpy*; Cheney-Lippold, "Jus Algoritmi" and *We Are Data*; Chun, *Control and Freedom*; Eubanks, *Automating Inequality*; Lessig, *Code*; Noble, *Algorithms of Oppression*; Vivienne et al., "Digital Citizenship as Fluid Interface."

17   Henry Jenkins in Jenkins and Carpentier, "Theorizing Participatory Intensities"; Fenton and Barassi, "Alternative Media and Social Networking Sites"; Juhasz, "Learning the Five Lessons of YouTube"; Papacharissi, *A Private Sphere*.

18   Mercea et al., "Protest Communication Ecologies"; Fenton and Barassi, "Alternative Media and Social Networking Sites."

19   Cornwall, "Unpacking 'Participation,'" 278.

20   Shirky, *Here Comes Everybody*, 20–21.

21   Uribe Neira, *Jóvenes y Acción Colectiva*, 36.

22   Ito et al., "Learning Connected Civics," 11, 25, original emphasis. See also Bennett and Segerberg, "The Logic of Connective Action"; Nico Carpentier in Jenkins and Carpentier, "Theorizing Participatory Intensities," 13–14.

23   Servaes and Hoyng, "The Tools of Social Change," 268.

24   Checkoway, "What Is Youth Participation?" 342.

25   Uribe Neira, *Jóvenes y Acción Colectiva*, 68.

26 Carpentier, *Media and Participation*, 125.
27 Nico Carpentier in Jenkins and Carpentier, "Theorizing Participatory Intensities."
28 Oliver Gordon, "Behind the Medellín Miracle: Why the Smart Kids are Going to Hip Hop," *The Guardian*, November 20, 2017, https://www.theguardian .com/cities/2017/nov/20/medellin-miracle-hip-hop-school-gangs.
29 Reguillo, *Culturas Juveniles*, 150.
30 See, e.g., Gumucio Dagron, "Playing with Fire."
31 For relevant debates on some of the problems of participatory culture/ politics, see the series "Participatory Politics in an Age of Crisis," accessed June 27, 2019, http://henryjenkins.org/archives-html.
32 Franz, "Urban Governance and Economic Development in Medellín."
33 *Q'Viva! The Chosen*, season 1, episode 1, directed by Jamie King, aired January 28, 2012 (Los Angeles, CA: SO3 Projects, King Productions).
34 *Q'Viva! The Chosen*, season 1, episode 1, directed by Jamie King, aired January 28, 2012 (Los Angeles, CA: SO3 Projects, King Productions).
35 *Q'Viva! The Chosen*, season 1, episode 4, directed by Jamie King, aired February 12, 2012 (Los Angeles, CA: SO3 Projects, King Productions).
36 Jenkins, *Convergence Culture*. See also Andrejevic, *Reality TV*; Murray and Ouellette, *Reality TV*.
37 *Q'Viva! The Chosen*, season 1, episode 8, directed by Jamie King, aired February 18, 2012 (Los Angeles, CA: SO3 Projects, King Productions).

Acosta Valencia, Gladys Lucía, and Ángela Garcés Montoya. *Colectivos de Co-munación y Apropiación de Medios.* Medellín, Colombia: Universidad de Medellín, 2013.

Acosta Valencia, Gladys Lucía, and Ángela Garcés Montoya. "Prácticas de Comunicación y Apropiación de Medios en Colectivos de Comunicación Juveniles en Medellín." In *Cátedra UNESCO de Comunicación: Encuentro Nacional de Investigación*, edited by José Miguel Pereira, 78–88. Bogotá, Colombia: Pontificia Universidad Javeriana, 2013.

Acosta Valencia, Gladys Lucía, and Ángela Garcés Montoya. *Proyecto Comunicación, Juventud y Ciudadanía: Informe Final.* Medellín, Colombia: Universidad de Medellín, 2012.

Alcaldía de Medellín. *ABC de Planeación Local y Presupuesto Participativo.* Medellín, Colombia: Alcaldía de Medellín, 2011. Accessed July 10, 2018. https://www.medellin.gov.co/irj/go/km/docs/wpccontent/Sites/Subportal%20del%20 Ciudadano/Desarrollo%20Social/Secciones/Plantillas%20Gen%C3%A9ricas /Documentos/2011/CARTILLA%20PP%20Final-WEB%202011.pdf.

Alcaldía de Medellín. *Del Miedo a la Esperanza: Alcaldía de Medellín 2004/2007.* Medellín, Colombia: Alcaldía de Medellín, 2008.

Alcaldía de Medellín. *La Participación en Medellín.* Medellín, Colombia: Alcaldía de Medellín, 2007.

Alcaldía de Medellín. *Plan de Desarrollo 2004–2007: Medellín Compromiso de Toda la Ciudadanía.* Medellín, Colombia: Alcaldía de Medellín, 2004.

Alcaldía de Medellín. *Programa Paz y Reconciliación: Modelo de Intervención Regreso a la Legalidad.* Medellín, Colombia: Alcaldía de Medellín, n.d.

Allagui, Ilhem, and Johanne Kuebler. "The Arab Spring and the Role of ICTs." *International Journal of Communication* 5, no. 8 (2011): 1435–1442.

Allen, Danielle, Moya Bailey, Nico Carpentier, Natalie Fenton, Henry Jenkins, Alexis Lothian, Jack Linchuan Qui, Mirko Tobias Schaefer, and Ramesh

Srinivasan. "Participations: Dialogues on the Participatory Promise of Contemporary Culture and Politics. Part 3: Politics." *International Journal of Communication* 8 (2014): 1129–1151.

Altieri, Miguel A. *Agroecology: The Science of Sustainable Agriculture*. Boca Raton, FL: CRC Press, 2018.

Ames, Morgan G. "Learning Consumption: Media, Literacy, and the Legacy of One Laptop per Child." *The Information Society* 32, no. 2 (2016): 85–97.

Andrejevic, Mark. *iSpy: Surveillance and Power in the Interactive Era*. Lawrence: University Press of Kansas, 2007.

Andrejevic, Mark. *Reality TV: The Work of Being Watched*. Lanham, MD: Rowman and Littlefield, 2004.

Arnstein, Sherry R. "A Ladder of Citizen Participation." *Journal of the American Institute of Planners* 35, no. 4 (1969): 216–224.

Ball-Rokeach, Sandra J., Yong-Chan Kim, and Sorin Matei. "Storytelling Neighborhood Paths to Belonging in Diverse Urban Environments." *Communication Research* 28, no. 4 (2001): 392–428.

Banet-Weiser, Sarah, and Charlotte Lapsansky. "RED Is the New Black: Brand Culture, Consumer Citizenship and Political Possibility." *International Journal of Communication* 2 (2008): 21.

Bar, François, Matthew S. Weber, and Francis Pisani. "Mobile Technology Appropriation in a Distant Mirror: Baroquization, Creolization, and Cannibalism." *New Media and Society* 18, no. 4 (2016): 617–636.

Barber, Benjamin R. "Participatory Democracy." In *Encyclopedia of Democracy*, Vol. 3, edited by Seymour Martin Lipset, 921–924. London: Routledge, 1995.

Barranquero, Alejandro. "Latinoamérica: La Arquitectura Participativa de la Comunicación para el Cambio." *Dialogos de la Comunicación* 78 (2009): 1–14.

Beltrán, Luis Ramiro. "Adeus a Aristóteles: Comunicação Horitzontal." *Revista Comunicação e Sociedade do Programa de Comunicação* 16 (1981): 5–35.

Benkler, Yochai. "Practical Anarchism: Peer Mutualism, Market Power, and the Fallible State." *Politics and Society* 41, no. 2 (2013): 213–251.

Bennett, W. Lance, ed. "Changing Citizenship in the Digital Age." In *Civic Life Online: Learning How Digital Media Can Engage Youth*, 1–24. Cambridge, MA: MIT Press, 2008.

Bennett, W. Lance, Deen Freelon, and Chris Wells. "Changing Citizen Identity and the Rise of a Participatory Media Culture." In *Handbook of Research on Civic Engagement in Youth*, edited by Lonnie R. Sherrod, Judith Torney-Purta, and Constance A. Flanagan, 393–423. Hoboken, NJ: Wiley, 2010.

Bennett, W. Lance, and Alexandra Segerberg. "The Logic of Connective Action: Digital Media and the Personalization of Contentious Politics." *Information, Communication and Society* 15, no. 5 (2012): 739–768.

Bernal Medina, Jorge Arturo. "Contexto: Características de Medellín en los Años Noventa." In *Democracia y Ciudadanías: Balance de Derechos y Libertades en Medellín*, edited by Jorge Arturo Bernal Medina and Luz Stella Álvarez Castaño, 27–46. Medellín, Colombia: Corporación Región, 2005.

Beyer, Jessica L., and Fenwick McKelvey. "You Are Not Welcome Among Us: Pirates and the State." *International Journal of Communication* 9 (2015): 19.

Bivens, Rena, and Oliver L. Haimson. "Baking Gender into Social Media Design: How Platforms Shape Categories for Users and Advertisers." *Social Media + Society* 2, no. 4 (2016): 2056305116672486.

Boal, Augusto. *Theater of the Oppressed.* Translated by Charles A. and María-Odilia Leal McBride. London: Pluto Press, 1979.

Bordenave, Juan Díaz. "Participative Communication as a Part of Building the Participative Society." In *Participatory Communication: Working for Change and Development*, edited by Shirley A. White, K. Sadanandan Nair, and Joseph R. Ascroft, 35–48. Thousand Oaks, CA: Sage, 1994.

Botero, Fernando. *Medellín 1890–1950: Historia Urbana y Juego de Intereses.* Medellín, Colombia: Editorial Universidad de Antioquia, 1996.

Boyd, Andrew, and Dave Oswald Mitchell, eds. *Beautiful Trouble: A Toolbox for Revolution.* New York: OR Books, 2012.

boyd, danah. *It's Complicated: The Social Lives of Networked Teens.* New Haven, CT: Yale University Press, 2014.

boyd, danah. "White Flight in Networked Publics? How Race and Class Shaped American Teen Engagement with MySpace and Facebook." In *Race after the Internet*, edited by Lisa Nakamura and Peter Chow-White, 203–222. New York: Routledge, 2012.

boyd, danah, Karen Levy, and Alice Marwick. "The Networked Nature of Algorithmic Discrimination." In *Data and Discrimination: Collected Essays*, edited by Seeta Pena Ganghadaran, Virginia Eubanks, and Solon Barocas, 53–57. Washington, DC: Open Technology Institute.

Brough, Melissa. "Analytical Antidotes to Technological Determinism: Learning from (Digital) Citizenship and Participation in Medellín, Colombia." In *Technological Determinism and Social Change: Communication in a Tech-Mad World*, edited by Jan Servaes, 213–242. Lanham, MD: Lexington, 2014.

Brough, Melissa. "Participatory Culture." In *The Johns Hopkins Guide to Digital Media*, edited by Marie-Laure Ryan, Lori Emerson, and Benjamin J. Robertson, 382–387. Baltimore: Johns Hopkins University Press, 2014.

Brough, Melissa, Charlotte Lapsansky, Carmen Gonzalez, Benjamin Stokes, and François Bar. "Mobile Voices: Design as a Method to Explore the Possibilities and Limitations of Community Participation." *Mobile Media and Communication* 6, no. 2 (2018): 247–265.

Brough, Melissa, and Sangita Shrapnel. "Fandom Meets Activism: Rethinking Civic and Political Participation." *Transformative Works and Cultures* 10 (2012).

Bruns, Axel. *Blogs, Wikipedia, Second Life, and Beyond: From Production to Produsage.* New York: Peter Lang, 2008.

Burgess, Jean, Elija Cassidy, Stefanie Duguay, and Ben Light. "Making Digital Cultures of Gender and Sexuality with Social Media." *Social Media + Society* 2, no. 4 (2016): 2056305116672487.

Burgess, Jean, Marcus Foth, and Helen Klaebe. "Everyday Creativity as Civic Engagement: A Cultural Citizenship View of New Media." Paper presented at the Communications Policy and Research Forum, Sydney, Australia, September 25–26, 2006.

Butler, Judith. "Giving an Account of Oneself." *Diacritics* 31, no. 4 (2001): 22–40.

Cabannes, Yves. "The Impact of Participatory Budgeting on Basic Services: Municipal Practices and Evidence from the Field." *Environment and Urbanization* 27, no. 1 (2015): 257–284.

Cabannes, Yves. "Participatory Budgeting: A Significant Contribution to Participatory Democracy." *Environment and Urbanization* 16, no. 1 (2001): 27–46.

Cañas, Angarita, Pablo Emilio, Héctor Gallo, and Blanca Inéz Jiménez Zuluaga, eds. *Dinámicas de Guerra y Construcción de Paz: Estudio Interdisciplinario del Conflicto Armado en la Comuna 13 de Medellín.* Medellín, Colombia: Universidad de Antioquia, Universidad de Medellín, 2008.

Canclini, Néstor García. "El Malestar en los Estudios Culturales." *Revista Fractal* 6, no. 2 (1997): 45–60.

Carlsson, Ulla. "The Rise and Fall of NWICO." *Nordicom Review* 24, no. 2 (2003): 31–67.

Carpentier, Nico. *Media and Participation: A Site of Ideological-Democratic Struggle.* Chicago: Intellect, University of Chicago Press, 2011.

Castañeda Osorio, Elizabeth, and Natalia Botero Valencia. "Caracterización de la Participación Ciudadana en la Formulación y Ejecución de las Políticas Sociales de Educación en Medellín Entre 1998–2005." Thesis, Universidad EAFIT, Medellín, Colombia, 2007.

Castells, Manuel. "Communication, Power and Counter-Power in the Network Society." *International Journal of Communication* 1, no. 1 (2007): 29.

Castells, Manuel. *Communication Power.* Oxford: Oxford University Press, 2009.

Castells, Manuel. *End of Millennium.* 2nd ed. Vol. 3 of *The Information Age: Economy, Society, and Culture.* Malden, MA: Blackwell Publishers, 1998.

Castells, Manuel. *Networks of Outrage and Hope: Social Movements in the Internet Age.* Malden, MA: Polity Press, 2012.

Chambers, Robert. "Participatory Rural Appraisal (PRA): Challenges, Potentials and Paradigm." *World Development* 22, no. 10 (1994): 1437–1454.

Chan, Anita Say. "Balancing Design: OLPC Engineers and ICT Translations at the Periphery." In *Beyond Imported Magic: Essays on Science, Technology, and Society in Latin America,* edited by Eden Medina, Ivan da Costa Marques, Christina Holmes, and Marcos Cueto, 181–206. Cambridge, MA: MIT Press, 2014.

Chan, Anita Say. *Networking Peripheries: Technological Futures and the Myth of Digital Universalism.* Cambridge, MA: MIT Press, 2013.

Checkoway, Barry. "What Is Youth Participation?" *Children and Youth Services Review* 33, no. 2 (2011): 340–345.

Cheney-Lippold, John. "Jus Algoritmi: How the National Security Agency Remade Citizenship." *International Journal of Communication* 10, no. 22 (2016).

Cheney-Lippold, John. *We Are Data: Algorithms and the Making of Our Digital Selves*. New York: New York University Press, 2017.

Chernick, M. W. *Acuerdo Posible: Solución Negociada al Conflicto Armado Colombiano*. Bogotá, Colombia: Ediciones Aurora, 2008.

Chow, Rey. "Gender and Representation." In *Feminist Consequences: Theory for the New Century*, edited by Elisabeth Bronfen and Misha Kavka, 38–57. New York: Columbia University Press, 2001.

Chun, Wendy. *Control and Freedom*. Cambridge, MA: MIT Press, 2006.

Ciudad Comuna. *Proyectos Comunicativos Comuna 8*. Medellín, Colombia: Ciudad Comuna, 2010.

Ciudad Comuna. "Un Nuevo Mapa para la Comuna. Memoria y Territorio." In *Visión 8*, 6–7. Medellín, Colombia: Ciudad Comuna, 2010.

Clark, Lynn Schofield. "Theories: Mediatization and Media Ecology." *Mediatization: Concepts, Changes, Consequences*, edited by Knut Lundby, 85–100. New York: Peter Lang, 2009.

Clifford, James. "On Ethnographic Authority." *Representations* 2 (1983): 118–146.

Cohen, Cathy J., and Joseph Kahne. *Participatory Politics: New Media and Youth Political Action*. Chicago: MacArthur Foundation, 2012.

Connor, David J., Robert S. Loomis, and Kenneth G. Cassman. *Crop Ecology: Productivity and Management in Agricultural Systems*. New York: Cambridge University Press, 2011.

Convergencia Research. *Ranking Motorola de Ciudades Digitales*. Buenos Aires, Argentina: Convergencia Research and Motorola, 2009.

Cooke, Bill, and Uma Kothari, eds. *Participation: The New Tyranny?* London: Zed Books, 2001.

Cornwall, Andrea. "Historical Perspectives on Participation in Development." *Commonwealth and Comparative Politics* 44, no. 1 (2006): 62–83.

Cornwall, Andrea. *The Participation Reader*. New York: Zed Books, 2011.

Cornwall, Andrea. "Unpacking 'Participation': Models, Meanings and Practices." *Community Development Journal* 43, no. 3 (2008): 269–283.

Cornwall, Andrea. "Whose Voices? Whose Choices? Reflections on Gender and Participatory Development." *World Development* 31, no. 8 (2003): 1325–1342.

Cornwall, Andrea, and Rachel Jewkes. "What is Participatory Research?" *Social Science & Medicine* 41, no. 12 (1995): 1667–1676.

Coryat, Diana. "Challenging the Silences and Omissions of Dominant Media: Youth-led Media Collectives in Colombia." *Youth Media Reporter* 2, no. 4 (2008).

Couldry, Nick. *Why Voice Matters: Culture and Politics After Neoliberalism*. Thousand Oaks, CA: Sage, 2010.

Couldry, Nick, Hilde Stephansen, Aristea Fotopoulou, Richard MacDonald, Wilma Clark, and Luke Dickens. "Digital Citizenship? Narrative Exchange and the Changing Terms of Civic Culture." *Citizenship Studies* 18, no. 6–7 (2014): 615–629.

Dagnino, Evelina. "Citizenship: A Perverse Confluence." *Development in Practice* 17, no. 4–5 (2007): 549–556.

DANE and Municipio de Medellín. "Perfil Sociodemográfico 2005–2015: Comuna 13 San Javier." 2010. Accessed November 1, 2013. http://www.medellin.gov.co/irj/go/km/docs/wpccontent/Sites/Subportal%20del%20Ciudadano/Planeaci%C3%B3n%20Municipal/Secciones/Indicadores%20y%20Estad%C3%ADsticas/Documentos/Proyecciones%20de%20poblaci%C3%B3n%202005%20-%202015/Perfil%20Demografico%202005-2015%20Comuna%2013.pdf.

DANE and Municipio de Medellin. "Proyecciones de Población Municipio de Medellín por Grupos de Edad y Sexo por Comunas y Corregimientos: Años 1993, 2005–2015." 2010. Accessed December 2013. http://www.medellin.gov.co/irj/go/km/docs/wpccontent/Sites/Subportal%20del%20Ciudadano/Planeaci%C3%B3n%20Municipal/Secciones/Indicadores%20y%20Estad%C3%ADsticas/Documentos/Proyecciones%20de%20poblaci%C3%B3n%202005%20-%202015/03%20Proyecciones%20Poblaci%C3%B3n%20Medell%C3%ADn%20Grupos%20de%20Edad%202005-2015%20por%20comuna%20y%20correg.pdf.

De Certeau, Michel. *The Practice of Everyday Life*. Translated by Steven Rendall. Berkeley: University of California Press, 1984.

De la Peña, Carolyn. "Slow and Low Progress. Or Why American Studies Should Do Technology." *American Quarterly* 58, no. 3 (2006): 915–941.

Deleuze, Gilles, and Michel Foucault. "Les Intellectuels et le Pouvoir." *L'Arc* 49 (1972): 3–10.

Delwiche, Aaron. "The New Left and the Computer Underground: Recovering Political Antecedents of Participatory Culture." In *The Participatory Cultures Handbook*, edited by Aaron Delwiche and Jennifer Jacobs Henderson, 10–21. New York: Routledge, 2013.

Doyle, Caroline. "Explaining Patterns of Urban Violence in Medellin, Colombia." *Laws* 5, no. 1 (2016): n.p.

Enghel, Florencia, and Martín Becerra. "Here and There: (Re)Situating Latin America in International Communication Theory." *Communication Theory* 28, no. 2 (2018): 111–130.

Escobar, Arutro. *Encountering Development: The Making and Unmaking of the Third World*. Princeton, NJ: Princeton University Press, 1995.

Escobar, Arturo. *Territories of Difference: Place, Movements, Life, Redes*. Durham, NC: Duke University Press, 2008.

Escobar Arango, David. "Medellín Digital, una Ciudad para la Inclusión y el Salto a la Sociedad del Conocimiento." *Revista Colombiana de Telecomunicaciones* 15, no. 47 (2008): 32–36.

Eubanks, Virginia. *Automating Inequality: How High-Tech Tools Profile, Police, and Punish the Poor*. New York: St Martin's Press, 2018.

Everett, Anna, ed. *Learning Race and Ethnicity: Youth and Digital Media*. Cambridge, MA: MIT Press/MacArthur Foundation, 2008.

Fajardo, Sergio. "Medellín, la Más Educada." CEE *Participación Educativa* 6 (2007): 65–70.

Fals-Borda, Orlando. "The Application of Participatory Action-Research in Latin America." *International Sociology* 2, no. 4 (1987): 329–347.

Fals Borda, Orlando. "Grietas de la Democracia. La Participación Popular en Colombia." *Análisis Político* 28 (1996): 65–77.

Fals-Borda, Orlando, and Muhammad Rahman. *Action and Knowledge: Breaking the Monopoly with Participatory Action Research*. New York: Apex Press, 1991.

Fanon, Frantz. *Black Skin, White Masks*. New York: Grove Press, 1986.

Farrington, John, Anthony Bebbington, with Kate Wellard, and David J. Lewis. *Reluctant Partners: Non-Governmental Organizations, the State, and Sustainable Agricultural Development*. London: Routledge, 1993.

Fenton, Natalie, and Veronica Barassi. "Alternative Media and Social Networking Sites: The Politics of Individuation and Political Participation." *The Communication Review* 14, no. 3 (2011): 179–196.

Fierst, Sonya. "El Presupuesto Participativo en el Contexto de los Jóvenes de la Comuna 13 de Medellín." *Analecta Política* 3, no. 4 (2013): 113–137.

Fierst, Sonya. "Jóvenes y su Participación en la Política de Medellín: Retos del Presupuesto Participativo en la Comuna 13." Thesis, Universidad Pontificia Bolivariana, Escuela de Derecho y Ciencias Políticas, Facultad de Ciencias Políticas, Medellín, Colombia, 2013.

Fine, Janice. "Choose Tactics that Support Your Strategy." In *Beautiful Trouble: A Toolbox for Revolution*, edited by Andrew Boyd and David Oswald Mitchell, 112–113. New York: OR Books, 2012.

Firmino, Rodrigo Jose, Fernanda Bruno, and Nelson Arteaga Botello, eds. "Surveillance in Latin America." Special issue, *Surveillance and Society* 10, no. 1 (2012).

Fish, Adam, Luis F. R. Murillo, Lilly Nguyen, Aaron Panofsky, and Christopher M. Kelty. "Birds of the Internet: Towards a Field Guide to the Organization and Governance of Participation." *Journal of Cultural Economy* 4, no. 2 (2001): 157–187.

Foronda Cano, Jairo de Jesús. "Hacia una Estrategia de Desarrollo Participativo Para la Ciudad." *Mercatec* 433 (2007): 3.

Foucault, Michel. "Governmentality." *Ideology and Conscious* 6 (1979): 5–21.

Franco, Vilma Liliana. *Poder Regional y Proyecto Hegemónico: El Caso de la Ciudad Metropolitana de Medellín y su Entorno Regional, 1970–2000*. Medellín, Colombia: Instituto Popular de Capacitación.

Frank, Thomas. *The Conquest of Cool: Business Culture, Counterculture, and the Rise of Hip Consumerism*. Chicago: University of Chicago Press, 1997.

Franz, Tobias. "Urban Governance and Economic Development in Medellín: An 'Urban Miracle'?" *Latin American Perspectives* 44, no. 2 (2017): 52–70.

Freire, Paulo. "Education and Community Involvement." In *Critical Education in the New Information Age*, edited by M. Castells, R. Flecha, P. Freire, H. Giroux, D. Macedo, and P. Willis, 83–92. Lanham, MD: Rowman and Littlefield, 1999.

Freire, Paulo. *Pedagogy of the Oppressed*. Translated by Myra Bergman Ramos. 30th anniversary edition. New York: Continuum, 2003.

Friedland, Lewis A. "Communication, Community, and Democracy: Toward a Theory of the Communicatively Integrated Community." *Communication Research* 28 (2001): 358–391.

Fuchs, Christian. *Foundations of Critical Media and Information Studies*. New York: Routledge, 2011.

Fuchs, Dieter. "Participatory Democracy." In *The Participatory Cultures Handbook*, edited by Aaron Delwiche and Jennifer Jacobs Henderson, 163–170. New York: Routledge, 2013.

Galindo Cuesta, Jairo Alberto, "Ciudadanía Digital." *Signo y Pensamiento* XXVIII (2009): 164–173.

Garcés Montoya, Ángela. "De Organizaciones a Colectivos Juveniles: Panorama de La Participación Política Juvenil." *Ultima Década* 18, no. 32 (2010): 61–83.

Garcés Montoya, Ángela. *Nos-otros los Jóvenes: Polisemias de las Culturas y los Territorios Musicales en Medellín*. Medellín, Colombia: Universidad de Medellín, 2005.

Garcia Ávila, Susana. "Alfabetización Digital," *Razon y Palabra* 21 (2017): 66–81.

García Canclini, Néstor. "El Malestar en los Estudios Culturales." *Revista Fractal* 6 (1997): 45–60.

García Canclini, Néstor. *Hybrid Cultures: Strategies for Entering and Leaving Modernity*. Translated by Christopher L. Chiappari and Silvia L. López. Minneapolis: University of Minnesota Press, 2005.

García Guzmán, Nathalia, and Johrman Giraldo Obando. "HipHop y Educación: Aproximación a Los Procesos Culturales de Cuatro Coelctivos de HipHop de Medellin." Thesis, Facultad de Ciencias Sociales y Humanas, Universidad de Antioquia, Medellin, Colombia, 2011.

García Sánchez, Andrés, and Vladimir Montoya Arango. *Jóvenes Afrocolombianos en la Ciudad de Medellín: Identidades, Representaciones y Territorioalidades*. Medellín, Colombia: Universidad de Antioquia and Alcaldía de Medellín, 2009.

Gilbert, James. *A Cycle of Outrage: America's Reaction to the Juvenile Delinquent in the 1950s*. New York: Oxford University Press, 1986.

Gilman, Hollie Russon. *Democracy Reinvented: Participatory Budgeting and Civic Innovation in America*. Washington, DC: Brookings Institution Press, 2016.

Ginwright, Shawn, and Julio Cammarota. "Introduction." In *Beyond Resistance! Youth Activism and Community Change*, edited by Shawn Ginwright, Pedro Noguera, and Julio Cammarota, xiii–xxii. New York: Taylor and Francis Group, 2006.

Giroux, Henry. A. *Border Crossings: Cultural Workers and the Politics of Education*. New York: Routledge, 2005.

Gladwell, Malcolm. "Small Change." *The New Yorker* 4 (2010): 42–49.

Goldfrank, Benjamin. "Lessons from Latin American Experience in Participatory Budgeting." In *Participatory Budgeting*, edited by Anwar Shah, 91–126. Washington, DC: World Bank Institute, 2007.

Goldfrank, Benjamin. "The World Bank and the Globalization of Participatory Budgeting." *Journal of Public Deliberation* 8, no. 2 (2012): Article 7.

Gómez Hernández, Esperanza. "El Presupuesto Participativo Entre Democracia, Pobreza y Desarrollo." *Investigación y Desarrollo* 15, no. 1 (2007): 56–77.

Grupo de Memoria Histórica. *La Huella Invisible de la Guerra: Desplazamiento Forzado en la Comuna 13*. Bogotá, Colombia: Ediciones Semana, 2011.

Grupo de Trabajo de Medellín Digital. "Medellín Digital: Documento de Inversión para el Año 2008." Medellín, Colombia: Alcaldía de Medellín, 2008.

Guijt, Irene, Mae Arevalo, and Kiko Saladores. "Tracking Change Together." *PLA Notes* 31, no. 1 (1998): 28–36.

Guillén-Rascón, Gladys, Gerardo Ascencio-Baca, Javier Tarango. "Alfabetización Digital: Una Perspectiva Sociológica." *E-Ciencias de la Información* 6, no. 2 (2016): 1–20.

Gumucio Dagron, Alfonso. *Making Waves: Stories of Participatory Communication for Social Change*. New York: Rockefeller Foundation, 2001.

Gumucio Dagron, Alfonso. "Playing with Fire: Power, Participation, and Communication for Development." *Development in Practice* 19, no. 4–5 (2009): 453–465.

Gumucio Dagron, Alfonso, and Thomas Tufte, eds. *Communication for Social Change Anthology: Historical and Contemporary Readings*. South Orange, NJ: CFSC Consortium, 2016.

Hajdarowicz, Inga. "Does Participation Empower? The Example of Women Involved in Participatory Budgeting in Medellin." *Journal of Urban Affairs* (2018): 1–16.

Haraway, Donna. "Situated Knowledges: The Science Question in Feminism and the Privilege of Partial Perspective." In *Turning Points in Qualitative Research: Tying Knots in a Handkerchief*, edited by Yvonna S. Lincoln and Norman K. Denzin, 21–46. Walnut Creek, CA: AltaMira Press, 2003.

Hargittai, Eszter. "Digital Na(t)ives? Variation in Internet Skills and Uses Among Members of the 'Net Generation.'" *Sociological Inquiry* 80, no. 1 (2010): 92–113.

Hargittai, Eszter, and Gina Walejko. "The Participation Divide: Content Creation and Sharing in the Digital Age." *Information, Community and Society* 11, no. 2 (2008): 239–256.

Harvey, David. *A Brief History of Neoliberalism*. New York: Oxford University Press, 2005.

Heeks, Richard. "The Tyranny of Participation in Information Systems Learning from Development Projects." Development Informatics Working Paper Series. Manchester: Institute for Development Policy and Management, University of Manchester, 1999.

Herrera, Martha Cecilia, Raúl Acevedo, Alexis V. Pinilla Díaz, and Carlos J. Diaz Soler. *La Construcción de Cultura Política en Colombia*. Bogotá, Colombia: Universidad Pedagógica Nacional, 2005.

Hersh, Marion. "Science, Technology and Values: Promoting Ethics and Social Responsibility." *AI and Society* 29, no. 2 (2014): 167–183.

Hickey, Samuel, and Giles Mohan. *Participation: From Tyranny to Transformation? Exploring New Approaches to Participation in Development*. New York: Zed Books, 2001.

Horst, Heather. "Free, Social, and Inclusive: Appropriation and Resistance of New Media Technologies in Brazil." *International Journal of Communication* 5, no. 6 (2011): 437–462.

Huesca, Robert. "A Procedural View of Participatory Communication: Lessons from Bolivian Tin Miners' Radio." *Media, Culture and Society* 17, no. 1 (1995): 101–119.

Huesca, Robert. "Tracing the History of Participatory Communication Approaches to Development: A Critical Appraisal." In *Approaches to Development Communication*, edited by J. Servaes, chap. 8. Paris: UNESCO, 2002.

Human Rights Watch. *Smoke and Mirrors: Colombia's Demobilization of Paramilitary Groups*. New York: Human Rights Watch, 2005.

Internet World Stats. "Colombia: Internet Usage Indicators and Country Profile," 2011. Accessed October 2013. http://www.internetworldstats.com/sa/co.htm.

Isin, Engin, and Evelyn Ruppert. *Being Digital Citizens*. London: Rowman and Littlefield, 2015.

Ito, Mizuko, Sonja Baumer, Matteo Bittani, danah boyd, Rachel Cody, Becky Herr-Stephenson, Heather A. Horst, Patricia G. Lange, Dilan Mahendran, Katynka Z. Martinez, C. J. Pascoe, Dan Perkel, Laura Robinson, Christo Sims, and Lisa Tripp. *Hanging Out, Messing Around and Geeking Out: Living and Learning with New Media*. Cambridge, MA: MIT Press, 2010.

Ito, Mizuko, Kris Gutierrez, Sonia Livingstone, Bill Penuel, Jean Rhodes, Katie Salen, Juliet Schor, Julian Sefton-Green, S. Craig Watkins. *Connected Learning: An Agenda for Research and Design*. Irvine, CA: Digital Media and Learning Research Hub, 2013.

Ito, Mizuko, Elizabeth Soep, Neta Kligler-Vilenchik, Sangita Shresthova, Liana Gamber-Thompson, and Arely Zimmerman. "Learning Connected Civics: Narratives, Practices, Infrastructures." *Curriculum Inquiry* 45, no. 1 (2015): 10–29.

Jandrić, Petar, and Ana Kuzmanić. "Digital Postcolonialism." *LADIS International Journal on www/Internet* 13, no. 12 (2016): 34–51.

Jenkins, Henry. *Convergence Culture: Where Old and New Media Collide*. New York: New York University Press, 2006.

Jenkins, Henry. "Why Mitt Romney Won't Debate a Snowman." In *Satire TV: Politics and Comedy in the Post-Network Era*, edited by Jonathan Gray, Jeffrey P. Jones, and Ethan Thompson, 187–212. New York: New York University Press, 2009.

Jenkins, Henry, and Nico Carpentier. "Theorizing Participatory Intensities: A Conversation about Participation and Politics." *Convergence: The International Journal of Research into New Media Technologies* 19, no. 3 (2013): 265–286.

Jenkins, Henry, Ravi Purushotma, Margaret Weigel, Katie Clinton, and Alice J. Robison. *Confronting the Challenges of Participatory Culture: Media Education for the 21st Century*. Chicago: MacArthur Foundation, 2001.

Jenkins, Henry, and Sangita Shresthova, eds. "Transformative Works and Fan Fiction." Special issue, *Transformative Works and Cultures* 10 (2012).

Jenkins, Henry, Sangita Shresthova, Liana Gamber-Thompson, Neta Kligler-Vilenchik, and Arely Zimmerman. *By Any Media Necessary: The New Youth Activism*. New York: New York University Press, 2016.

Juhasz, Alexandra. "Learning the Five Lessons of YouTube: After Trying to Teach There, I Don't Believe the Hype." *Cinema Journal* 48, no. 2 (2009): 145–150.

Kahne, Joseph, and Benjamin Bowyer. "The Political Significance of Social Media Activity and Social Networks." *Political Communication* 35, no. 3 (2018): 470–493.

Kahne, Joseph, Nam-Jin Lee, and Jessica T. Feezell. "The Civic and Political Significance of Online Participatory Cultures Among Youth Transitioning to Adulthood." *Journal of Information Technology and Politics* 10, no. 1 (2013): 1–20.

Kahne, Joseph, Ellen Middaugh, and Danielle Allen. "Youth, New Media, and the Rise of Participatory Politics." In *From Voice to Influence: Understanding Citizenship in a Digital Age*, edited by Danielle Allen and Jennifer S. Light, 35–56. Chicago: University of Chicago Press, 2015.

Kassimir, Ronald, and Constance Flanagan. "Youth Civic Engagement in the Developing World: Challenges and Opportunities." In *Handbook of Research on Civic Engagement in Youth*, edited by Lonnie R. Sherrod, Judith Torney-Purta, and Constance A. Flanagan, 91–113. Hoboken, NJ: Wiley, 2010.

Kelty, Christopher M. "From Participation to Power." In *The Participatory Cultures Handbook*, edited by Aaron Delwiche and Jennifer Jacobs Henderson, 22–31. New York: Routledge, 2013.

Kelty, Christopher M. *Two Bits: The Cultural Significance of Free Software*. Durham, NC: Duke University Press, 2008.

Kelty, Christopher, Aaron Panofsky, Morgan Currie, Roderic Crooks, Seth Erickson, Patricia Garcia, Michael Wartenbe, and Stacy Wood. "Seven Dimensions of Contemporary Participation Disentangled." *Journal of the Association for Information Science and Technology* 66, no. 3 (2015): 474–488.

Kim, Yong-Chan, and Sandra J. Ball-Rokeach. "Community Storytelling Network, Neighborhood Context, and Civic Engagement: A Multilevel Approach." *Human Communication Research* 32, no. 4 (2006): 411–439.

Kleine, Dorothea. *Technologies of Choice? ICTs, Development, and the Capabilities Approach*. Cambridge, MA: MIT Press, 2013.

Kwon, Soo Ah. *Uncivil Youth: Race, Activism, and Affirmative Governmentality*. Durham, NC: Duke University Press, 2013.

Lankshear, Colin, and Michele Knobel. *New Literacies: Everyday Practices and Classroom Learning*. Maidenhead, UK: Open University Press, 2016.

Leal, Pablo Alejandro. "Participation: The Ascendancy of a Buzzword in the Neoliberal Era." *Development in Practice* 17, no. 4–5 (2007): 539–548.

Lemke, Thomas. "Foucault, Governmentality and Critique." *Rethinking Marxism* 14, no. 3 (2002): 49–64.

Leonard, Peter, and Peter McLaren, eds. *Paulo Freire: A Critical Encounter*. New York: Routledge, 2002.

León Gutiérrez, Alberto, Luis Alberto Hincapié, and Gloria María Villa. "Potencial Social y Político de la Planeación Local y el Presupuesto Participativo en Medellín (Colombia) Para Fortalecer la Democracia Latinoamericana." *EURE (Santiago)* 42, no. 125 (2016): 205–224.

Lessig, Lawrence. *Code and Other Laws of Cyberspace.* New York: Basic Books, 1999.

Levine, Peter. "A Public Voice for Youth: The Audience Problem in Digital Media and Civic Education." In *Civic Life Online: Learning How Digital Media Can Engage Youth*, edited by W. Lance Bennett, 119–138. Cambridge, MA: MIT Press/MacArthur Foundation, 2008.

Lévy, Pierre. *Collective Intelligence: Mankind's Emerging World in Cyberspace.* Translated by Robert Bonomo. New York: Perseus Publishing, 1999.

Leyva Botero, Santiago. "El Proceso de Construcción de Estatalidad Local (1998–2009): ¿La Clave Para Entender el Cambio de Medellín?" In *Medellín: Medio Ambiente, Urbanismo, Sociedad*, edited by Michel Hermelin Arbaux, Alejandro Echeverri Restrepo, and Jorge Giraldo Ramírez, 271–293. Medellín, Colombia: URBAM, Centro de Estudios Urbanos y Ambientales, Universidad EAFIT, 2010.

Light, Jennifer S. "Putting Our Conversation in Context: Youth, Old Media, and Political Participation, 1800–1971." In *From Voice to Influence: Understanding Citizenship in a Digital Age*, edited by Danielle Allen and Jennifer S. Light, 19–34. Chicago: University of Chicago Press, 2015.

Literat, Ioana, and Melissa Brough. "From Ethical to Equitable Social Media Technologies: Amplifying Underrepresented Youth Voices in Digital Technology Design." *Journal of Media Ethics* 34, no. 3 (2019): 132–145.

Literat, Ioana, Neta Kligler-Vilenchik, Melissa Brough, and Alicia Blum-Ross. "Analyzing Youth Digital Participation: Aims, Actors, Contexts and Intensities." *The Information Society* 34, no. 4 (2018): 261–273.

Livingstone, Sonia. *Children and the Internet: Great Expectations and Challenging Realities.* Cambridge: Polity, 2009.

Loader, Brian D., ed. *Young Citizens in the Digital Age: Political Engagement, Young People and New Media.* New York: Routledge, 2007.

Londoño, Juan Fernando. "Aproximación a la Democracia Participativa." In *Sociedad Civil, Control Civil y Democracia Participativa*, edited by Juan Fernando Londoño, Luis Alberto Restrepo, Mauricio García Villegas, Margarita Bonamusa, and María Teresa Uribe, 13–25. Bogotá, Colombia: Fundación Friedrich Ebert de Colombia, Fescol, 1997.

Longford, Graham. "Pedagogies of Digital Citizenship and the Politics of Code." *Techné* 9, no. 1 (2005): 68–96.

López, Antonio. "Circling the Cross: Bridging Native America, Education, and Digital Media." In *Learning Race and Ethnicity: Youth and Digital Media*, edited by Anna Everett, 109–126. Cambridge, MA: MIT Press/MacArthur Foundation, 2008.

Lowenthal, Abraham F., and Pablo Rojas Mejía. "Medellín: Front Line of Colombia's Challenges." *Americas Quarterly* (2010). Accessed November 20, 2013. http://www.americasquarterly.org/node/1310.

Maclean, Kate. *Social Urbanism and the Politics of Violence: The Medellín Miracle.* Basingstoke, UK: Palgrave MacMillan, 2015.

Martin, Gerard. *Medellín, Tragedia y Resurrección: Mafia, Ciudad y Estado, 1975–2012.* Bogotá, Colombia: Planeta, 2012.

Martin, Gerard, and Miguel Ceballos. *Bogotá, Anatomía de una Transformación: Políticas de Seguridad Ciudadana, 1995–2003.* Bogotá, Colombia: Pontificia Universidad Javeriana, 2004.

Martín Barbero, Jesús. *De los Medios a las Mediaciones.* Mexico: Gustavo Gili, 1987.

Martín Barbero, Jesús. "Esa Móvil y Excéntrica Identidad." In *Al Sur de la Modernidad: Comunicación, Globalización, y Multiculturalidad.* Pittsburgh, PA: Instituto Internacional de Literatura Iberoamericana, University of Pittsburgh, 2001.

Martín Barbero, Jesús. "Jóvenes: Des-Orden Cultural y Palimpsestos de Identidad." In *Viviendo a Toda: Jóvenes, Territorios Culturales y Nuevas Sensibilidades,* edited by H. Cubides, M. C. Laverde, and C. E. Valderrama, 22–37. Santa Fe de Bogotá: Fundación Universidad Central-Siglo del Hombre Editores, 1998.

Massanari, Adrienne. "#Gamergate and the Fappening: How Reddit's Algorithm, Governance, and Culture Support Toxic Technocultures." *New Media and Society* 19, no. 3 (2017): 329–346.

McCosker, Anthony, Sonja Vivienne, and Amelia Johns, eds. *Negotiating Digital Citizenship: Control, Contest and Culture.* Lanham, MD: Rowman and Littlefield, 2016.

Medellín Cómo Vamos. "Encuesta de Percepción Ciudadana, Medellín." Medellín, Colombia: Pregón Ltda, 2011.

Medellín Cómo Vamos. "Informe de Calidad de Vida de Medellín, 2017." Accessed July 2019. https://www.medellincomovamos.org/download/documento-informe-de-calidad-de-vida-de-medellin-2017/.

Medina, Eden, Ivan da Costa Marques, Christina Holmes, and Marcos Cueto, eds. *Beyond Imported Magic: Essays on Science, Technology, and Society in Latin America.* Cambridge, MA: MIT Press, 2014.

Medina Holguín, Jose David, and Natalia García Guzmán. "Crew Peligrosos: Un Viaje Para Reconocer Una Práctica Educativa Juvenil." *Revista Universidad de Medellín* 43, no. 86 (2008): 31–42.

Medina Holguín, José David, Lina Maria Castrillón Guzmán, Ángela Garcés Montoya, and J. D. Rincón Ochoa. *Somos Hip Hop: Una Experiencia de Resistencia Cultural en Medellín.* Medellín, Colombia: Alcaldía de Medellín, 2008.

Mefalopulos, Paolo. "Theory and Practice of Participatory Communication: The Case of the FAO Project *Communication for Development in Southern Africa.*" PhD diss., University of Texas at Austin, 2003. Accessed June 2013. http://hdl.handle.net/2152/776.

Melucci, Alberto. *Challenging Codes: Collective Action in the Information Age.* New York: Cambridge University Press, 1996.

Mercea, Dan, Laura Iannelli, and Brian D. Loader. "Protest Communication Ecologies." *Information, Communication and Society* 19, no. 2 (2015): 279–289.

Middaugh, Ellen. "Service and Activism in the Digital Age: Supporting Youth Engagement in Public Life." *DML Central Working Paper Series* (2012). Accessed June 2013. http://dmlhub.net/sites/default/files/Service_Activism_Digital_Age.pdf.

Middaugh, Ellen, and Ben Kirshner, eds. *#youthaction: Becoming Political in the Digital Age*. Charlotte, NC: Information Age Publishing, 2015.

Moncada, Eduardo. "Urban Violence, Political Economy, and Territorial Control: Insights from Medellín." *Latin American Research Review* 51, no. 4 (2016): 225–248.

Morozov, Evgeny. *The Net Delusion: The Dark Side of Internet Freedom*. New York: Public Affairs, 2011.

Mossberger, Karen, Caroline J. Tolbert, and Ramona S. McNeal. *Digital Citizenship*. Cambridge, MA: MIT Press, 2008.

Mouffe, Chantal. "Feminism, Citizenship and Radical Democratic Politics." In *Feminists Theorize the Political*, edited by Judith Butler and Joan W. Scott, 369–385. New York: Routledge, 1992.

Murray, Susan, and Laurie Ouellette, eds. *Reality TV: Remaking Television Culture*. New York: New York University Press, 2009.

Naranjo Giraldo, Gloria. *Entre Luces y Sombras. Medellín: Espacio y Políticas Urbanas*. Medellín, Colombia: Corporación Región, 1997.

Naranjo Giraldo, Gloria. *Medellín en Zonas. Monografías*. Medellín, Colombia: Corporación Región, 1992.

Negroponte, Nicholas. *Being Digital*. New York: Knopf, 1995.

Noble, Safiya Umoja. *Algorithms of Oppression: How Search Engines Reinforce Racism*. New York: New York University Press, 2018.

Novy, Andreas, and Bernard Leubolt. "Participatory Budgeting in Porto Alegre: Social Innovation and the Dialectical Relationship of State and Civil Society." *Urban Studies* 42, no. 11 (2005): 2023–2036.

Observatorio Legislativo del Instituto de Ciencia Política. "Ley Estatutaria de Participación Ciudadana." Boletín 203 (2012, June). Bogotá, Colombia: Instituto de Ciencia Política.

Olsson, Tobias. "From the Ecology of Broadcasting to the Ecology of Participation: Critical Reflections." *Nordicom Review* 31 (2010): 95–104.

Ouellette, Laurie, and James Hay. *Better Living Through Reality TV*. Oxford: Blackwell, 2008.

Papacharissi, Zizi. *A Private Sphere: Democracy in a Digital Age*. Malden, MA: Polity Press, 2010.

Pateman, Carole. *Participation and Democratic Theory*. Cambridge: Cambridge University Press, 1970.

Pateman, Carole. "Participatory Democracy Revisited." *Perspectives on Politics* 10, no. 1 (2012): 7–19.

Patiño Lemos, María Ruth, and Mercedes Vallejo Gómez. "Caracterización de Prácticas con TIC Por Actores Diferenciados en Cuatro Comunas de la Ciudad de Medellín: Un Abordaje Para El Reconocimiento De La Apropiación Tecnológica." *Revista Q* 5, no. 10 (2011): 1–31.

Pécaut, Daniel. *Crónica de Cuatro Décadas de Política Colombiana*. Bogotá, Colombia: Grupo Editorial Norma, 2006.

Pécaut, Daniel. "From the Banality of Violence to Real Terror: The Case of Colombia." In *Societies of Fear: The Legacy of Civil War, Violence and Terror in Latin*

America, edited by Kees Koonings and Dirk Krujit, 141–167. New York: Zed Books, 1999.

Peixoto, Tiago. "Beyond Theory: E-participatory Budgeting and its Promises for Participation." *European Journal of ePractice* 7 (2009): 55–63.

Pettingill, Lindsay. "Engagement 2.0? How The New Digital Media Can Invigorate Civic Engagement." In *GoodWork Project Paper Series*, edited by Howard Gardner, 1–22. Accessed January 2010. http://www.thegoodproject.org/pdf/50-Engagement-2.0.pdf.

Pimienta Betancur, Alejandro. "Escenarios de Educación Informal Como Proceso de Formación Ciudadana: El Caso del Presupuesto Participativo en Medellín." *Unipluriversidad* 8, no. 3 (2008).

Pimienta Betancur, Alejandro. "La 'Ciudad Educadora' y el Presupuesto Participativo en Medellín: Qué Ciudad(anía) Enseña?" *Boletim Paulista de Geografia* 89 (2017): 33–49.

Postman, Neil. "The Humanism of Media Ecology." In *Proceedings of the Media Ecology Association*, Vol. 1, 2000. Accessed March 2020. https://www.media-ecology.org/resources/Documents/Proceedings/v1/v1-02-Postman.pdf.

Proyecto Gestores Culturales Comuna 13. "Caracterización de los y las Jóvenes Gestores Culturales de la Escuela de Hip Hop Kolacho: Pasos Que No Son en Vano." Medellín, Colombia: Secretaría de Cultura Ciudadana, Alcaldía de Medellín, 2010.

Putnam, Robert. *Bowling Alone: The Collapse and Revival of American Civic Life*. New York: Simon and Schuster, 2000.

Quarry, Wendy, and Ricardo Ramirez. *Communication for Another Development: Listening Before Telling*. London: Zed Books, 2009.

Quodling, Andrew. "Platforms are Eating Society: Conflict and Governance in Digital Spaces." In McCosker et al., *Negotiating Digital Citizenship*, 131–146.

Ramírez Gallegos, Franklin. "El Espacio Público como Potencia. Controversias Sociológicas desde la Experiencia Participativa de Medellín." *Iconos* 13, no.3 (2008): 61–73.

Reguillo, Rossana. "Ciudadanías Juveniles en América Latina." *Ultima Década* 11, no. 19 (2003): 11–30.

Reguillo, Rossana. *Culturas Juveniles: Formas Políticas del Desencanto*. Buenos Aires, Argentina: Siglo Veintiuno Editores, 2013.

Restrepo, Adrián. "Los Jóvenes y Sus Luchas por El Reconocimiento." *Nómadas* 32 (2010): 179–192.

Restrepo Mesa, Clara Inés. "El Presupuesto Participativo y la Transformación de Medellín." *Mercatec* 43 (2007): 4–15.

Rheingold, Howard. *Smart Mobs: The Next Social Revolution*. Cambridge, MA: Basic Books, 2002.

Rheingold, Howard. "Using Participatory Media and Public Voice to Encourage Civic Engagement." In *Civic life Online: Learning How Digital Media Can Engage Youth*, edited by W. Lance Bennet, 97–118. The John D. and Catherine T. MacArthur Foundation Series on Digital Media and Learning. Cambridge, MA: MIT Press, 2008.

Riaño, Pilar. *Women in Grassroots Communication: Furthering Social Change.* Thousand Oaks, CA: Sage, 1994.

Riaño-Alcalá, Pilar. *Dwellers of Memory: Youth and Violence in Medellín, Colombia.* New Brunswick, NJ: Transaction, 2006.

Ribble, Mike S., Gerald D. Bailey, and Tweed W. Ross. "Digital Citizenship." *Learning and Leading with Technology* 13, no. 2 (2004): 34–51.

Robins, Melinda B. "Are African Women Online Just ICT Consumers?" *Gazette* 64, no. 3 (2002): 235–249.

Rodríguez, Clemencia. *Citizens' Media against Armed Conflict: Disrupting Violence in Colombia.* Minneapolis: University of Minnesota Press, 2001.

Rodríguez, Clemencia. *Fissures in the Mediascape: An International Study of Citizens' Media.* Cresskill, NJ: Hampton Press, 2001.

Rojas, Christina. *Civilización y Violencia. La Búsqueda de la Identidad en la Colombia del Siglo XIX.* Bogotá, Colombia: Norma, 2001.

Roldán, Mary. "Wounded Medellín: Narcotics Traffic against a Backdrop of Industrial Decline." In *Wounded Cities: Destruction and Reconstruction in a Globalized World,* edited by J. Schneider and I. Susser, 129–148. New York: Berg, 2003.

Rosaldo, Renato. *Culture and Truth: The Remaking of Social Analysis.* Boston: Beacon Press, 1993.

Rose, Nicholas. "Government and Control." *British Journal of Criminology* 40, no. 2 (2000): 321–339.

Rose, Nicholas, Pat O'Malley, and Mariana Valverde. "Governmentality." *Annual Review of Law and Social Science* 2 (2006): 83–104.

Rose, Tricia. *Black Noise: Rap Music and Black Culture in Contemporary America.* Middletown, CT: Wesleyan University Press, 1994.

Ross, Andrew. "In Search of the Lost Paycheck." In *Digital Labor: The Internet as Playground and Factory,* edited by Trebor Scholz, 13–32. New York: Routledge, 2013.

Sáez, Mari, and Víctor Manuel. "El Enfoque de la Comunicación Participativa para el Desarrollo y su Puesta en Práctiva en los Medios Comunitarios." *Razón y Palabra* 15, no. 71 (2010).

Salazar, Alonso. *No Nacimos pa' Semilla.* Medellín, Colombia: Cinep, 1990.

Salazar, Alonso, and Ana Maria Jaramillo. *Medellín: Las Subculturas del Narcotráfico.* Santafé de Bogotá, Colombia: Cinep, 1992.

Scott, James C. *Weapons of the Weak: Everyday Forms of Peasant Resistance.* New Haven, CT: Yale University Press, 1985.

Seiter, Ellen. "Practicing at Home: Computers, Pianos, and Cultural Capital." In *Digital Youth, Innovation and the Unexpected,* edited by Tara McPherson, 27–52. Cambridge, MA: MIT Press, 2008.

Servaes, Jan. *Communication for Development: One World, Multiple Cultures.* Cresskill, NJ: Hampton Press, 1999.

Servaes, Jan. "Participatory Communication (Research) from a Freirian Perspective." *Africa Media Review* 10 (1996): 73–91.

Servaes, Jan, and Rolien Hoyng. "The Tools of Social Change: A Critique of Techno-Centric Development and Activism." *New Media and Society* 19, no. 2 (2017): 255–271.

Servaes, Jan, and Patchanee Malikhao. "Participatory Communication: The New Paradigm?" In *Media and Glocal Change: Rethinking Communication for Development*, edited by Oscar Hemer and Thomas Tufte, 91–103. Buenos Aires, Argentina: NORDICOM/CLACSO.

Sey, Araba, Chris Coward, François Bar, George Sciadas, Chris Rothschild, and Lucas Koepke. *Connecting People for Development: Why Public Access ICTs Matter*. Seattle: University of Washington, 2013.

Shah, Anwar, ed. *Participatory Budgeting*. Washington, DC: The World Bank, 2007.

Shah, Dhavan V., Kjerstin Thorson, Chris Wells, Nam-jin Lee, and Jack McLeod. "Civic Norms and Communication Competence: Pathways to Socialization and Citizenship." In *The Oxford Handbook of Political Communication*, edited by Kate Kenski and Kathleen Hall Jamieson, 467–482. Oxford: Oxford University Press, 2017.

Sherrod, Lonnie R., Constance Flanagan, and James Youniss. "Dimensions of Citizenship and Opportunities for Youth Development: The What, Why, When, Where, and Who of Citizenship Development." *Applied Developmental Science* 6, no. 4 (2001): 264–272.

Shifman, Limor. "Meme" In *Digital Keywords: A Vocabulary of Information Society and Culture*, Vol. 8, edited by Benjamin Peters. Princeton, NJ: Princeton University Press, 2016.

Shirky, Clay. *Here Comes Everybody: The Power of Organizing Without Organizations*. New York: Penguin Books, 2008.

Sierra Caballero, Francisco, and Tommaso Gravante. "Ciudadanía Digital y Acción Colectiva en América Latina: Crítica de la Mediación y Apropiación Social por los Nuevos Movimientos Sociales." *La Trama de la Comunicación* 20, no. 1 (2016): 163–175.

Singhal, Arvind, and Kanta Devi. "Visual Voices in Participatory Communication." *Communicator* 37 (2003): 1–15.

Spivak, Gayatri C. "Can the Subaltern Speak?" In *Colonial Discourse and Postcolonial Theory: A Reader*, edited by Patrick Williams and Laura Chrisman, 66–111. New York: Columbia University Press, 1994.

Srinivasan, Ramesh, and Adam Fish. *After the Internet*. Medford, MA: Polity Press, 2017.

Staples, William G. *Everyday Surveillance: Vigilance and Visibility in Postmodern Life*. Lanham, MD: Rowman and Littlefield, 2013.

Stiefel, Matthias, and Marshall Wolfe. *A Voice for the Excluded: Popular Participation in Development: Utopia or Necessity?* London: Zed Books, 1994.

Takhteyev, Yuri. *Coding Places: Software Practice in a South American City*. Cambridge, MA: MIT Press, 2012.

Tarrow, Sidney. *The New Transnational Activism*. Cambridge: Cambridge University Press, 2005.

Terranova, Tiziana. "Free Labor." In *Digital Labor: The Internet as Playground and Factory*, edited by Trebor Scholz, 41–65. New York: Routledge, 2013.

Third, Amanda, Delphine Bellerose, Urszula Dawkins, Emma Keltie, and Kari Pihl. "Children's Rights in the Digital Age: A Download from Children Around the World." Melbourne: Young and Well Cooperative Research Centre and UNICEF, 2014. Accessed July 14, 2018. https://www.unicef.org /publications/files/Childrens_Rights_in_the_Digital_Age_A_Download_from _Children_Around_the_World_FINAL.pdf.

Third, Amanda, and Philippa Collin. "Rethinking (Children's and Young People's) Citizenship through Dialogues on Digital Practice." In McCosker et al., *Negotiating Digital Citizenship*, 41–60.

Thomas, Pradnip Ninan. *Digital India: Understanding Information, Communication and Social Change.* Thousand Oaks, CA: Sage, 2012.

Torney-Purta, Judith, and Jo-Ann Amadeo. *Fortalecimiento de la Democracia en las Américas a Través de la Educación Cívica: Un Análisis Empírico que Destaca las Opiniones de los Estudiantes y los Maestros.* Washington, DC: Organization of American States, Social Development and Education Unit, 2004.

Torney-Purta, Judith, Carolyn Henry Barber, and Wendy Klandl Richardson. "Trust in Government-related Institutions and Political Engagement among Adolescents in Six Countries." *Acta Politica* 39, no. 4 (2004): 380–406.

Treré, Emiliano. "Social Movements as Information Ecologies: Exploring the Coevolution of Multiple Internet Technologies for Activism." *International Journal of Communication* 6 (2012): 2359–2377.

Tubb, Daniel. "Narratives of Citizenship in Medellín, Colombia." *Citizenship Studies* 17, no. 5 (2013): 627–640.

Tufte, Thomas, and Paolo Mefalopulos. *Participatory Communication: A Practical Guide.* Washington, DC: World Bank, 2009.

Tufte, Thomas, Cicilia M. Krohling Peruzzo, and Jair Vega Casanova. *Trazos de Una Otra Comunicación en América Latina: Prácticas Comunitarias, Teorías y Demandas Sociales.* Barranquilla, Colombia: Editorial Universidad del Norte, 2013.

Turner, Fred. *From Counterculture to Cyberculture: Stewart Brand, the Whole Earth Network, and the Rise of Digital Utopianism.* Chicago: University of Chicago Press, 2006.

UNICEF. "Adolescent and Youth Engagement Strategic Framework," March 2017. http://www.unicefinemergencies.com/downloads/eresource/docs /Adolescents/63792683.pdf.

Universidad de EAFIT and Universidad de Medellín. "Reporte Breve No. 3: Presupuesto Participativo." Medellín, Colombia: Consejo de Medellín. Accessed July 8, 2018. http://oppcm.concejodemedellin.gov.co:8090/oppcm_site/index .php?option=com_k2&view=item&task=download&id=73_130a20def858a228 2c2328e1aa7c5d42.

Uran, Omar. "Medellín Participatory Creativity in a Conflictive City." In *Participation and Democracy in the Twenty-first Century City*, edited by Jenny Pearce, 127–153. London: Palgrave Macmillan, 2010.

Urán, Omar. "Participación Ciudadana y Espacio Popular Urbano en Medellín: Entre Ciudadanía Insurgente y Programas de Planeación Participativa y Urbanismo Social—Comuna 1 y Comuna 13, Una Reflexión Comparativa." *e-Metropolis* 3, no. 8 (2012): 32–43.

Uribe, Maria T. "La Territorialidad de los Conflictos y de la Violencia en Antioquia." In *Realidad Social I*, edited by Tirando Mejiía et al., 51–157. Medellín, Colombia: Gobernación de Antioquia, Edinalco Ltda, 1990.

Uribe Neira, G. P., ed. *Jóvenes y Acción Colectiva: Caracterización y Diagnóstico de las Expresiones Juveniles Asociativas en la Ciudad de Medellín.* Medellín, Colombia: Federación Antioqueño de ONG, 2009.

Vaidhyanathan, Silva. *The Googlization of Everything (and Why We Should Worry).* Berkeley: University of California Press, 2011.

Veeduría Plan de Desarrollo de Medellín. *Balance de la Gestión de los Planes de Desarrollo de Medellín 1995–2011*, 2012. Accessed December 2012. http://www.bapp-eafit.info/uploads/docs/Balance%20de%20la%20Gesti%C3%B3n%20de%20los%20planes%20de%20desarrollo%20de%20Medell%C3%ADn%20completo,%20con%20car%C3%A1tula[1].pdf.

Vega, Jair. "Tecnologías de la Información y la Comunicación, Subjetividad y Cambio Social." In *Comunicación, Desarrollo y Cambio Social: Interrelaciones Entre Comunicación, Movimientos Ciudadanos, y Medios*, edited by J. Pereira and A. Cadavid, 349–360. Bogotá, Colombia: Editorial Javeriana, 2011.

Vega Casanova, Jair, Monica Pérez Marín, German Arango Rendón, and Camilo Pérez Quintero. "'Pasolini en Medellín': Jóvenes, Transferencia de Medios y Esferas Públicas Locales." In *Trazos de Una Otra Comunicación en América Latina: Prácticas Comunitarias, Teorías y Demandas Sociales*, s283–300. Barranquilla, Colombia: Editorial Universidad del Norte, 2011.

Vega Casanova, Manuel Jair, and Keila Saray Escalante Orozco. "Organizaciones Juveniles: ¿Espacios de Formación Ciudadana?" *Signo y pensamiento* 26, no. 51 (2007): 150–159.

Velásquez, Fabio, and Esperanza González. *¿Qué Ha Pasado con la Participación Ciudadana en Colombia?* Bogotá, Colombia: Fundación Corona, 2003.

Verba, Sidney, Kay Lehman Schlozman, and Henry E. Brady. *Voice and Equality: Civic Voluntarism in American Politics.* Cambridge, MA: Harvard University Press, 1995.

Vilchis, Mitzi, Kimberly A. Scott, and Courtney Besaw. "COMPUGIRLS Speak: How We Use Social Media for Social Movements." In Middaugh and Kirshner, *#youthaction*, 59–79.

Villa Martínez, Marta Inés. "Medellín: De Aldea a Metrópoli: Una Mirada al Siglo XX Desde el Espacio Urbano." In *Historia de las Ciudades e Historia de Medellín como Ciudad*, edited by Ramón Moncada Cardona, 98–118. Medellín, Colombia: Corporación Region, 2007.

Villa Martínez, Marta Inés, Luz Amparo Sánchez Medina, and Ana María Jaramillo Arbeláez. *Rostros del Miedo: Una Investigación Sobre los Miedos Sociales Urbanos.* Medellín, Colombia: Corporación Región, 2003.

Vivienne, Sonja, Anthony McCosker, and Amelia Johns. "Digital Citizenship as Fluid Interface: Between Control, Contest and Culture." In McCosker et al., *Negotiating Digital Citizenship*, 1–18.

Vodanovich, Shahper, Brad McKenna, and Wenjie Cai. "Cultural Values Inherent in the Design of Social Media Platforms: A Case Study of WeChat." In *Bled 2017: Proceedings of the 30th Bled eConference Digital Transformation—From Connecting Things to Transforming Our Lives*, 2017. Accessed January 2020. http://aisel.aisnet.org/bled2017/8.

Watkins, Samuel Craig. *The Young and the Digital: What the Migration to Social Network Sites, Games, and Anytime, Anywhere Media Means for Our Future*. Boston: Beacon Press, 2009.

White, Sarah C. Depoliticizing Development: The Uses and Abuses of Participation. *Development in Practice* 6, no. 1 (1996): 6–15.

White, Shirley A., ed. *Participatory Video: Images that Transform and Empower*. Thousand Oaks, CA: Sage, 2003.

Williams, Raymond. "Culture is Ordinary." In *Cultural Theory: An Anthology*, edited by Imre Szeman and Timothy Kaposy, 53–59. Malden, MA: Wiley-Blackwell, 2011.

Williams, Raymond. *Television: Technology and Cultural Form*. 2nd ed. New York: Routledge, 1990.

Winner, Langdon. "Do Artifacts Have Politics?" *Daedalus* 109, no. 1 (1980): 121–136.

Youniss, James, Susan Bales, Verona Christmas Best, Marcelo Diversi, Milbrey McLaughlin, and Rainer Silbereisen. "Youth Civic Engagement in the Twenty-First Century." *Journal of Research of Adolescence* 12, no. 1 (2002): 121–148.

Youniss, James, Jeffrey A. McLellan, and Miranda Yates. "What We Know About Engendering Civic Identity." *American Behavioral Scientist* 40, no. 5 (1997): 620–631.

Yúdice, George. "Afro Reggae: Parlaying Culture into Social Justice." *Social Text* 19, no. 4 (2001): 53–65.

Yúdice, George. *The Expediency of Culture: Uses of Culture in the Global Era*. Durham, NC: Duke University Press, 2003.

Zuboff, Shoshana. "Big Other: Surveillance Capitalism and the Prospects of an Information Civilization." *Journal of Information Technology* 30, no. 1 (2015): 75–89.

Zuckerman, Ethan. "New Media, New Civics? My Bellwether Lecture at the Oxford Internet Institute." ethanzuckerman.com (blog). December 6, 2013. http://www.ethanzuckerman.com/blog/2013/12/06/new-media-new-civics-my-bellweather-lecture-at-the-oxford-internet-institute/.

Zukin, Cliff, Scott Keeter, Molly Andolina, Krista Jenkins, and Michael X. Delli Carpini. *A New Engagement? Political Participation, Civic Life, and the Changing American Citizen*. Oxford: Oxford University Press, 2006.

INDEX

Page numbers in italics indicate illustrations.

discourses of participation, 10, 19, 23, 29
DJs (disc jockeys), 80, 89
Don Berna (crime boss), 14, 17, 156n57

ecology of participation, 48, 68, 88, 140–48; definitions of, 160n43; ecology of broadcasting versus, 160n43; horizontal organization in, 95; participatory budgeting and, 117; youth power and, 35–43
Egypt, 2, 44
Ejército de Liberación Nacional (ELN), 10–12
El Circular Digital (Digital Circuit), 53, 54
Elite Hip Hop Network. *See* La Red de Hip Hop la Elite
El Perro (graffiti artist Daniel Felipe Quiceno Fernández), 6, 75
Enghel, Florencia, 19
entrepreneurship, 46, 52–53, 132
Escobar, Arturo, 104
Escobar, Pablo, 5, 10; biopics of, 153n28; community projects of, 12; death of, 13; Mafia partnership with, 11
Esk-lones (rap group), 78; "Esta es la 13" of, 74
"Esta es la 13" (song), 74

Facebook, 45, 68, 136–38; growth of, 27; internet service of, 157n2
"Facebook Revolution," 2
Fajardo, Sergio, 14–16, 46, 82, 170n36; administration of, 17, 112–13, 128–30, 131; citizen participation and, 38–39, 108–9; digital initiatives of, 71; slogan of, 83
Fals Borda, Orlando, 5, 159n24
FARC. *See* Fuerzas Armadas Revolucionarias de Colombia
Foucault, Michel, 109
Franz, Tobias, 146

free/libre and open-source software (FLOSS), 2–3, 50, 68, 164n15; Microsoft versus, 67, 164n15
Freire, Paulo, 32, 58, 89, 170n34
Friedland, Lewis, 156n63
fronteras invisibles. See invisible borders
Fuchs, Christian, 65
Fuerza Joven (Youth Power), 127–28
Fuerzas Armadas Revolucionarias de Colombia (FARC), 10–12, 154n36; public protests against, 2

Galán, Luis Carlos, 110
Gallo, Héctor, 78–79
Galtung, Johan, 76
Garcés Montoya, Ángela, 162n67, 168n3; on *colectivos juveniles*, 76–77; on hip-hop groups, 169n20
García Canclini, Néstor, 80
Gaviria, Aníbal, 135
Gaviria, César, 14
Geertz, Clifford, 21–22
gender issues, 33, 143; indigenous women and, 18; La Elite and, 89–90, 93; participatory budgeting and, 114, 123–24; Son Batá and, 120
gestores culturales juveniles (youth cultural advocates), 80–81
Gilman, Hollie Russon, 129
Giroux, Henry, 22
Global North/South, 1, 31, 44, 145; definitions of, 151n12; digital divide between, 5, 51; economic development programs in, 44; governments' role in, 112; neoliberalism and, 29, 49; young people in, 158n20
Goldfrank, Benjamin, 112
Gonzalez, Esperanza, 110
governmentality, 126, 139, 140; "affirmative," 171n4; of budgeting process, 36; participation and, 109
government services, on Internet, 53, 65

graffiti artists, 6, *7*, 21, 75, 80, 86–90, *87*
Gumucio Dagron, Alfonso, 69
Gutiérrez Zuluaga, Federico, 128

Habermas, Jürgen, 44
Harry Potter Alliance, 34–35
Hay, James, 157n7
Hewlett-Packard, 5, 46, 52
Hickey, Samuel, 43–44
hip-hop artists/activists, 35, 74–80, 91, 96, 170n29
hip-hop groups, 79–80, 145; elements of, 80; Garcés Montoya on, 169; schools for, 81, 88–91, 127–28, 145
horizontal decision making, 91–96
horizontal governing, 76–77
horizontality, 59–60, 135; of digital communication, 48, 50, 51, 73, 135; of Medellín Digital, 54
horizontal learning, 88, 91. *See also* popular education
Hoyng, Rolien, 33, 73, 143
Huesca, Robert, 33
human rights, 63, 79

ICTS (information communication technology services), 52, 54, 165n22
India, 44
Indignados movement, 35
Information and Communication Technology (ICT), 46, 52, 54, 73
Information and Communication Technology for Development (ICT4D), 51
Instagram, 44–45
International Monetary Fund, 110
invisible borders (*fronteras invisibles*), 40, 82–84, 86–87, 124
Isin, Engin, 47, 65
Ito, Mizuko, 88, 142

Jaramillo, Ana María, 12, 152n26
JEIHHCO (hip-hop artist), 6–8, 75

Jenkins, Henry, 66; on participatory culture, 34
Jewish Colombians, 9
Jiménez Zuluaga, Blanca Inés, 78–79
Juntas Administradoras Locales (Local Administrative Councils, JALS), 119
Juntas de Acción Comunal (Communal Action Councils, JACS), 119

Kelty, Christopher, 2, 29–30, 67, 93, 160n35
King, Jamie, 148
Kirshner, Ben, 66–67
Kleine, Dorothea, 66
Kolacho School of Hip Hop, 81, 88–91, 127–28, 145
Kothari, Uma, 43
Kwon, Soo Ah, 36, 171n4

Lara Bonilla, Rodrigo, 11, 39
La Red de Hip Hop La Elite, 6, 24, 78–96, 132, 140; Facebook use by, 136–38; formation of, 80; graffiti artists of, 86–88; Kolacho School of, 81, 88–91, 127–28, 145; membership of, 81; mission of, 80–81, 106; participatory activism by, 87–88, 90; participatory budgeting by, 117–20, 126–27; participatory decision making of, 91–96; Son Batá and, 75–77, 105–7, 118–20, 126–29. *See also* Revolución Sin Muertos
La Sierra (documentary film), 57
La 13. *See* Comuna 13 of Medellín
La Violencia (1946–1958), 10–12, 153n29
Library Parks, 5–6, *7*, 82, 133
literacy, media, 66–67, 139
Londoño, Juan Fernando, 125
Longford, Graham, 67, 164n15
Lopez, Jennifer, 103, 148, 150

Maclean, Kate, 16
Mafia (U.S.), 11

malnutrition, 78, 169n16
March For Our Lives (2018), 2, 35
Martin, Gerard, 12, 153n28
Martín Barbero, Jesús, 5, 161n46
McLuhan, Marshall, 160n43
Medellín: demographics of, 9; homicide rates in, 5, 10, 13–14, 78, 134, 154n46; "miracle" of, 131; as model city, 4–8, 7
Medellín Ciudad Inteligente (Medellín A Smart City) program, 47
Medellín Digital, 47–49, 51–56, 54, 165n38; Ciudad Comuna and, 56, 57, 64–73, 138–39
media literacy, 66–67, 139
mentorship, 81, 89–91, 142. See also referentes
Mesa Interbarrial (neighborhood network), 167n57
methodological notes, 18–23
Me Too movement, 2, 35
Metrojuventud (municipal youth programs), 8, 128
Microsoft Corporation, 46, 52, 65, 67; FLOSS software versus, 67, 164n15
Middaugh, Ellen, 66–67
"Mi Identidad" (song), 96
militia groups, 11–12, 41, 162n67
M-19 (19th of April Movement), 11
Mohan, Giles, 43–44
Motorola Corporation, 53
Mouffe, Chantal, 22–23, 45, 65
Myanmar, 44

narco-culture, 39, 76, 127, 133–34
National Liberation Army (ELN). See Ejército de Liberación Nacional
Negroponte, Nicholas, 51
neoliberalism, 29, 33, 49, 112; Couldry on, 33; economic restructuring and, 9
net neutrality, 47

New World Information and Communication Order (NWICO), 159n24
19th of April Movement (M-19), 11

Occupy Movement, 2, 34–35
Olsson, Tobias, 160n43
One Million Voices Against FARC, 2
Operation Orion (2002), 13, 74, 78, 154n45, 169n17
O'Reilly, Tim, 1
Ouellette, Laurie, 157n7

paisas (people of Antioquia), 9, 76; chocoanos and, 99
Palenque, Colombia, 171n43
parainstitutionality, 12
paramilitary groups, 12–14
Park Libraries, 5–6, 7, 82, 133
participation: agency from, 72–73, 160n43; children's right to, 29; content-related, 56; definitions of, 28, 45; as form of governmentality, 109; history of, 29; "ladders" of, 33–34; "pseudo," 65; recuperating of, 43–45; structural, 56; tactics of, 81–96, 106–7, 147; "transformative," 34. See also ecology of participation
participatory administration, 63
participatory budgeting (PB), 5, 36, 108–26, 121, 132, 144–45; Cabannes on, 115; digital communication technologies for, 55; gender issues with, 114, 123–24; Gilman on, 129; La Elite and, 117–20, 126–27; outcomes of, 122, 125–27; process for, 113–14; reform of, 128–29; Shah on, 112, 174n33; Son Batá and, 117–20, 121, 124, 126–27, 133; weakening of, 135; World Bank on, 112
participatory communication, 32, 49–51; Medellín Digital and, 54; studies of, 20
participatory culture, 75–76, 126; Jenkins on, 34

Secretaría de Cultura Ciudadana (Department of Civic Culture), 8, 128, 137, 169n27, 170n36
Secretaría de Gobierno (Department of the Government), 127
self-defense groups, 13, 154n45
Servaes, Jan, 33, 73, 142–43
Shah, Anwar, 112, 174n33
Shirky, Clay, 141
Situationism, 29
"slacktivism," 44
Snapchat, 45
Snowden, Edward, 28, 44
social cleansing campaigns, 11–12
social justice issues, 5, 65, 96
"social urbanism," 16, 146
socioeconomic status, 152n20, 169n16
sociopolitical ecology, 20
Son Batá (Afro-Colombian collective), 24, 75–77, 96–107, 97, 102, 132–33; Facebook use by, 136–38; La Elite and, 75–77, 105–7, 118–20, 126–29; "Mi Identidad" of, 96; mission of, 101, 106; participatory activism by, 80, 91–96; participatory budgeting by, 117–20, 121, 124, 126–27; political influence of, 8; reterritorialization by, 82–83; school of, 98, 101, 136; on U.S. television show, 148–50
South Africa, 145
Sri Lanka, 44
Stop Online Piracy Act, 34–35

Tarrow, Sidney, 137–38
techno-elites, 25, 30, 73
techno-fundamentalism, 51
technological determinism, 35, 48, 65, 71, 163n1
technology gap. See digital divide
"technosocial literacy," 66, 139
techno-utopianism, 48, 51
Third, Amanda, 46–47
Toqueville, Alexis de, 161n51
Torres Restrepo, Camilo, 42
Twitter, 2, 44–45, 137

Ukraine, 2
UN Children's Fund (UNICEF), 139
UN Convention of the Rights of the Child (1989), 29, 37
UN High Commissioner for Refugees (UNHCR), 153n30
Urban Land Institute, 4–5
urban militias, 11–12, 41
Uribe, Álvaro, 13, 169n17
Uribe, María Teresa, 99
Uribe Neira, Gloria Patricia, 143, 168n9, 169n14

Vallejo Gómez, Mercedes, 66, 166n44
Velásquez, Byron de Jesús, 39
Velásquez, Fabio, 110
Venezuela, 145
Vietnam War, 42
Vilchis, Mitzi, 66
violence, 10–14; culture of, 39, 76, 127; representational, 79, 95, 98; rhetoric of, 106; structural, 79, 99
Visión 8 (newspaper), 58–60, *61*, 166n51
Voces de la 8 (radio station), 59

war on drugs, 37, 153n32, 154n36, 154n43
Web 2.0, 18–19, 53; Fuchs on, 65; Olsson on, 160n43; O'Reilly on, 1
WikiLeaks, 28, 44
Wikipedia, 50, 164n15
Williams, Raymond, 51, 76
Winner, Langdon, 51
World Bank, 43, 110, 112

YMCA (Young Men's Christian Association), 80
young people, 11–12; adults' relationships with, 76, 90–91, 118–19, 122, 144; demographics of, 36, 38; indigenous, 107; mentorship of, 81, 89–91, 142
youth citizenship, 14, 17, 75, 129; resignification of, 101–6

youth collectives. See *colectivos juveniles*
Youth Network (Red Juvenil), 167n57
youth power, 36–43
youth subculture, 76

YouTube, 18–19, 44–45, 59, 68
Yúdice, George, 28, 111

Zapatistas, 18
Zinagoga Crew, 78
Zuckerberg, Mark, 27, 28